SCENE-WRITING FOR FILM AND TV

Focusing on an integral aspect of screenplays, this book takes students and writers at all levels through the process of understanding and writing better scenes. It interrogates the functions of a scene and how writers can then apply this knowledge to their own film and television scripts.

Author Simon van der Borgh familiarises the screenwriter with the aspects of a scene, looking at what a scene is, the characters involved, the action depicted, dialogue, setting, and style. Featuring original scenes that show the practice of scene-writing and the application of ideas and approaches alongside in-depth analysis and critique, the book explores the process and approach to scene-writing and how to learn and improve methods of telling dynamic, engaging, and moving stories of diverse types and formats on screen. With a strong focus on practice-based advice, the book includes exercises at every step to enable writers to build on and extend their knowledge and skills with confidence and clarity chapter by chapter.

Exploring the film and TV scene with its different types, forms, and functions, it is the ideal book for aspiring screenwriters and students of screenwriting and filmmaking at all levels, as well as directors, producers, and actors looking to better understand the contextual and subtextual motivations intended by the writer.

Simon van der Borgh has worked globally for 40 years, gaining an international reputation as a produced screenwriter, screenwriting teacher, and script consultant. He has delivered his practical scene-writing lectures, masterclasses, and workshops to thousands of students, screenwriters, and filmmakers worldwide. Many of the ideas in this book were developed during his time as Senior Lecturer in Screenwriting at the University of York.

SCENE-WRITING FOR FILM AND TV

Simon van der Borgh

Routledge
Taylor & Francis Group

LONDON AND NEW YORK

Designed cover image: ©Frances van der Borgh

First published 2025
by Routledge
4 Park Square, Milton Park, Abingdon, Oxon OX14 4RN

and by Routledge
605 Third Avenue, New York, NY 10158

*Routledge is an imprint of the Taylor & Francis Group, an informa
business*

© 2025 Simon van der Borgh

British Library Cataloguing-in-Publication Data
A catalogue record for this book is available from the British Library

Library of Congress Cataloging-in-Publication Data
Names: Borgh, Simon van der, author.
Title: Scene-writing for film and TV / Simon van der Borgh.
Description: London ; New York : Routledge, 2025. | Includes
    bibliographical references and index.
Identifiers: LCCN 2024019565 (print) | LCCN 2024019566 (ebook) |
    ISBN 9781032277561 (hardback) | ISBN 9781032277554
    (paperback) | ISBN 9781003293927 (ebook)
Subjects: LCSH: Television authorship. | Motion picture authorship.
Classification: LCC PN1992.7 .B67 2025 (print) | LCC PN1992.7
    (ebook) | DDC 808.2/25—dc23/eng/20240618
LC record available at https://lccn.loc.gov/2024019565
LC ebook record available at https://lccn.loc.gov/2024019566

ISBN: 978-1-032-27756-1 (hbk)
ISBN: 978-1-032-27755-4 (pbk)
ISBN: 978-1-003-29392-7 (ebk)

DOI: 10.4324/9781003293927

Typeset in Sabon
by Apex CoVantage, LLC

CONTENTS

ACKNOWLEDGEMENTS

One of the outcomes of enjoying a 40+ year career in the entertainment industry and in education is that there are a lot of people to thank for their part in the origins, development, and writing of this book:

In the theatre – Christopher Denys, Peter Cheeseman, John Dexter, Jocelyn Herbert, Nick Barter, Bryony Lavery, Chris Fisher, Clive Wolfe, James Mansfield.

At the NFTS – Jan Fleischer, Sandy Lieberson, Dick Ross, Philip Palmer, Stephen Frears, Jeremy Webb.

At the MBFI, Amsterdam and North by Northwest, Denmark – Jeanne Wickler, David Howard, Martin Daniel, Ken Dancyger, Eva Svenstedt, Anette Funch Thomassen, Ted Braun, Beth Serlin, Tom Abrams, and Dave Weber (also my sometime writing partner in LA).

At Arista – Stephen Cleary, Colin Young, Hannah Kodicek, Peter Speyer, Bella Roe.

In London and Los Angeles – Peter Medak, Davina Belling, Clive Parsons, Alistair Cameron, Abdul Latif Salazar, Haroon Sugich, Tom Roberts, David Warner, Paul Iacovou.

At AFTRS, Sydney – Ross Grayson Bell, Allen Palmer, Nell Greenwood, Samantha Lang, Marty Murphy, Catherine Millar, Cathryn McConaghy.

In Australia and New Zealand – Mike Cowap, Martha Coleman, Alan Payne, ScreenWest, Film Victoria, Screen Australia, Screen NSW, NT Film Office, NZ Film Commission.

Screenwriting teachers – Frank Daniel, Michael Hauge, Steve Kaplan, Chris Vogler, Robert McKee, John Truby, Linda Seger.

Agents and managers – Candy Thorpe, John Rush, Emily Hayward-Whitlock, Emma Woolley, Charlotte Knight, Stacey Testro.

In the UK – Alby James OBE, Hugo Heppell, Helen Bingham, Ann Tobin, and Jonathan Rawlinson, who supported my screenwriting and teaching from the outset.

At the University of York – Andrew Higson, Ed Braman, Jimmy Richards, Kristyn Gorton, Jonathan Carr, Colin Ward, John Mateer, Lisa Peschel, Mike Cordner, Áine Sheil, my colleagues, and my undergraduate, masters, and PhD students since 2012.

My York colleagues Duncan Petrie, Andrew Vickers, and David Barnett read chapters of the book and gave feedback, advice, and encouragement at key stages.

Julian Lyons, Peter Boswell, Rod Moore, Angie Hobbs, Graham and Juliet Smith, Jill Smith, Bruce Martin, Daniel Luscombe, Richard Branczik, Marius Grose, Roger Hampson, Peter Litten, Gary Fitzpatrick, Oliver and Katie Close, for their enduring support and friendship.

All the students, writers, filmmakers, and storytellers around the world that I've worked with, taught, learnt from, continue to learn from.

My brothers Peter, James, Adam, and Matthew, with whom I discovered characters, stories, scenes, action, dialogue, and drama in the first place.

My parents Sarah and Jonathan, who have always encouraged us to follow our dreams and be guided by our hearts.

My children Lucy, Molly, and Felix, who grew up living with a screenwriter.

And Frances, who sat down next to me on a beach towel in Antibes in 1986 and told me I should be a writer. Without her, nothing since would have been possible.

Simon van der Borgh, York 2024

INTRODUCTION

There are dozens of books on screenwriting. There are very few books about scene-writing. And yet scenes are the common denominator in every stage and screen story ever written, from *The Persians*[1] by Aeschylus,[2] first staged in Athens in 472 BCE and one of the oldest surviving play texts, to the latest films and TV dramas.

Scenes are everywhere. Literally. Each of us plays out our lives in a series of scenes, involving events that happen in real time in a single location in the present tense.

I am currently writing this:

INT. HOME OFFICE, YORK, UK — DAY

So far today, I have already been in:

INT. BEDROOM — NIGHT
INT. BEDROOM — DAY
INT. BATHROOM — DAY
INT. STAIRS — DAY
INT. HALLWAY - DAY

---

1 "Scene: Before the Council-Hall of the Persian Kings at Susa. The tomb of Darius the Great is visible. The time is 480 B.C., shortly after the Battle of Salamis." (Translated by R. Potter, *The Persians by Aeschylus*).
2 Aeschylus (c.525–456 BCE), Greek playwright and soldier, wrote about what he knew: he was a soldier in the Persian Wars and fought at the Battles of Marathon (490 BCE) and Salamis (480 BCE).

DOI: 10.4324/9781003293927-1

```
INT. KITCHEN — DAY
EXT. BACKYARD — DAY
EXT. STREET - DAY
```

You get the picture . . .

So it is little wonder that scenes form an integral *sine qua non*[3] part of all the dramatic spectacles that we watch, participate in, engage in.

We understand scenes because we live them every day. Perhaps, it is this familiarity with them and their ubiquitous nature in our lives that makes us so blasé towards them. Even screenwriters. Especially screenwriters!

This book explores the film and TV scene and its different types, forms, and functions and relocates it front and centre in our consciousness as we consider and improve our ability to tell dynamic, engaging, moving stories of diverse types and formats on screen.

Scenes are the component parts that make up the engine of a dramatic story and drive it forward – interlinked, involving, intricate. Memorable scenes stay with us forever, defining our response to a particular film, TV show, or 'short': that scene when . . . that moment when . . . and so on. Mediocre scenes can confuse, disengage, and undermine the story and its meaning. A better understanding of scenes and how they work results in better-written scenes and, thereby, better scripts.

Writing Better Scenes

This book is aimed at anyone with an interest in writing for the screen, whether you're writing a short film script for the very first time as part of your course, you're an aspiring screenwriter who wants to understand the craft of dramatic writing better, or you're a produced screenwriter who is interested in refreshing your knowledge and skills in this fundamental part of writing professionally.

The ideas in it have formed a key part of my ongoing practice-based scholarship and research inside and outside the classroom since 1997 when I became an optioned[4] screenwriter and a screenwriting teacher. As I continue to discover every day, effective scene-writing and how writers at all levels might approach this has a tangible, potentially exponential effect on improving the standard of a script of any length, genre, or type and the impact it can make.

Clearer scenes, with well-defined dramatic tensions and active dramatic questions, can aid readers, directors, and actors to understand better the

---

3 *sine qua non* = 'without which not', or something that is essential, an indispensable element.
4 An option is a contractual agreement between a screenwriter and producer that assigns the rights to a project (generally a script) to that producer for an agreed period of time to develop the project, raise the finance, cast it, and move it into production.

contextual and subtextual motivations intended by the writer through the behaviour of their characters and the strategies these characters adopt to get what they want, thereby resulting in more involving and engaging performances on screen.

Scenes give dramatic stories form, structure, location, time, shape, diversity, familiarity, contrast, juxtaposition, tone, genre, mood, atmosphere, context, subtext, and meaning. This meaning can be obvious, overt, immediately clear to the narrative and its action, or it can be covert, hidden, initially confusing to the narrative and its action. It can direct the reader or viewer, or it can intentionally misdirect them. Scenes can reinforce and support the plot and narrative, or they can offer juxtaposition and contrast to them.

Depending on the position of the scene in the script and its purpose and function in the ongoing dramatic action, a scene's meaning can feel primary, provocative, dominant at a particular moment in the plot or secondary, supportive, subservient in it. Well-crafted scenes ensure reader and audience understanding and provide clarity, complexity, texture, and thematic resonance both in real time and to the overall arc of the story. Well-written scenes that fuse action and dialogue in the right measure for the particular point in the plot help create tension, conflict, emotion, and audience affect. They provide evidence on the page of that most elusive and desirable of elements in all dramatic writing: the writer's voice.

This book aims to help you reconsider and improve your approach to understanding, developing, or writing scenes for short films and different forms of TV scripts and feature films, whatever your level of experience, your role, or the medium you are writing or working in.

Identifying a common clear approach to the process of scene-writing will help reframe the way we go about looking at, constructing, understanding, and interpreting dramatic stories on screen. Its incorporation of my relatable practical approach, examples of scene-writing practice, and customised writing exercises will enable the reader to build on and extend their knowledge and skills with confidence and clarity chapter by chapter.

The Approach

There is a range of screenwriting software on the market that enables the writer to lay out and format their work so that it looks like a script. Tabs automatically create "Scene Heading", "Action", "Character", "Dialogue", "Parentheses", Transition", "DAY/NIGHT", "INT/EXT", and so on.

However, looking like a script is one thing. Being a script – the evolving, involving blueprint for a screen story that engages the reader and elicits their participation to turn this virtual proposition into a tangible, physical creative work – is quite another.

Despite the evident creative, industrial, and technical differences that exist between, say, a no-budget 'short' to be shot on a film course or over a weekend, a returnable TV sit-com, a low-budget 'Indie' film, a multi-season TV drama, or a hi-concept franchise movie, the approach in this book deliberately focuses on the scenes we are writing. Improving these will inevitably improve the particular type of script they are integral to, scene by scene, page by page.

The traditional dividing lines between feature films and TV dramas that meant that writers were pigeonholed[5] and wrote one or the other have become increasingly invisible to the point where they no longer exist. Writers now write scripts for both – and for all the other types of films and TV outlets that are available, too. This flexibility and crossover are reinforced even as I write this introduction by the fact that Wes Anderson, nominated for seven Academy Awards from 2001–18,[6] won at the eighth attempt in 2024 for his live-action short *The Wonderful Story of Henry Sugar* (2023).[7]

This book draws together my own experience as a produced writer, script consultant, teacher, and director and reveals the overt and hidden core elements that exist in every scene. It identifies the key questions that apply to every scene we write and offers answers and ideas for these, such as

- Whose scene is it?
- What is the specific dramatic question of the scene?
- What strategies does the character use to get what they want?
- What are the key events or beats in the scene?
- How does this scene fit into a sequence of scenes?
- How is the story's theme incorporated into the scene?

The emphasis of this book's approach is on clarity, best practice, and the application of skills and tools to aid writers at any level to improve their scene-writing knowledge and understanding and enable them to write better dramatic scenes.

This book hopefully acts as a complement and extension to the existing practice of writing for the screen and to the many texts about this that exist and are yet to come.

---

5 On the NFTS Screenwriting programme (1994–96), we were advised we should write either for films or for TV.
6 Nominated for Best Original Screenplay: *The Royal Tenenbaums* (2001), *Moonrise Kingdom* (2012), *The Grand Budapest Hotel* (2014); Best Animated Picture: *Fantastic Mr. Fox* (2009), *Isle of Dogs* (2018); Best Director and Best Picture: *The Grand Budapest Hotel* (2014).
7 Adapted from the 1977 short story of the same name by Roald Dahl (1916–90).

A Change of Plan . . .

Most screenwriting books and approaches to screenwriting teaching involve the use of clips or examples from produced films and TV programmes to support the particular craft point being made. As a teacher, I regularly use entire films and TV shows, sequences, individual scenes, and passages in scenes to explain, illustrate, and enhance my teaching. And it was my intention to do the same with this book. Indeed, the proposal I initially wrote for the book mentions a broad range of produced film and TV work in my locker that I planned to draw from and refer to.

Then I started writing the book. And this plan changed.

In the movie *Jerry Maguire* (1996), Cameron Crowe's comedy about sports agent Jerry Maguire (Tom Cruise) who gets fired by the management company he works for and faces a race against time to try and retain his sports star clients, there is an iconic seduction scene early in the film. Maguire is on the phone desperately trying to convince NFL receiver Rod Tidwell (Cuba Gooding, Jr) to stay with him before Maguire's erstwhile colleague now rival agent Bob Sugar gets through to him and signs him up. It is often referred to as the "Show Me the Money" scene because the crux of the scene is that Tidwell won't agree to Jerry's proposal until Jerry has repeated the Tidwell "family motto" to "Show Me the Money". The scene revolves around Jerry's goal of trying to convince Tidwell to stay with him as his – as it turns out – one and only client, and enjoyably, Tidwell is playfully countering this by trying to get Maguire to repeat the Tidwell family motto.

In the scene in the produced film, the phrase "show me the money" is said 13 times in 25 exchanges of dialogue from Tidwell's initial, "It's a very personal, very important thing. It's a family motto" to the climactic, "Congratulations. You're still my agent". Their 'call and response' exchange lasts for 1'30", with Tidwell saying the phrase three times, and Maguire repeating it ten times. It's funny, revealing, and characterful. It explores and uses character and status to set up the relationship between Maguire and Tidwell. Conflict and comedy create an engaging scene that has been much used by teachers of screenwriting and scene-writing since the movie was released.

However, in the original script, the phrase "show me the money" is presented in a markedly different way. On the page, we see the same characters, same settings intercut on the phone (Tidwell's home / Maguire's office), same objective for Maguire, same response by Tidwell, similar action and dialogue. However, "show me the money" is said only three times: twice by Tidwell, and only once by Maguire. It covers seven exchanges of dialogue in 6/8th of a page, approximately 45" of screen time.

Cameron Crowe was the writer and the director of the movie, so it is perfectly understandable that on set shooting the scene, he and his team may have realised the power of the "Show Me the Money" exchange and encouraged his excellent actors to improvise around this. But the difference between the original scene and the scene that made it into the finished film points up one of the major issues when using clips like this to make scene-writing points for screenwriters.

Script to Screen

Scenes in produced movies can be unreliable guides when it comes to representing what was originally written in the script. As the *Jerry Maguire* example indicates, magic happens in the process of making a film or TV drama – during the shoot, in performance, in direction and filming, in the edit. Indeed, if the scenes we write are doing their job, they facilitate, encourage, inspire this magic.

There is an additional and equally significant challenge, too, in relying on produced film and TV content to exemplify, illustrate, and explain the teaching points in this book, and that is that it requires you actually to have seen – or be able to access and see – the scene being referenced and referred to in the text. A lot of film and TV scenes are available to be viewed on the internet. But many aren't, and access and accessibility should never be barriers to learning.

Taken out of context and presented in their film or TV form, I began to question the value of the produced scene approach for the aspiring or working screenwriter on their own outside the classroom. And since this book is fundamentally about the process of writing scenes, either before any official script development or at some stage during that script development, and often a long time before production becomes a possibility let alone an actuality, I began to realise that relying on produced film or TV scenes to demonstrate the points I am intending to make risked adding a significant and unwelcome degree of separation from the actual scene-writing process and the ideas I am sharing in this book.

Discovering this almost inadvertently as I was writing an early draft of a chapter, I then looked around for another source of scenes to complement, illustrate, reflect, and test the ideas being introduced and proposed.

Eventually, I realised what that source was. Is.

Me.

Simon van der Borgh
York 2024

1

APPROACH

What Is a Scene?

Introduction

```
INT. LECTURE HALL — DAY

UP ON A SCREEN: PowerPoint title - "Scene-writing" Pt.1

Standing below the large screen:

SIMON (60s)

And sitting in front of him:

EIGHTY STUDENTS...

                    SIMON
          Morning, everyone. Good to see you all.
          Today's lecture gets us started on my
          favourite topic: scene-writing!
               (beat)
          Now then, tell me. What is a scene?

Simon smiles at the Students. Encouraging. Desperate?

SOME stare back. OTHERS avoid his eye. Silence........
```

At the beginning of my introductory lecture on scene-writing, I always ask the participants the same question: "What is a scene?" The silence this simple question often generates is deafening. And revealing.

DOI: 10.4324/9781003293927-2

After all, we know what a scene is. Instinctively. Innately. At a basic level. Because film and TV content is all around us and the variety of this content is huge, from franchise movies to indie films, lo budget to no budget to short films, TV series to soaps to sit-coms, and more besides, on a plethora of platforms. Regardless of the medium, genre, running time, budget, or audience, this content has one thing in common.

It all contains scenes.

So what is a film or TV scene? How would you define what it is? What key elements make up a scene and are integral to it?

Here are some of the answers I've had over the years:

"Scenes have characters in them".
"A scene is where stuff happens".
"You have to have scenes, it's one of the rules".
"Scene time is a sort of version of our time."
"Scenes happen inside. Except ones that happen outside".

Think about a film or TV scene you love: that scene when . . . that moment when . . . that dialogue when . . . Better still, think of a scene that you have written or are thinking about writing. What key elements make up your scene? What elements are integral to it? What makes it a scene? How? Why?

What Is a Scene?

In its simplest form – in its essence, if you like – a film or TV scene is a unit of dramatic action that takes place in one location in real time, day or night.

Like all rules, in as much as this is a rule, there may be times when elements of it are challenged, changed, or broken. But as a starting point for each scene I write or read, it provides me with a useful early checklist:

- Does this scene have a unit of dramatic action?
- Does it take place in one location?
- Does it take place in a version of real time – (e.g., our time)?
- Does it take place in the day or at night?

I find this simple definition of a scene helpful because it reflects the classical notion of the *Three Unities,* the cornerstones of the principles of drama derived from Aristotle's *Poetics*[1] that have underpinned most approaches to writing for the stage and the screen and informed our understanding of this process.

---

1 The earliest surviving text articulating dramatic theory, and still the most influential, *Poetics* was written by Aristotle (384–322 BCE) circa 335 BCE.

The *Three Unities* in Drama

Action – there is one main unit of action
Place – that action takes place in one main location
Time – that action takes place within 24 hours

The plots of TV dramas such as police procedurals, soaps, and sit-coms continue to draw on these three 'unities' and use them as a framework to varying degrees. But they also feature at some level in most of the film and TV scenes we write:

Action – a scene involves a central unit of dramatic action
Place – that scene takes place in one location
Time – that scene takes place in a defined period of time

Just as Aristotle's classical principles for a dramatic work as a whole are reflected in some way in each scene, so our overall approach to writing a film or TV script is also reflected in our approach to writing every scene in that script.

To help us understand the structural components of a scene and how these work, we need to understand the structural components of the larger screen story that our scenes are contained within. As we will see in this chapter, the key components of a scene can also be found in the structure of the story and plot as a whole. This shouldn't come as a surprise to us. After all, if we are doing our job as screenwriters and approaching the writing of scenes in the most productive and effective way, then it stands to reason that the overall script is reflective of the scenes, and vice versa.

A lot of time in development is spent looking at elements of the overall script – its theme, tone, genre, style, atmosphere, character arcs, and so on. Much less time is spent looking at these elements in each scene and how they are reflected or inherent in the dramatic action scene by scene.

The importance of core dramatic theory principles, like character Want and Need in creating a story and the associated Six Key Beats or plot events evolving from that specific Want and Need to create the core structure of that story, are equally applicable to our script as a whole and to each scene that's in that script.

What Does Your Character Want?

A Want is the conscious, external, physical, objective, or active goal of your main character that is established and identified in Act 1 and which then drives them on through the middle part of your story (Act 2).

At the centre of a screen story is a character of some sort, generally referred to as the protagonist or the main character. If we go along with the idea that screen stories tend to have three parts to them – often called acts – then the protagonist is introduced in some way in the first part. We locate them in their ordinary world, existing in their *status quo*. They may be happy or sad, engaged with their world or far removed from it, hopeful or fearful, active, frozen or catatonic, a mistress or a servant, depending on who they are and what you the writer have in store for them.

Midway through Act 1, something happens. A character and or an event makes itself known in the story and intrudes in some way. This can be a major interruption – the declaration of war, a zombie invasion, realising someone is trying to kill you – or a seemingly minor one – spilling coffee on someone, finding a stray dog, missing the bus – but it affects the protagonist and changes their *status quo*, creating a new situation or dilemma for them. It's often as a consequence of this intrusion that the main antagonist – the character that stands in opposition to our protagonist in some way, emotionally and/or physically – makes their presence felt in the story, too.

As a result of these events, by the end of Act 1, the main goal of our protagonist is established for the audience. This so-called Want of the protagonist articulates the external physical objective that they are going to pursue through Act 2, the main story act of complication and confrontation, creating conflict, tension, obstacles, and increasing physical and emotional difficulty for them. The decisions and actions taken by our main character in pursuit of their Want create the plot of your story.

Act 2 culminates when our protagonist has gone as far as they can in pursuit of this Want, a goal or objective that ends in success or failure. Often a low point for the main character, they enter the final part of the story: Act 3, the act of Need.

What Does Your Character Need?

A Need is the internal emotional desire of our main character. Buried, ignored, avoided, it is what the character comes to recognise as a result of the Act 2 Want story and is compelled to respond to – or ultimately fails to respond to – in Act 3.

This so-called Need is different from our protagonist's Want. Ideally, it should be directly opposed to it, thereby maximising the potential for conflict and tension. The Need often creates a new dramatic tension for the main character in Act 3, articulated by a new dramatic question.

Although it often manifests later in the story than the Want, a character's Need exists within them before the screen story and its events begin. Unlike their Want, which is a new goal initiated and incited in this particular screen story, the protagonist arrives in this story with their Need already *in situ*. A character's internal emotional Need can relate to a past event, wound, or flaw[2] that has been hard-wired into them long before the story of your film or TV show starts and their specific Want in that is activated.

In many respects, the main function of the external physical Want story is to provoke, unearth, expose, drag to the surface and into the action of the plot the character's internal emotional Need to enable its resolution. Or not. Many of our most beloved characters in our favourite long-running TV series are caught forever within the confines of their opposing Wants and Needs. The unresolved tension between these acts as a potent productive story engine, creating dynamic plots season by season.

The bigger the gap between the character's external physical Want and their internal emotional Need, the more opportunities there are for us to create drama, embodied in conflict, tension, tragedy, and comedy. If our character's external Want and internal Need feel too similar – they want and need to survive, they want and need to love, they want and need money, they want and need to find someone – it can be hard to create requisite nuance and depth to make our characters and stories compelling.

As we will see, the function and importance of the gap between a character's Want and their Need is particularly true when it comes to writing scenes.

Six Key Story Beats

Allied to the Wants and Needs of our characters, the notion that in all stories there are six associated key beats or plot events that are unique to each particular story and provide its core structure remains the most useful and applicable screenwriting element that I've been introduced to as a writer and teacher.[3]

They form the cornerstone of my own screenwriting teaching – so much so that a cohort of my students once inscribed "The 6 Key Beats" on a medal and gave it to me at their leaving do. In my view, there are worse things to be remembered for!

It is worth investigating these Six Key Beats in a little more detail because they are going to be hard-wired into our approach to developing and writing scenes.

Every story – an anecdote at dinner, a tale in the pub or on the bus, a short film, a TV drama or sit-com episode, or a feature film – has six key moments within it that ideally involve the protagonist of that story in some way. This applies to factual stories, too, such as documentaries, which are often structured to a high level.

---

2 Aristotle uses the term *hamartia* in *Poetics* to define this notion of the defects and flaws in our characters.
3 I was introduced to the concept of Six Key Beats as they relate to screenwriting at the MBFI (Amsterdam) by teachers David Howard and Martin Daniel from the USC Graduate Screenwriting program in September 1996.

Since our ancestors started telling stories to one another around a fire, there has been a pattern to these stories. We know what a story sounds like. We know what a story feels like. We know when we hear a good story. We know when we hear a bad story. We just *know*. Because our story knowledge is hard-wired into our DNA.[4]

These Six Key Beats are also fundamental to our screenwriting:

1. Someone starts telling a story. We're introduced to a character and their world. To their situation. Before we get bored (!), something happens.
2. Whatever happens changes the character's status quo. It creates a new situation. They face a new problem, creating conflict and difficulty for them.
3. The character has to take action willingly or unwillingly to try and fix this ever-increasing problem. Success and failure are always close by.
4. Taking action raises the stakes, creates greater conflict, more tension, bigger obstacles, even more difficulty. The character succeeds or fails.
5. Either way, this creates a new situation for them that they have to face.
6. By the end, they may lose everything yet still win, or win everything and yet still lose.

Whatever happens, this outcome is in the gift of the storyteller and the way we choose to tell our particular story. That is the power of telling stories.

Our DNA Meets Our Screen Story

This is the schema laying out the Six Key Beats for film and TV that I share with students. I find this approach to be helpful for writers at any stage of their writing journey,[5] from first time students attempting to write their first short film script to experienced and produced screenwriters:

I – Beginning: Introduction and Set Up

We establish the undisturbed status quo of our main character / protagonist.

1. The **Inciting Incident** is the moment mid Act 1 when the dramatic conflict of the story announces itself, often the first intrusion of the predicament to come for the main character. A new *status quo* is created, building the

---

4 Deoxyribonucleic acid (DNA) is the molecule that carries genetic information for the development and functioning of an organism. (National Human Genome Research Institute website).
5 "The DNA from any two people is 99.9% identical, with that shared blueprint guiding our development and forming a common thread across the world. The differing 0.1% contains variations that influence our uniqueness, which when combined with our environmental and social contexts give us our abilities, our health, our behavior". (National Human Genome Research Institute website).

dilemma for the main character and often leading to the 'collision' with the antagonist.

We create a new situation or problem for our protagonist.

2. The **Main Tension** confirms the external physical Want of the main character and is established by the end of the first part / act and clearly articulated to the audience. This Main Tension can ideally be stated as a question: "*Will the main character . . . (or won't they)?*" generating hopes and fears in the audience and engagement throughout the second part or act of our story.

II – Middle: Complication / Confrontation / Culmination / Crisis

We introduce new characters and subplots (if there are any).
The first serious obstacle is faced and overcome by the main character.

3. The **Midpoint** is when the main character is closest to or furthest away from getting what they want in the story. As a consequence of the midpoint, there is often a turning point / pivotal moment / reversal for the main character soon afterwards that is indicative of their internal emotional Need.
4. The **Main Culmination** denotes the end of Act 2. The Want story is effectively over. The main character has gone as far as they can in trying to get what they want and has either succeeded or failed.

Their Need creates a new tension in Act 3, which can be expressed as a new, dramatic "*Will the main character . . . (or won't they)?*" question in the final act.

III – End: Consequences / Climax / Resolution

Revolves around what the main character has or hasn't learnt.
What's going to happen at the end? How will things turn out?

5. The **Twist, False Resolution or Sacrifice** can initially look like a potential solution for the main character but turns out not to be one. They have still further to go. Recognising and responding to their Need often requires the sacrifice by the main character of the thing they felt most strongly about at the beginning of the story.
6. The **Resolution** reveals how things turn out for the main character, that is, what actually happens and the outcome of the story for the main character and other characters.

If a character fails to get what they want but recognises and responds to their Need in Act 3 and thereby changes, the story generally ends 'in balance' for the main character and the audience.

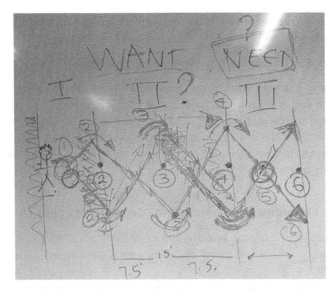

IMAGE 1.1 Diagram drawn during a class to explain the Six Key Beats in a 30-minute script. One line on it shows the rising and falling and rising action for an 'in balance' story; the other line shows the falling and rising and falling action for an 'out of balance' story.

However, failure to change, failure to recognise and respond to their Need generally results in an 'out of balance' ending for the main character, the essence of tragedy. A character may get what they want, but it is at the expense of the resolution of their Need. As the traditional cautionary tale warns us, be careful what you wish for.

Jack and the Beanstalk in Six Key Beats

Using a fairy tale is a good way of identifying the Six Key Beats in a story as illustrated in the diagram:

1. Jack and his widowed mother are poor. She tells him to sell their only cow at the market. But Jack decides to exchange the cow for some magic beans.
2. Angry, his mother throws away the beans. Overnight, they grow into a giant beanstalk. Jack decides to climb up it to see if there might be food at the top.
3. Up in the clouds, Jack explores. He discovers a Giant's castle. In it, he finds a magic hen and gold coins.
4. While the Giant sleeps, Jack steals the hen and gold coins. But the Giant wakes up and chases after him, determined to eat him.

5. In mortal danger, Jack climbs down the beanstalk. The Giant follows him down too – towards Jack's home and his mother.
6. At the bottom, Jack uses an axe to cut down the beanstalk. The Giant falls and is killed. Jack and his mother are reunited.

These Six Key Beats act as stepping stones for our characters and for us through our story. They are also called 'tent-pole' moments because they stick up out of our story like tent-poles, giving it a structure and enabling us to hang the 'canvas' – which can be any form, shape, colour, fabric, pattern – of our story from them.

This notion of the Six Key Beats enabling us to step through the story and see it is also helpful and instructive when it comes to the scenes we write.

The Structure of a Film or TV Scene

All film and TV scenes start with a *status quo* for the characters in the story no matter where the particular scene is located in the script.

Unlike the *status quo* that exists at the start of a story, the *status quo* in each scene changes.

Depending on what has happened in the previous scene or scenes, a character arrives in the new scene with a new *status quo*.

Sometimes this change in *status quo* will be monumental and life-changing for the characters. At other times, it will be delicate and barely perceptible.

Once the new *status quo* for the character in the scene is established, the conflict within the scene needs to be established.

I SET UP	II CONFLICT	III CONSEQUENCES

IMAGE 1.2 A character arriving in a new scene with a new *status quo*.

This conflict is either external, or internal, or both. It creates the tension – the drama – in the scene.

At the end of the first part of the scene – the set up – the specific goal or objective for the character in middle part of the scene is established.

The clearer and more specific to the particular scene this goal is, the better.

This goal also activates the principle of rising and falling action: as the character acts, the consequences of their actions make things more difficult for them.

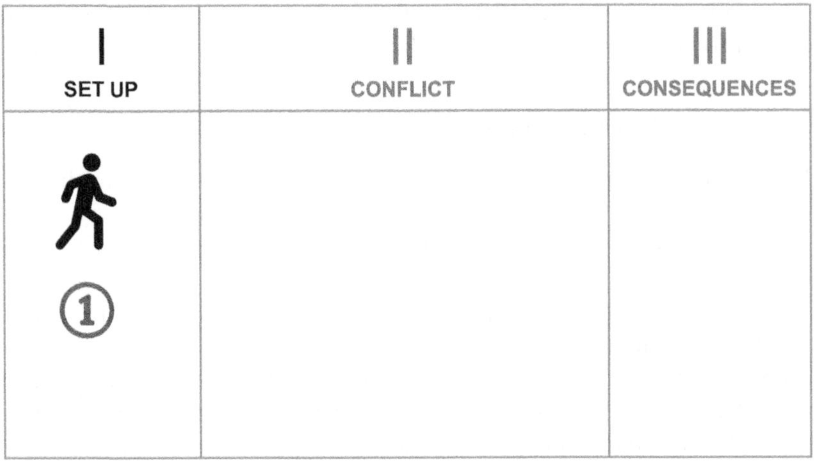

IMAGE 1.3 Scene beat 1: introduction of conflict in the scene.

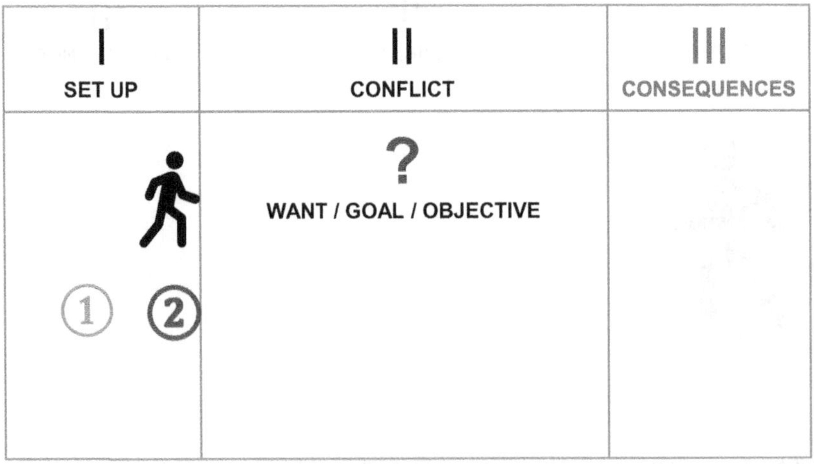

IMAGE 1.4 Scene beat 2: tension and dramatic question established – end of part I.

Rising and falling action activates our hopes and fears for the characters in the scene.

Characters have to come up with a variety of strategies to enable them to pursue their goal and keep it on track.

There is often a midpoint in the scene, the moment that the character is closest or furthest away from achieving their goal in the scene.

The character's objective in the scene culminates at the end of the second part.

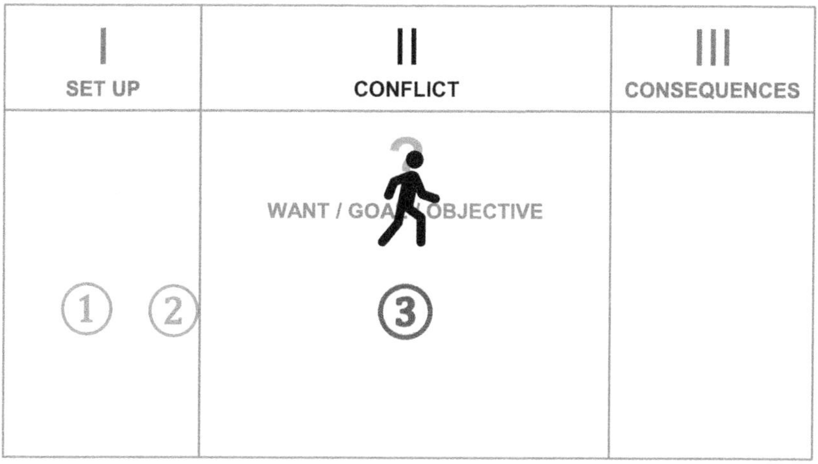

IMAGE 1.5 Scene beat 3: midpoint – often results in a change of strategy.

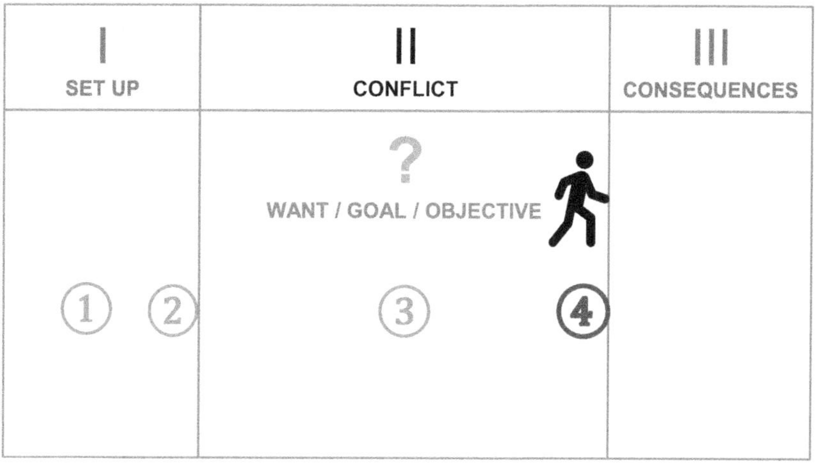

IMAGE 1.6 Scene beat 4: culmination of scene's dramatic question – end of part II

This is the point at which the character has achieved – or failed to achieve – what they want in the scene.

In the third part, we see the consequences of the character's actions in the scene.

This final part can be very short or drawn out depending on the extent of these consequences.

There is sometimes a twist, an unexpected development that emerges logically out of the action of the scene.

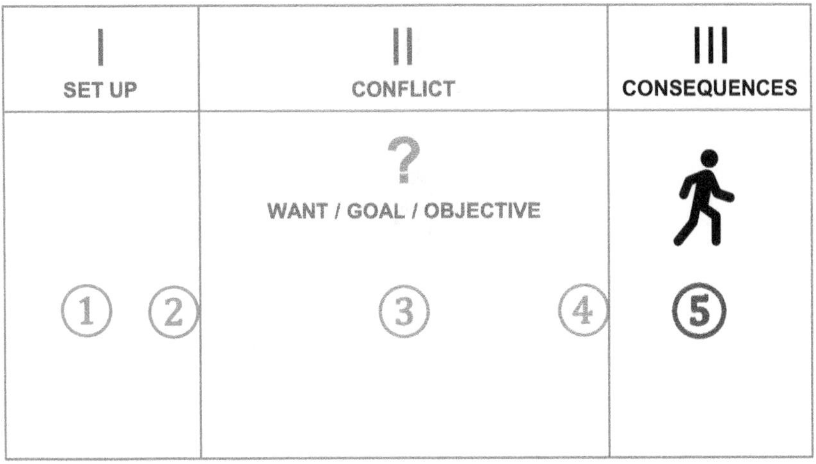

IMAGE 1.7   Scene beat 5: twist or reversal spinning us into the next scene.

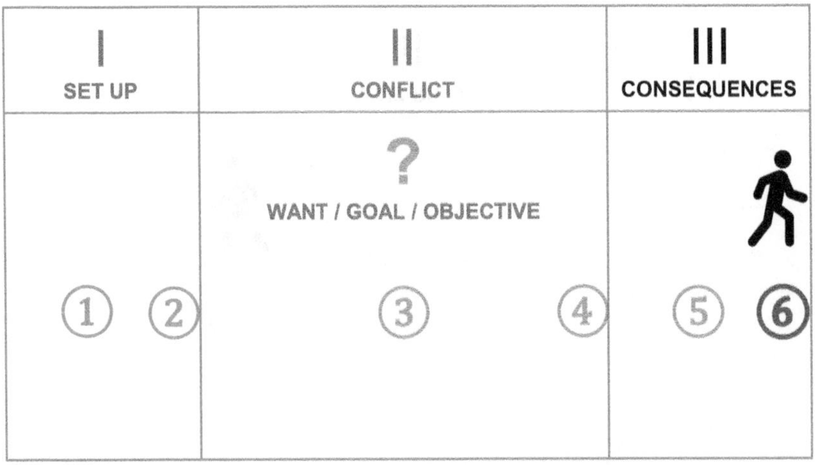

IMAGE 1.8   Scene beat 6: resolution – consequence of some kind

Failure to achieve the objective in the scene at the end of the middle part leads to a twist that opens the door for the character – leading to another scene.

Success in achieving the objective in the scene at the end of the middle part leads to a twist and closes the door for them – necessitating another scene.

The characters and plot are propelled into the next scene – with a new *status quo*.

NB: Beats 5 and 6 can often merge into one. Or there may be no resolution as such at all, just a twist that propels us into the next scene.

Putting This Into Practice

So how does this approach work in practice? How should one try and apply the ideas in it in one's own scene-writing?

In the middle of the night after I wrote the previous section of this chapter, I woke up with an idea for a scene in my head. Turns out, I literally dreamt up an idea so that I could show you how I follow this approach.

I jotted it down in bed, went back to sleep, and reviewed it the next day. As the photograph on the front cover indicates, I use pen and paper to do a lot of my initial writing of new ideas and new scenes. I find this frees me up from limitations that can be imposed by involving technology too early in the creative process. So I wrote the scene fast and with energy from start to finish. Then I moved this work onto my computer. On my screenwriting software, the scene I dreamt up covers 2 and 6/8 pages – about 2'45" of screen time. It took me about an hour to write, type and revise (a little) in one go.

EXT. TOP OF DIVING PLATFORM, POOL - DAY

Two hands grip the top of the ladder: ELLIE (16) emerges
up onto the 10-metre diving board.

OTHER GIRLS are in front of her along the railings in the
queue: MARSHA, EVE, KASIA (all 16)

And in front of them: MR. PALMER (50, coach, mean-faced).

DOWN BELOW — IN THE STADIUM SEATS

Ellie can see her MOTHER (40s) and GRANDMOTHER (70s), packing
up to leave. Her Grandmother stops, stares up.

BACK TO SCENE

Ellie steps forward. Past Marsha and co.

                    MARSHA
          Whast you doing?

                    ELLIE
          I have to go first.

                    MARSHA
          No.

                    ELLIE
          Please.

                    MARSHA
          Why?

                    ELLIE
          I just do.

Mr. Palmer notices the commotion. Moves towards them.

                    MR. PALMER
          What's going on?

                    MARSHA
          Ellie's trying to push in...

Mr. Palmer gazes at Ellie.

                    MR. PALMER
          Are you now. Why?

               ELLIE
I just have to.

               MR. PALMER
No.

               ELLIE
Please, sir.

               MR. PALMER
You know the rules. You dive in the order
I give you.

               ELLIE
My grandma's having to leave.

               MR. PALMER
Not my problem.

               ELLIE
She's... She's sick.

               MR. PALMER
Sorry.

He's not.

               ELLIE
Really sick. It's the last time she'll be
able to come watch me dive.

Silence. Marsha and the Other Girls eye one another. Nod.

               MARSHA
She can go ahead of us, sir. We don't
mind.

               MR. PALMER
            (curt)
I mind. You all know the rules too.

Ellie stares at Palmer. Takes a deep breath.

               ELLIE
My grandma's been there for me all my
life. When my dad died, she moved in with
us. Looked after me when my mum had to
work. She bought me my first swim suit.
Taught me how to swim. Taught me to dive.
It's because of her that I got good at

> diving. That I'm up here now. She's been
> there for me all my life. And soon, she
> won't be there anymore.

Silence.

All the Girls on the board are staring at Mr. Palmer.

>   MR. PALMER
>   It's still no.

He turns on his heels. Walks back to the open end of the
10-metre board. Consults his list.

>   MR. PALMER (CONT'D)
>   Next...

Ellie looks at him. Then ROARS. Moves along the board with
speed and agility. Straight at Mr. Palmer.

She reaches him. Arms outstretched. Connects with him full in
the midriff.

He loses his balance. Tries to stay on the high board. Loses
the battle. Topples out over the edge. SCREAMS.

Marsha and the Girls stare down through the railings. Shocked.

>   MARSHA
>   I think he missed the water.

>   ELLIE
>   That'll be a 0 out of 10 then.

Marsha and the Other Girls LAUGH.

>   ELLIE (CONT'D)
>   I'm going to dive now. For my grandma.

>   MARSHA
>   (nods)
>   Good luck, Ellie.

Ellie steps forward to the edge of the high board. Settles
herself. Checks her breathing. Listens to her HEART BEAT as
it slows.

When she is ready, she launches herself off the board, out into
the air, towards the pool below.

The Structure of "The Diver" Scene

All film and TV scenes start with a *status quo* for the characters in the story no matter where the particular scene is located in the script. Unlike the *status quo* that exists at the start of a story, the *status quo* changes scene by scene. Depending on what has happened in the previous scene or scenes, a character arrives in the new scene with a new *status quo*.

This scene could come anywhere in a longer script. It could be the opening scene of a screen story, for example, an "Introduction to Main Character" scene to hook us into Ellie and her world. It could be the inciting incident scene mid Act 1, or the end of Act 2 scene, or maybe even the final scene of the script in Act 3.

But wherever it comes, Ellie enters the scene with a particular *status quo* that is unique to the specific scene and where it is in her story.

Part One – Set Up

Ellie arrives at the top of the 10-metre diving platform during a diving competition. There is a queue of divers ahead of her. Looking down, she realises that her mother and grandmother below are having to leave the dive meet before she has taken her dive.

Sometimes this change in *status quo* will be monumental and life-changing for the characters. At other times, it will be delicate and barely perceptible. Once the new status quo for the character in the scene is established, the conflict within the scene needs to be established.

Scene Beat 1 – Inciting Incident: Introducing the Conflict

Ellie decides to try and move up the queue so that she can take her dive before her mother and grandma leave. But Marsha, one of the other divers ahead of her in queue, complains about this.

This conflict is either external, or internal, or both. It creates the tension – the drama – in the scene.

There is plenty of external conflict in the scene for Ellie: the other divers, the queue, the location they're on, the realisation that her mother and grandma are leaving, and, of course, Mr. Palmer.

At the end of the first part of the scene – the set up – the specific goal or objective for the character in middle part of the scene is established.

Scene Beat 2 – Scene Tension: Establishing the Want/Goal

When Marsha blocks Ellie from jumping the queue, Mr. Palmer spots the commotion and comes along the board to see what's going on. He reinforces the obstacles to Ellie jumping the queue.

The specific and unique question of the scene is: Will Ellie convince Mr. Palmer to let her jump the queue and get her dive in before her grandma leaves?

The clearer and more specific to the particular scene this goal is, the better.

Part Two – Conflict: Complication / Confrontation

Ellie's goal in the scene also activates the principle of rising and falling action: as the character acts, the consequences of their actions make things more difficult for them.

There is evidently no love lost between Ellie and Mr. Palmer. Although we don't know their back story or what has preceded this scene, they seem to have some history.

Rising and falling action activates our hopes and fears for the characters in the scene. Characters have to come up with a variety of strategies to enable them to pursue their goal and keep it on track.

Ellie tries different strategies to get what she wants in the second part of the scene.

- She says she has to go first and defers to Mr. Palmer, calling him sir.
- This doesn't work so she mentions her grandma is having to leave.
- This doesn't work so she says her grandma is sick to try and gain his sympathy.
- This doesn't work so she reveals her grandma is really sick (dying). This will be her last chance to be able to watch Ellie dive. This strategy wins around Marsha and the other girls, enlisting them as allies. They are now in agreement with Ellie jumping the queue. But Palmer still isn't.
- Ellie decides to tell the truth. She owes everything to her grandma and wants to make sure her grandma knows that Ellie recognises this. Even this is not enough for Mr. Palmer.
- So Ellie resorts to taking physical action – her last strategy.

There is often a midpoint in the scene, the moment that the character is closest or furthest away from achieving their goal in the scene.

Scene Beat 3 – Midpoint + Midpoint Reversal

The closest Ellie gets to her goal – wanting Mr. Palmer to let her jump the queue so she can dive before her grandma leaves – is when Marsha and the Other Girls agree she can jump ahead of them and tell Mr. Palmer this is okay with them. The reversal of this moment is when Palmer refuses to agree to this and rounds on them, too.

The character's objective in the scene culminates at the end of the second part.

This is the point at which the character has achieved – or failed to achieve – what they want in the scene.

Scene Beat 4 – Culmination of Part Two

Once Ellie has made her big speech and Palmer again refuses to let her move ahead in the dive queue and turns his back on her, the goal of the scene and its dramatic tension is effectively over. Ellie has failed to persuade Palmer to let her jump the queue, and he reinforces this culmination by turning his back on her and moving back to the front of the dive queue.

Part Three – Consequences

In the third part, we see the consequences of the character's actions in the scene.

This final part can be very short or drawn out depending on the extent of these consequences.

There is sometimes a twist, an unexpected development that emerges logically out of the action of the scene.

Scene Beat 5 – Twist / False Resolution

Enraged, Ellie runs at Palmer, effectively pushing him off the 10-metre platform.

Failure to achieve the objective in the scene at the end of the middle part leads to a twist that opens the door for the character – leading to another scene.

Success in achieving the objective in the scene at the end of the middle part leads to a twist and closes the door for them – necessitating another scene.

Scene Beat 6 – Resolution of the Scene

Ellie fails in her goal in the scene. But her anger as a consequence of Palmer's intransigence leads to her confronting him and pushing him off the board. This opens up the door for her to have another go. She composes herself. Marsha wishes her good luck – With the dive? Or with what is going to await Ellie down below? – and Ellie launches herself into the air.

The characters and plot are propelled into the next scene – with a new *status quo*.

Ellie evidently has a new status quo to take into the next scene – Dive champion? Murderer? Both? – wherever and whatever that scene might be.

Questions to Ask About Each Scene

The following questions can also be helpful to ask when we're working on a scene whether we're the writer of the scene or working with the writer on it. Again, I've used "The Diver" scene to indicate how these can be used.

What is the character's status quo at the start of the scene?
Ellie arrives at the top of the 10-metre diving platform during a diving competition and there is a queue of rival divers ahead of her.

Whose scene is it?
It is Ellie's scene. She has the biggest goal (want) in the scene and it is this goal / objective that creates the scene and its events and action.

Is it your protagonist's scene or another character's?
It is Ellie's scene, but she may or may not be the protagonist of the larger story. We often learn more about a protagonist when we see them having to respond to and react to the actions of someone else. What if Mr. Palmer is, in fact, the protagonist, and the next scene finds him in traction in a hospital bed? What would we then learn about him from "The Diver" scene? That he's dogmatic, unreasonable, not prepared to break the rules, unfeeling, unsympathetic, unempathetic, and the victim of a misfortune because of this.

What does the character want in the scene?
Ellie wants Mr. Palmer to let her jump the queue and get her dive in before her grandma leaves.

What is the specific question of the scene?
Will Ellie convince Mr. Palmer to let her jump the queue and get her dive in before her grandma leaves?

How does the character go about pursuing this goal / objective?
Ellie tries to convince the girls ahead of her in the queue and then the coach marshalling the queue to let her jump the queue.

Who or what is the conflict in the scene?
The location of the 10-metre diving platform; the competition; her grandma leaving early; Marsha and the other girls; Mr. Palmer and his rules; Ellie's own nature.

What is the type of conflict?
External and physical as represented by the other characters in the scene and the setting; there is also internal and emotional conflict, represented by Ellie's history with her grandmother, her father's death, and maybe also her previous history with Mr. Palmer and the other girls.

What strategies does the character use or have to use to get what they want?
*Ellie tries six different strategies to try and get what she wants in the second
part of the scene.*

- She says she has to go first and defers to Mr. Palmer, calling him sir.
- She mentions her grandma is having to leave.
- She says her grandma is sick to gain his sympathy.
- She reveals her grandma is dying, winning around Marsha but not Palmer.
- Ellie says she owes everything to her grandma. Palmer is still unmoved.
- Ellie resorts to taking physical action – her last strategy.

Who wins the scene?
*Ellie wins the scene in that she overcomes Mr. Palmer to make her dive. But
the next scene will reveal at what cost she has 'won'.*

What are the Six Key Beats in the scene?
1. Ellie is in the queue and sees Grandma is leaving the dive meet.
2. Ellie wants to jump the queue to dive for her.
3. Ellie wins over Marsha and the other divers.
4. Ellie fails to convince Mr. Palmer to let her jump the queue.
5. Ellie resorts to taking physical action.
6. Ellie makes her dive

What do we learn about the characters and plot?
*Ellie owes a lot to her grandma. Ellie is perceived as an outsider. Ellie likes
diving. Ellie and Mr. Palmer don't get on. Ellie is quick-witted, clever, can
make a good argument; Ellie can snap if she doesn't get her own way.*

What do we find out in the scene that's new?
*Given this scene is a one-off, written to illustrate our approach to writing a
scene, everything we find out in it is new to us and the reader.*

How does the main character change in some way?
*Ellie changes from being a teen diver to (potentially) being a murderer.
This invokes ideas of genre and tone. Is this story a drama or a comedy?
A comedy-drama or a black comedy? Contextual considerations like these
are relevant in scene-writing at every stage of a scene's development.*

How is the story revealed to us without dialogue?
*The setting – the top of a 10-metre diving platform – is a visual one. The
outdoor diving pool suggests we are in a place with a warm climate. Ellie's
physical action in the final part is shocking and violent.*

What dialogue can you replace with action?
*The ratio of action to dialogue in the scene is 60% action / 40% dialogue.
A typical ratio for a scene in this type of screen story is 65% action /*

35% dialogue. So this ratio is something I would look at in a rewrite of the scene to try and reduce the dialogue where possible and increase the action.

What spins the story, plot, and characters into the next scene and their new status quo?

Ellie pushing Mr. Palmer off the 10-metre board and then calmly undertaking her dive creates a new status quo for her and spins the story into the next scene. It also changes the way Ellie is viewed by Marsha and the other girls, which may pay off in scenes to come.

Conclusion

"The Diver" scene was a lot of fun to write. Having been able to immerse myself in my approach to scene-writing and think deeply about it while I was working on this chapter, it is encouraging to see how a spontaneous idea for a scene involving a main character and a situation that I literally dreamt up for this purpose is able to help me exemplify and illustrate the relevant points in the chapter.

Ellie's scene-specific external physical Want and the glimpses she gives us about her deeper internal emotional Need give rise to the scene's Six Key Beats to create and structure the action and dialogue to promising effect.

Remember, this is only a first draft of the scene, and it took me less than an hour to write. Given that the art of writing is rewriting, additional contextual and subtextual elements and information would be developed in further drafts.

It also confirms the continual existence and importance to us of Aristotle's *Three Unities* in our scene-writing:

Action: a scene involves a central unit of dramatic action
– Ellie wanting to jump the diving competition queue
Place: that scene takes place in one location
– On the 10-metre platform above the diving pool
Time: that scene takes place in a defined period of time
– Its action covers 2–3 minutes of real time

Now that we have established a shared approach to writing a typical dramatic scene for film and TV, we are ready to start our journey through the core elements that can be found in these scenes:

- character
- action

- dialogue and sound
- setting
- formatting and layout

As is so often the case in screenwriting and scene-writing, we begin this journey with character.

Approach – Scene-Writing Exercise

"Scene Analysis" Exercise

Core dramatic principles like character Want and Need and the Six Key Beats emerging from these provide us with a way of structuring our stories and our scenes, ensuring that each scene is a particular, specific, inherent part of the overall narrative of our screen story. Use this scene exercise to explore some of the ideas in the chapter.

Step 1 – *Choose a scene that is memorable to you from a film or TV show you know well. Watch this scene and study it against the following questions:*

    a. What is the character's status quo at the start of the scene?
    b. Whose scene is it?
    c. Is it the protagonist's scene or another character's?
    d. What does the character want in the scene?
    e. What is the specific question of the scene?
    f. How does the character go about pursuing this goal / objective?
    g. Who or what is the conflict in the scene?
    h. What is the type of conflict? External? Internal? Both?
    i. What strategies does the character use or have to use to get what they want?
    j. Who wins the scene?
    k. What are the Six Key Beats in the scene?
    l. What do we learn about the characters and plot?
    m. What do we find out in the scene that's new?
    n. How does the main character change in some way?
    o. How is the story revealed to us without dialogue?
    p. What dialogue could you replace with action?
    q. What spins the story, plot, and characters into the next scene and their new status quo?

Step 2 – *Now choose one of your own scenes and test it against these questions.*

Notes:

As you watch or read the scene, how are Aristotle's *Three Unities* used / evident?

- *Action*: the scene involves a central unit of dramatic action
- *Place*: the scene takes place in one location
- *Time*: the scene takes place in a defined period of time

2

CHARACTER

Whose Scene Is It? Who Is in the Scene and Why?

Introduction

Creating memorable characters lies at the heart of the development of memorable stories, plots, and story worlds – and at the heart of the creation and development of memorable scenes.

Writers can get distracted during the process of development. The desire to be original is a strong one. Reimagining elements like a story's type or genre can be a useful part of its development process. It can also be counter-productive. We get so bound up in the intellectual exercise of genre reinvention or genre hybridisation (the bringing together of two or more genres in one story)[1] that our original intention of writing dynamic engaging character-driven stories for the screen gets subsumed and even lost.

When I'm teaching, I sometimes joke that Aristotle once said that there were only seven basic plots – then he inconveniently died before he'd written down what they were. Storytellers have been trying to work out what these basic plots are ever since, from the earliest story types about fratricide, regicide, quests, monsters, and so on.[2]

---

1 A highly enjoyable and successful example of a genre hybrid is zom-rom-com *Shaun of the Dead* (2004).
2 For a consideration of this, check out Christopher Booker's *The Seven Basic Plots* (Continuum, 2004). Soviet folklorist and formalist Vladimir Propp (1895–1970) also analysed Russian folktales, identifying seven character types and the narrative structure resulting from these in *Morphology of the Folktale* (1928. Translated by L. Scott; 1968).

DOI: 10.4324/9781003293927-3

As it happens, there is a much closer and more readily available means of story refreshment and reinvention that we can apply scene by scene. Yet it is one that we frequently ignore.

Ourselves.

Character and the Scene

When I lecture to students, I see individual faces looking back at me from the subdued light, each with their own lives and experiences no matter what their age, background, gender, nationality. This unique lived experience, translated by them in some way into a facet of their own screen characters and played out accordingly in their stories and plots, is what can really revive and refresh elements like genre.

Each character enters a screen story at the beginning of their life within that story and is introduced to us with a particular *status quo*, informed by what has happened to them before this story starts. In the same way, they enter each scene in that story with a particular *status quo* informed by what has happened to them previously in that story and evolving accordingly along the way.

The change in this *status quo* in the character from scene to scene can be monumental or imperceptible, or anywhere in between, depending on a number of key factors:

- where we are in the plot
- what stage the character has reached in their personal drama
- the type of story
- the genre that is at work
- the external physical objective (Want) that the character may be pursuing
- what is at stake
- the resulting obstacles and conflict they are facing
- the state of their internal emotional Need at the particular moment

But whether the change in their *status quo* as they enter the new scene from the previous one is profound or slight, life-changing or superficial, the function of that scene remains the same: to push the character, story, and plot forward in some way.

One of the first lessons to keep in mind when we begin to work on new characters is that no matter how ambitious, imaginative, or contemporary they may be, if those characters don't face challenges, if they don't face tangible obstacles, if they aren't confronted by stakes and jeopardy in every scene on their journey, if they're not forced to make life-and-death decisions, then the likelihood is that we won't be revealing enough about these characters to the audience. We deny the audience reasons to be able to engage with them and want to go on the journey scene by scene with them.

Think of our own lives and the lives of people we know. Our own characters are shaped and revealed by the obstacles and the conflicts that we face and the decisions that we consequently have to make whatever these may be. Why should it be any different with the characters we are creating, who are often our cyphers and avatars, the proponents and advocates for our ideas and beliefs?

One of the reasons I became a screenwriter in the first place is because it enabled me to put my characters in situations and story worlds that I was unlikely ever to be put in and to make decisions that I could only imagine or dream about – heroic, antiheroic, life-changing, psychotic, life-affirming, murderous, noble, sociopathic, brave.

As a result, I've written stories about characters as diverse as the first man in space, a young girl on the world's most remote island who befriends its notorious new arrival, a put-upon undertaker on a body recovery job in the so-called "Wild East", a female doctor in a Soviet women's transit camp at the end of World War II, and so on. None of them is me. All of them are different from me, from different origins, time periods, story worlds, countries. Yet all of them contain a little bit of me and my worldview, my likes and dislikes, my hopes and fears, my preoccupations and my flaws, activated in them and what they do and say scene by scene.

We often think of drama and the way a character goes through that drama as a journey, an arc. This implies that they're following a prescribed linear path. But in reality, throughout this journey, they keep coming to a series of junctions and crossroads. At each of these junctions – scenes, if you like – the character has to be active in some way and make a decision. Are they (and the plot) going to go left? Are they going to go right? Are they going to go straight on? Are they even going to have to go backward? After all, sometimes we have to reverse to be able to then go forward again.

Each of these decisions will have ramifications. They will have an effect in some way on the character, their journey, and the arc of that journey. The decisions they make at each junction point – in each scene – reveal character through cause and effect.

Faced with a choice, a character has to make a decision of some sort. Even not making a decision is a decision! This decision is causative. It has an effect, in some way, on the action of the plot, creating consequences for the character and the story. It sets up another obstacle and another causative choice, producing another effect, and so on. These physical and emotional decisions and this external and internal decision-making process, scene by scene, enable the audience to realise what's at stake for the main character, what they're trying to hide from, run away from, run towards, find out, avoid, and so on.

Inevitably, if we're creating characters that are making decisions within the story, this is going to, in turn, create the story of our film. It's going to increase the tension, conflict, stakes, and jeopardy in the plot. And it's going to increase the reader's involvement and engagement in this.

A Character Is Someone Who . . .

A helpful and dynamic way of looking at the basic requirements of a screen story of any length or type is via the deceptively simple paradigm that screen stories are generally about:

Someone who wants something badly and is having difficulty getting it.

I was introduced to this paradigm by screenwriting teachers from the University of Southern California (USC),[3] and I continue to return to it whenever I am working on a new story of my own or helping a student or writer with their story. It is particularly helpful in the early stages of story development because it encourages the writer to ask some core story questions about their idea:

- *Who is the someone?*
- *What do they want?*
- *How badly do they want it?*
- *What kind of difficulty are they having getting it?*

These questions are deceptively simple, which is why I like them. Because, in reality, they are asking writers to focus on, identify, investigate, and define the most fundamental elements of character and story development.

- **Who is the someone?** is a <u>character</u> question that opens up a myriad of potential follow-up questions that can then be asked about the particular someone in order to build up their biography.
- **What do they want?** introduces the notion of some kind of <u>story</u>, enabling the storyteller to start to ask more and more questions that will drill down into the specifics and nuances of that story and begin to build the <u>plot</u>.
- **How badly do they want it?** suggests <u>stakes</u>, the notion that characters are in life-and-death situations in their world regardless of story type or genre. After all, not many people go to the cinema or commit to a long-running

---

3 David Howard and Martin Daniel from the University of Southern California Graduate Screenwriting program, at the Maurits Binger Film Institute, Amsterdam, September 1996. I was the first UK screenwriter selected for the first 5-month feature film lab (1996–97) with my original project *Boney and Betsy*.

TV series to watch stories about people who want things quite badly. Generally, characters want what they want in their particular story world to the exclusion of everything – and often, everyone – else. Even in a comedy. *Particularly* in a comedy.

- **What kind of difficulty are they having getting it?** proposes <u>conflict, obstacles, and antagonists</u>. These can be a spectrum of things depending on the story type, genre, and story world, from tangible external factors like other characters or aliens or monsters to deep internal factors that have remained long ignored and long hidden until the story starts – the monsters within.

When I shared this paradigm with a group of writers at one of my workshops at The Screenwriters' Festival[4] in the early 2000s, one of the participants, Julian Fellowes,[5] Academy Award–winning writer of *Gosford Park* (2001) and subsequently the creator of *Downton Abbey* (2010), suggested an additional fifth question to me and the group based on his, then relatively new, experience of writing in and for Hollywood:

- **Why are we rooting for them** (i.e., for the character)? which introduces the idea of the <u>audience</u> being a focal point of the creative process.

Thanks to Julian's insightful intervention, I have incorporated this fifth question ever since, not least because it reflects one of the cornerstones of my approach in early story and character development. You have to know how your story ends and your intended effect of this on the audience, even in the most basic terms – my character lives or dies, is happy or unhappy, their internal emotional Need is resolved or unresolved, the audience feels happy or sad, and so on.

In reality, character and story development is a process of reverse engineering, in which you come up with a character and a basic story – impulsive, thematic, philosophical, emotional, situational, event-driven, biographical – reflect on how that story might end, and then go back to the beginning and install a series of events, twists, and turns that will convey the character(s) and the audience to that end.

4 Screenwriters' Festival Cheltenham, 2006–2009, Festival Director: David Pearson.
5 Julian also said that you're not a professional writer until you've been fired by Hollywood. I don't necessarily agree with that, though I was fired by Hollywood via fax a week after the director told me how good my new draft of his movie was.

A Character in a Scene Is Also . . .

Someone who wants something badly and is having difficulty getting it.

Over the years, I've found that this simple paradigm works for scene-writing, too.

Choose a favourite scene from a film or TV show. Better still, choose a scene from something you're working on. As you contemplate or work on this scene, ask yourself:

- Who is the someone in the scene?
- What does this someone want in that scene specifically?
- How badly do they want it?
- What kind of difficulty in the scene are they having getting what they want?
- Why are we the audience rooting for them in some way?

The more we understand our characters and the more we are able to invest in them, the deeper the work we are able to do on them. The more we can think about their life up to the beginning of the story, the more likely they are to inhabit that story when it starts and live in it and its scenes. And if we understand our characters, then there's a good chance that the audience – and for most screenwriters that 'audience' is in reality a reader – is likely to engage with them and understand them, too.

If we don't understand them, if we don't have a clear view about them, if we're uncertain about key things – and this is inevitable in early stages of development – if we never clarify those things, if we never make key decisions about them, if we never undertake the work to define the character and make them deep and meaningful and functioning and everything else, it is very hard for us then to create vivid, believable, engaging, and compelling characters.

"The Diver" Scene

Let's return to the scene that I shared in the Approach chapter involving our character Ellie up on the 10-metre diving platform and apply this paradigm:

Who is the someone? Ellie. She has the biggest goal in the scene and makes the key decisions that create the scene and its action.

What does she want? She wants Mr. Palmer to let her jump the queue of divers ahead of her on the diving platform and make her dive before her grandma has to leave the competition.

How badly does she want this? Badly enough to reveal the truth to Marsha, the other divers, and Mr. Palmer that her grandma is dying and Ellie wants to acknowledge her debt to her. And ultimately, badly enough to push Palmer off the 10-metre platform.

What kind of difficulty is she having getting it (i.e., jumping the queue and diving)? The setting, situation, her grandma leaving, the other divers, the rules, and Mr. Palmer create varying degrees of difficulty for Ellie in pursuit of her Want / goal / objective in the scene.

Why are we rooting for her? Hopefully, we feel sympathy for Ellie and her situation. Mr. Palmer is unreasonable, especially so given the situation Ellie shares with him. She is quick-witted, determined, seemingly the victim of an undeserved misfortune,[6] up against it, an outsider, prepared to take direct – extreme – action. We begin to have empathy for her.

All this is created and activated in one scene, in less than three minutes of the script.

"The Diver" Story Scene By Scene

Ellie's propensity to take direct action against whomever or whatever stands in her way is common knowledge in her story world right from the moment we first meet her in this scene. If we were to use Ellie and this scene as the starting point or inspiration to develop a longer screen story, such as a short film, a feature, or a TV drama pilot, this might help us understand who Ellie is or could be, how she functions as the main character of her story, how she creates that story, and what decisions she makes that begin to reveal her character and create the plot.

Ellie's character, therefore, has a core function in determining the genre of the scene and the script she may be located in. Equally, the genre we decide to use, in turn, influences character construction and development and the type of scenes that character is in. Depending on the way we choose to present this character and her story, the subject-matter and its scenes could be those of a social drama, a horror, a tragedy, or a black comedy. We might elect to create scenes in which Ellie is forced to face and make life-changing decisions as a consequence of pushing her coach off the high-diving platform.

But this may not be the type of character or situation that we want to tell the reader about and share with them. It might be more enjoyable to subvert the story and celebrate Ellie's spontaneity and the fact that she doesn't care. Ellie's decisions, good or bad, should create the story, forcing her to make a series of escalating decisions scene by scene that have consequences for her and everyone else involved all the way through the film.

---

6 c.f. Michael Hauge's steps for creating empathy in a character, *Writing screenplays that sell* (Hauge, M; Collins, 1988).

Why Does This Story Start Today?

Early on in development, I ask my students and writers a key question:

Why does your story start today?

Again, the silence that this simple question can cause is deafening. And revealing.
If the writer is unsure how to answer this, I follow up:

Why didn't your story start yesterday? Why doesn't it start tomorrow?

Let's apply this to Ellie as if she was a character we were developing in a screen story:

Why does Ellie's story start today? Why not yesterday? Why not tomorrow?

My answer is: this story starts today because this is the day that she is driven to push Mr. Palmer off the 10-metre board. At the moment, it happens in the opening scene *in media res*,[7] right up front. Whatever has been going on in her life before this scene and no matter how much she has been trying to ignore things up till now, what happens in this scene is incontrovertible: pushing Palmer off the diving board is going to have consequences. And it potentially means she will have to take more action. Yesterday? She didn't push him off the platform yesterday. Tomorrow? She would have already pushed him off the day before. Her *status quo* would be different. The plot – *her* plot – a different plot – would already be underway.

This scene presents Ellie from the get-go of her story as her own person. Perceived by the other girls in the scene as an outsider, this would be reinforced in scenes to come by the attitude of people in her community towards her, depending on the direction in which we choose to take her story and her character forward – as victim, rebel, murderer, etc. On the basis of this scene – like the best screen characters – Ellie is undaunted. When she sets her mind on something, it becomes the most important thing in her life. She wants it to the exclusion of everything else. As my first screenwriting teacher[8] once told me: "The man with the fire at his back jumps the widest river". By pushing Palmer off the 10-metre board, Ellie now has the fire at her back.

The more your character has the fire at their back, the more heat they're feeling, the more heat we can expose them to in every scene, then the bigger the decisions they have to make and the bigger the obstacles they have to

7 *In media res* – in the middle of things. Usually the best place for a screen story to start.
8 Summer 1994. Jan Fleischer, Head of Screenwriting, NFTS, UK.

overcome. In this way, Ellie will be driven on – propelled – through the film to make decisions, to make choices.

If this were to be the opening scene of a longer screen story, from the outset, Ellie's character is presented to us in a particular way in her world – initially as the biggest outsider, the most desperate to dive for her grandma, the most antagonistic to Mr. Palmer, and the most unexpectedly violent person in that world.

Scenes as a Character Development Tool

Writing scenes like this can be a helpful way of developing your protagonist and other key characters in even the very earliest stage of development. I became much more interested in Ellie once I'd written her scene for this book, got her up on her feet in the story, and presented her with an antagonistic situation and characters. To chart the movement and change of your characters from scene to scene through their story, ask yourself the following about your characters:

- Who changes?
- Who is going to change?
- Who has to change?
- Who doesn't have to change?
- Who doesn't change?

The nature of your characters' change and the degree to which they do or don't change will inform core story elements like plot, genre, tone, atmosphere, and style.

An unrepentant Ellie who rampages through life scene by scene taking pleasure in sorting out in increasingly extreme ways the people who oppose her or stand in her way – and scaring us and / or making us laugh in the process – will be a very different character to a repentant Ellie who sets out to change the direction of her life in some way as a consequence of her actions that afternoon on the 10-metre diving platform.

Depending on the way the writer sees the world and the type of characters and stories they are interested in creating to share that worldview, one of these two approaches – or a totally different approach – will appeal more as a starting point for a story. This begins to inform the decisions we make about the Want and Need of our character, the key beats that character's particular story requires, and the scenes that will show and tell the plot of this in the most effective, compelling, memorable, and meaningful way.

Allied to this notion of character change are other investigative questions:

- How is the character going to change?
- What are they going to change?

- Where are they going to change?
- When are they going to change?
- Why are they going to change?

The Forces of Opposition

At the start of her story, Ellie has a pretty confrontational approach to her world. Whatever her Want in Act 2 turns out to be and whatever she is trying to do in the scenes in that act will create the plot in the middle of the story and shape it. Her decisions and actions will mean she herself creates major obstacles and forces of opposition for her character to overcome.

Initially, Marsha and Mr. Palmer are forces of opposition to Ellie, presenting as archetypal teen-drama antagonists: the rival girl diver, the bullying sports coach. But maybe this script is not actually going to be about that archetypal story. Depending on our chosen genre, tone, and story type, there may well be bigger, more dangerous forces of opposition just around the corner for Ellie in the scenes to come, characters who will stand in her way, thwart her, force her to change her plan, and create conflict, obstacles, difficulty for her.

As she pursues her main goal in Act 2, there will need to be a lot of twists, turns, ups and downs in the scenes along the way to create rising and falling action in the plot and escalating hopes and fears in the audience. Ranged against Ellie in every scene will be her forces of opposition, embodied in characters that are opposed to her and her goal or Want in some way and create antagonisms and conflict for her. Their existence and presence in the story will create significant obstacles that she has to overcome. After all, the character with the fire at her back jumps the widest river.

Different Character Types and Their Functions in Scenes

Another way of looking at the characters that are needed in your scenes to help or hinder the progress of your main character is to divide them up into character types and archetypes. As you begin to map out your story and scenes, various kinds of characters are available to you:

PROTAGONIST / MAIN CHARACTER / HERO[9] – the protagonist creates the story and plot of your film or TV idea through the existence of their Want and Need. The so-called 'hero', they are the main character of the story but not always the main character of every scene. Indeed, we often learn more about a main character from the way they behave and react in someone else's scene.

---

9 Terms like *hero* and *antihero* are non-gendered ones in this book.

ANTAGONIST – the antagonist is generally the character who stands in opposition to your main character or protagonist in the plot. Depending on the Want and Need of your main character and the type of story or genre you are developing, this antagonist may be the main love interest, an archetypal 'baddie', supernatural, monstrous, extra-terrestrial, or a confronting force for good for a flawed antihero.

ENEMY – the antagonist may or may not be an enemy *per se* of your protagonist, but an enemy in a scene is always a force of opposition and remains an enemy throughout – unless they are transformed for some reason from an enemy into a friend (see next).

ENEMY WHO BECOMES A FRIEND – This character fulfills the same function as the enemy in your story until the scene in which they change sides. This is usually prompted by some kind of insightful recognition that occurs within them because of their Need coming into contact with the main character. Often someone who has been wronged in some way, their change of sides frequently results in an heroic sacrifice in order to save the protagonist and the quest and ensure victory.

BEST FRIEND – usually the confidant of the main character. In certain genres, the best friend is often a solitary character. In that respect, they can also function as a warning to the main character about the future that may await them if they do not recognise, respond to, and resolve their internal emotional Need.

FALSE FRIEND / BETRAYER – starts their story as a confidant of the main character but ends up betraying them in a scene that is always shocking because it imperils the protagonist, their plan, and their 'family'.

LOVE INTEREST – the love interest may or may not also be the protagonist's main antagonist, again depending on the main genre you are working in.

MENTOR – the mentor is generally the character that the protagonist seeks advice from and confides in. They can incorporate one or more of our other character types here.

RAISONNEUR[10] – the character who keeps recapping the story and its themes in scenes; often the truth-teller for the audience, if not always for the other characters around them.

ONE-STRING CHARACTER – with no character arc to speak of, the one-string character generally only appears in one scene or a short sequence of scenes, fulfilling a specific function in the scene(s), either obstructing or helping the key character(s) in it.

MUSCLE – similar to the one-string character and, as the name suggests, fulfilling a specific role in the scene.

---

10 A character in a dramatic work who acts as a mouthpiece for the opinions of the play's author, usually displaying a superior or more detached view of the action than the other characters. *The Oxford Dictionary of Literary Terms*.

STORY WORLD CHARACTER – often overlooked in development, these characters have a vital function, helping to reinforce the veracity and authenticity of the genre, tone, and atmosphere of our chosen story world scene by scene.

This is not an exhaustive list and you may well be able to identify other character types and archetypes that fulfil a specific role in a scene and are useful to the progression of our main character and our stories. The key point is these types exist and activating them in our scenes adds variety, depth, and contrast to those scenes.

The Importance of Character to the Architecture of a Scene

By now, we have a clear sense of the importance of character – and different character types and archetypes – in building our story and its scenes. Because character helps us to determine key elements of every story and scene we write:

1. Character has a core **function**: enabling the story to exist scene by scene.
2. Character provides **form**: creating the shape of our story and scenes through the Want or Need of the main character and the specific goals and objectives of the other characters in each scene.
3. Character creates **structure**: enabling us to organise the parts of our story and reflect and confirm these – plot beats, genre, tone – in each scene.
4. Character requires **research**: verifying the world of our story and ensuring the veracity of this world and its characters moment by moment, scene by scene.

So how does all this come together and work in practice?

Learning to Play

Early in my career when I was training to be an assistant theatre director, I spent 18 months at the Unicorn Theatre for Children at the Arts Theatre, London.[11] The company commissioned new plays from leading writers such as Adrian Mitchell, Penny Casdagli, Bryony Lavery (*Sore Points*)[12] and David Wood (*The Meg and Mog Show*).[13] It considered itself to be the UK's national

---

11 1985–86.
12 I commissioned and co-directed *Sore Points* (Unicorn Summer Tour, 1986).
13 I was an assistant director to David Wood on *The Meg and Mog Show* (Arts Theatre, 1985–86).

theatre for children – a national theatre whose main audience just happened to be children – and its ethos and work were driven by this, employing the best writers, directors, actors, and crew to deliver new work for its audience. It was a wonderful place to learn about character and story – and to understand the importance of play in the development of these.

As the assistant director, my duties included attending rehearsals of each play with its director and cast. Such were the financial pressures on the company in the mid-1980s that we found ourselves short of an actor for one play, and I was inveigled by Artistic Director Nick Barter to act in it, making an unexpected West End debut in Nigel Townsend's *Younger Brother Son*, a new play for 8–12-year-olds that ran at the Arts Theatre from 12 October to 10 November 1985. In rehearsals, I learnt to juggle, do a self-propelled headstand from lying flat on the floor, mime and puppetry, and *tai chi*. I was also introduced to a fundamental aspect of story-telling that I retain and use to this day and which lies at the heart of my teaching of character, story, and scene-writing.

Character Status

Status has been integral to drama since its earliest origins because it has been integral to human society since our earliest origins. Regardless of gender, ethnicity, nationality, culture, class, country, century, or era, status has existed in and been inherent to all of these.

For the writer, status exists in every character group, situation, and set up – in every scene we are likely to be in, let alone write. Plays by writers as diverse as Aeschylus, Shakespeare, Beckett, or Kane; movies as diverse as those by Akira Kurosawa, Alfred Hitchcock, Chloé Zhao, or Bong Joon-ho; and TV series as diverse as *Breaking Bad* (2008–13), *Squid Game* (2021-), *Fleabag* (2016–19), *Bridgerton* (2020-), or *Dad's Army* (1968–77) depend on, revolve around, explore, and present status in each scene as an integral part, reflection, and exploration of the human condition.

Indeed, during my interview with theatre director John Dexter for my first job after drama school to be his assistant on his production of Jean-Paul Sartre's 4-hour historical epic *The Devil and the Good Lord*[14] at the Lyric Theatre, Hammersmith[15] in July 1984, Dexter concluded by declaring: "I believe in the Master / Servant relationship. I'm the Master, you're the Servant."

I accepted the job on that basis. And so it proved. Paid in luncheon vouchers, my servant duties included carrying Dexter's briefcase to meetings in the West End, driving him to the countryside to see his dogs (recently arrived

14 Written in 1951, translated by Frank Hauser 1984.
15 Opened 26 September 1984, Lyric Theatre, Hammersmith.

IMAGE 2.1 Bristol Old Vic Theatre School, 1984 ©Lisa Bowerman.

from New York) in quarantine, and running his bath. They also involved rehearsing scenes of the play with the cast in Hammersmith when he was unable to undertake this due to his ongoing ill health. Thus, by the time I was introduced to a more appropriate exploration of status at the Unicorn, I was already well-acquainted with it at a personal level.

One of the 'bibles' I was introduced to at the Unicorn was *Impro* by Keith Johnstone,[16] his book on theatre craft and, in particular, the improvisatory techniques and exercises that he evolved at The Royal Court Theatre to foster spontaneity, play, and narrative skills in theatre-making when he ran the Writers' Group there.

Grouped around four sections – *Status, Spontaneity, Narrative Skills,* and *Masks and Trance* – Johnstone's ideas and propositions about status, in particular, remain as fundamental to my ideas on character, story, and scene-writing today as they were when I first encountered them in 1985:

> Status is a confusing term unless it's understood as something one *does*. You may be low in social status, but play high, and vice versa. For example:
>
> ```
> TRAMP: 'Ere! Where are you going?
> DUCHESS: I'm sorry, I didn't quite catch...
> TRAMP: Are you deaf as well as blind?
> ```
>
> Audiences enjoy a contrast between the status played and the social status. We always like it when a tramp is mistaken for the boss, or the boss for a tramp. Hence plays like *The Inspector General.*[17] Chaplin liked to play the person at the bottom of the hierarchy and then lower everyone.
>
> I should really talk about dominance and submission, but I'd create a resistance. Students who will agree readily to raising or lowering their status may object if asked to 'dominate' or 'submit'.
>
> Status seems to me to be a useful term, providing the difference between the status you are and the status you play is understood.[18]

This is, of course, as true for real life as it is for fiction, make-believe, and story-telling. But for the screenwriter, the difference between the status a character may have and the status that character actually plays from scene

---

16 *Impro: Improvisation and the Theatre*, Keith Johnstone, Faber & Faber 1979; Routledge 1981.

17 *The Inspector General (also known as The Government Inspector)* by Nikolai Gogol (Premiered 1 May 1836, St. Petersburg, Russia).

18 *Status* (p. 28), *Impro* by Keith Johnstone (1979).

to scene is a fundamental part of character creation and story development. Movies and TV shows as diverse as *Toy Story* (1995), *Parasite* (2019), *The Crown* (2016–23), *The Office* (2001–3), *Breaking Bad,* and *Little Miss Sunshine* (2006) revolve around characters and the stories and plots that emanate from these characters' perceived, assumed, and actual statuses; the favourite toy and the new toy; the poor family in the slum and the rich family on the hill; the Queen and everyone else; the paper boss and his paper team; the new meth[19] maker, the drug cartels, and the DEA;[20] the father desperate to be a winner and his loser family.

Status in Scenes

Armed with my newfound knowledge of and passion for status, a desire to play, and a bunch of rolled-up newspaper truncheons, I first put my status ideas into practice in a workshop with a group of students in Swansea[21] at the 1986 National Student Drama Festival (NSDF) in a series of playful exercises – effectively, scenes.

The stage actor Roger Rees,[22] who played the title character in the Royal Shakespeare Company's renowned adaptation[23] of Charles Dickens' novel *The Life and Adventures of Nicholas Nickleby*, was also a teacher at that year's festival. He generously offered to participate in the workshop with me. I knew I was onto something when Roger, one of the most notable classical actors of his generation, ended up sitting on a 'throne' in the centre of the room wearing a newspaper crown – the supposed master with several student servants hitting him on the head with their paper whackers.

Just as status influences the way a character acts and behaves, it influences the way they talk and interact with other characters.

The status of a character at any moment in a screen-story influences and affects how core facets of that character, such as behaviour, attitude, perception, portrayal, goals, stakes, and conflict, are presented to the audience and interpreted scene by scene.

In archetypal 'Master / Servant'[24] stories, the actual status that exists between the master and servant characters from scene to scene is often

---

19 Methamphetamine.
20 Drug Enforcement Agency.
21 The 1986 National Student Drama Festival was hosted by the University of Swansea.
22 Roger Rees, actor, director, writer (1944–2015).
23 Adapted by David Edgar and co-directed by Trevor Nunn and John Caird, *The Life and Adventures of Nicholas Nickleby* opened at the Aldwych Theatre, London, in June 1980 initially for eight weeks. A sell-out, it ran for two years in London and on Broadway.
24 The terms *Master/Servant* are non-gendered in this book.

more complex, complicated, and less obvious than it appears at first sight. There is:

Perceived Status – conferred by birth, rank, age, gender, ethnicity, class, education, etc. It reflects how the character is viewed by other people.

Assumed Status – reinforced by birth, rank, age, gender, ethnicity, class, education, etc. It reflects how the character views themselves.

Earned Status – achieved by merit, collaboration, understanding, talent, etc. The character's actual, factual, truthful status.

Depending on the story you are wanting to tell, these different versions of status play out in the characters and their behaviours and actions from scene to scene.

The King's Speech (2010)

Status dominates every scene in the archetypal master / servant story *The King's Speech*.[25] Set predominately in the UK in the 1930s, in the lead up to the outbreak of World War II, everything in the story and its scenes serves to accentuate the difference in status between Prince Bertie (soon to become King George VI) and commoner Lionel Logue. And yet, status-wise, things are rarely what they first seem, as the following three scenes in the film reveal:

Perceived Status / Seduction Scene – "Opening Speech" 1924–25. Bertie is preparing to make a speech at Wembley Stadium. A royal prince, he has the perceived status to match the formal occasion, conferred on him by the people there. After all, giving speeches is what royals do. However, as soon as Bertie starts to speak, his stammer is evident. We see the reaction of the people around him (including his wife Elizabeth), and we realise the extent of his problem. His perceived status transforms into his actual status – one of pity and embarrassment from the very people he is, in theory, looked up to by and leads as a member of the royal family.

In this scene, Bertie tries to 'seduce' his willing audience in a suitable setting for a royal speech but fails miserably. The scene sets up vividly the rest of the film and its central dilemma.

Assumed Status / Seduction Scene – "First Meeting" 1925. Bertie's wife Elizabeth is desperate to find someone to help him with his speech impediment

---

25 Written by David Seidler (1937–2024) who won the 2011 Academy Award for Best Original Screenplay.

(stammer). None of the prince's knighted doctors have been able to, so in desperation, the couple visit speech doctor Lionel Logue, an Australian with unconventional methods. In their first meeting, Bertie assumes that he has the higher status. After all, he always does. However, Logue soon puts him right. He calls him Bertie and tells him he can't smoke. He tells the prince: "My place, my rules". Bertie's assumed status is somewhat different from Logue's perceived status, the actual status (for now, at least), creating comedy, conflict, and tension.

In this scene, the reluctant Bertie is 'seduced' unwillingly and unwittingly by the unconventional Logue into becoming his patient.

Earned or Achieved Status / Seduction Scene – "The King's Speech" 1939. Britain is at war with Germany. Bertie (now King George VI) has to address his people throughout the British Empire. Lionel is there, helping Bertie, conducting him as he delivers the speech of his life. Both men present as equals – the new king and the man who has enabled him to assume the mantle of that king. Bertie has earned the status of a king, with Logue's help. But he no longer needs to impose this status on Logue. King George VI has earned his place – achieved his place – as one of Britain's most beloved monarchs in its history, reinforced by the speech he is now able to make.

In this scene, at the British Empire's greatest moment of crisis, Bertie 'seduces' his global audience into believing that they are ready to face together whatever is to come. He does this with the help and support of Lionel.

As you can see in my previous summaries, scenes in which one character is trying to 'seduce' another character into agreeing to do something are common in screenwriting. Seduction has been an archetypal situation in storytelling on stage and screen since the beginning of drama. Indeed, since Adam, Eve, the serpent, and the apple.

Status in "The Diver" Scene

On the surface, our teen diver character Ellie is low status, a 16-year-old schoolgirl who is trying to push her way to the front of the diving queue against the wishes of her fellow competitors – higher status due to superior numbers if nothing else – and the rules imposed by higher status adult and coach Mr. Palmer. This could be viewed as the epitome of low status – a teen girl coming up against her peer group and the male patriarchy – reinforced by the antagonistic characters and the situation and setting in Ellie's story world. In the typical story of this type, the young outsider in their *status quo* at the start can generally only be low status compared to their parents, rivals, enemies, teachers, community, and society.

However, Ellie delights in subverting our preconceptions by her actions in the scene, effectively reframing and re-presenting the character and story type. As we see in the scene, Ellie takes action to raise her status, winning over Marsha and her contemporaries in the process, and ultimately overcoming Mr. Palmer by pushing him off the platform, removing him from her world and that of the other girls.

Only time – and events in the scenes to come – will tell how long Ellie's newly established high status lasts and what may threaten and change it.

Solo Characters in Scenes and Their Status

It is relatively straightforward to understand and activate the concept of status between two or more characters in scenes. Differences in status are inherent, built into human existence and behaviour.

But my ongoing work in this area reveals that there is also status in scenes in which there is only one character. Because settings, story worlds, genres, props, and ongoing action and events by their nature impose, create, and reinforce status, too.

The solitary astronaut orbiting Earth in a stricken ship, the single rower crossing the ocean in a Force 10 storm, the teenager imprisoned in a locked space all exist in some kind of status created by the world they find themselves in, and their response to this and their reaction to their specific situation reveals character.

When working on a scene with a single character in it, how are you using the elements in that scene for or against your character to enhance, deepen, confirm their status?

How does the character's status help determine:

- the action and events in the scene?
- the arc of the character through the scene?
- the key beats and events of it?
- the turning point(s)?
- how the scene culminates?

Vice versa, how is the character's status determined by each of these listed?

Ultimately, who wins the scene? The setting or story world? Or the character? What is the consequence of this, and how does it create a new *status quo* to convey the character and their story into a new scene? We will return to these questions throughout this book, in particular in Chapter 9, when we look at a sequence of scenes.

Conclusion

As this chapter has proposed, characters are fundamental to the creation of effective dramatic scenes at every stage of story and plot development.

The specific type of character and their intended function at a particular moment in the script is integral to the dramatic action in the specific scene. Throughout a script, its character or characters influence what's going on in each scene, and, in turn, what is going on in each scene influences and affects the character or characters.

The notion of status, its ever-presence and its fluidity and ever-changing nature when it comes to our characters, is key to this.

Screenwriting teaching approaches often refer to the *status quo* that the main character has coming into the story. But as we have seen, characters enter each scene with a *status quo* that should ideally be evolving and changing along with their status from scene to scene as a result of the dramatic action of the plot, the conflict they face, and the decisions they have to make.

Bertie in *The King's Speech* enters the final scenes of his story with a particular and distinctive *status quo*, but this *status quo* is very different – should be very different – to the *status quo* he first entered the story world with. The movement of a character through the plot is aided and affected by the movement of their *status quo* from scene to scene, and this will also be reflected in the level of their status.

Key to this for the screenwriter is how we want the reader to view a character in each scene. For example:

- What *status quo* do they enter the scene with?
- How is this reflected in their current status at the start of the scene?
- What are they trying to do in the scene?
- Where are they doing it?
- When are they doing it?
- Why are they doing it?
- How are they doing it?
- Who is trying to stop them doing it? Why? How?
- Who is trying to help them do it? Why? How?
- What is different for them in some way by the end of the scene?
- What is their new *status quo*?
- How has their status changed?

Now that we have looked at a number of the key elements and core aspects that are involved in developing characters scene by scene and we've begun to think about our own characters in relation to these ideas, it is time to look at the dramatic action that is integral to our characters in every scene of a script and shows us their stories.

Character – Scene-Writing Exercise

"Introduction to Main Character Scene" Exercise

The first time we meet a character like Ellie in a story is vital. What do we learn about them the first time we see them? What words come to mind to describe them? What is their 'Most' quality? What does the reader learn and take away about them?

Now take a character, situation, and scene you're working on or come up with a new character and a situation and scene they might be in. Locate them in some kind of story world.

- What words come to mind to describe them when we first see them?
- What is their 'Most' quality – (i.e., what are they the "most" in their world)?
- What do we learn about them the first time we see them?
- What is their *status quo* at the start of the scene? What is their status during it? How do these fluctuate and change?
- What do we take away about them?
- What do you want us to learn and take away?

3

ACTION

What Is the Scene About? What Do We See Happening in the Scene and Why?

Introduction

"Ever tried. Ever failed. No matter. Try again. Fail again. Fail better".[1] Playwright Samuel Beckett's provocative quote about the process of writing applies equally to our own lifelong journeys as screenwriters as well as to the journeys of our film and TV characters as they strive to take action because of – often in spite of – their Wants and Needs.

Two fundamental components are at work for the writer and the audience throughout every scene in a screen story:

1. What we are *seeing* via the screen at any given moment
2. What we are *hearing* via the screen at any given moment

This presentation of image and sound and their mode of presentation scene by scene in the ongoing evolving dramatic action are integral to the way we tell our stories. Their synthesis on screen can be harmonious, dissonant, or anywhere in between.

Most often, the presentation of images on screen is conveyed by some kind of action. We see someone and they are doing something or reacting to something. Or we are shown something or witness something that makes us privy to new information. Or we are deliberately misdirected about the plot in some way. Or we have something revealed to us which the character

---

1 Samuel Beckett, Nobel Laureate author and playwright (1906–89). Originally published in Beckett's short prose work *Worstward Ho!* (1983).

DOI: 10.4324/9781003293927-4

doesn't know and this new knowledge involves us and makes us complicit in the visual storytelling in some way.

Likewise, sound. Sound for the screenwriter predominately involves a) the dialogue of our characters –what they are saying and / or what we are hearing – and b) the key sounds that reflect the action in the scene and add to the narrative, the storytelling, and our understanding or interpretation of that action. The next chapter looks specifically at dialogue and explores related ideas arising from our work on action in this chapter.

What Is Action?

Action in film and TV is a term most of us are familiar with, from the notion of characters taking action in screen stories and doing something for a particular purpose, to the so-called action[2] movie itself, with its related genres such as action-adventure and action-thriller and tropes and obligatory scenes that the audience expects in these types of films.

'Action!' is also traditionally called on a film or TV set in conjunction with a clapperboard to alert the crew and instigate the start of the filming of a designated shot or 'take'.

As far as the screenwriter is concerned, we generally consider action to be all the written content in a scene that reveals what we are proposing the audience will see on screen moment by moment in our story.

But, in its most basic form, what actually is action? How does it operate in dramatic storytelling? What is its function?

Put simply: what does action do and how does it do it? How does action work?

How Action Works

Action in scenes happens in the present tense, in real time, as we are watching it:

EXT. CITY — DAY

Malek walks along the busy street looking for the diner.

---

2 Arista Special: 'Genre', London, July 2004 defined the action movie as: An active heroic protagonist struggles against evil through a clash of almost entirely physical, external force. The kind of force required from the hero will not change but will become more and more amplified as time passes. The middle of the plot will be a war of attrition and the hero will go through two false dawns in the final part before they finally emerge victorious.

As this basic line of action indicates, action is most often a fusion of the fundamentals of screenwriting – the subject, a verb, and an object:

Subject – what we're looking at, usually a character
Verb – what the subject is doing
Object – the parameters in which they are doing it

```
EXT. CITY — DAY

Malek (SUBJECT) walks along (VERB) the busy street looking for
the diner (OBJECT).
```

Note how the use of adjectives and adverbs – so-called descriptive words – is kept to a minimum. The only ones in my example are ALONG and BUSY.

Bear in mind that there are a number of verbs that could replace WALK and be more active and descriptive and add to the character, for example, STRIDE, SAUNTER, SWERVE, STAGGER. It all depends on how the writer sees Malek and what we want the reader to understand or infer from the way we posit the action of him walking.

Even a simple line of action works subliminally on the reader and can be indicative. The arrangement and presentation of the subject / verb / object in Malek walks along the busy street, looking for the diner suggest further key information to the reader about the action and how it might be filmed. For example:

- We are showing Malek (the subject) in the context of the busy street, which suggests a wide shot rather than a close-up.
- Malek's movement and its mode (the verb) could be captured by a static shot. Or it might suggest to a director / director of photography (DoP) that they track the camera with him.
- Looking for the diner (the object) is Malek's goal. This could be incorporated into the establishing shot or a director / DoP might want to change the frame / shot here to accentuate Malek's specific, known objective.

Action = Cause + Effect

For the screenwriter, action is intended to show us the story and advance the plot. An analysis of action as it happens scene by scene in any medium of writing for the screen looks something like this – our 12 steps of action, if you like:

I. *We see a character in a scene with some kind of physical goal* (**WANT / DESIRE / OBJECTIVE**)

  II. *who is facing difficult circumstances (**OBSTACLES**)*
 III. *and increasing opposition (**CONFLICT / ANTAGONISTS**)*
  IV. *so they have to make a decision to do something (**DRAMA**) to pursue this goal.*
   V. *The decision they make has a consequence (**CAUSE**)*
  VI. *changing the story (**EFFECT**)*
 VII. *moving it and the plot forward (**ACTION**)*
VIII. *and establishing a new situation (**NEW SCENE**)*
  IX. *As a result, the character is now in a new scene facing even more difficult circumstances (**OBSTACLES**)*
   X. *and even greater forces of opposition (**CONFLICT / ANTAGONISTS**)*
  XI. *and still has a goal (**WANT / DESIRE / OBJECTIVE**)*
 XII. *causing them – forcing them – to have to make another decision, and so on.*

In your script, whatever its intended medium or length, its action shows your story to us. As we read the action through a scene, we are being encouraged to imagine the story in our heads from the way you are describing it to us and what you are making your character do or putting them through. The action you create through the behaviour and decisions of your characters pushes forward the plot.

We read a scene, we follow your character(s) in it, and we engage with them and their story. All the while, the plot is being pushed forward as we discover new information about the characters and the story.

As well as creating action, the decisions our characters make scene by scene to overcome the conflicts they face also reveal character. Whatever the decision your character makes, it is causative in some way. Good decision or bad decision, the consequent action this creates has an effect on the decision-maker, their story, other characters, and the plot.

For example, a character in a story is explicitly warned never to go into that wood, or else. So what do they do? Better still in drama, what do they <u>have to do</u> for some reason? They are compelled to go into that wood, and the audience is left thinking, that's a bad decision. And it is not going to end well.

Good or bad, their decision reveals some sort of aspect of their character. It might reveal stupidity. It might reveal stubbornness. It might initially reveal arrogance but, ultimately, reveal hidden depths of strength or bravery. As the writer, you decide what you want it to reveal. But, rest assured, it reveals something – all because the character has made a decision.

It has a consequence that affects the story and pushes the plot forward. It may advance it in a way the character doesn't want. It pushes and pushes, and the character might be trying to resist and resist. But they can't. Ultimately, action is inexorable, relentless, unstoppable. Like the tide rising on a beach, there is nothing we can do to stop it or hold it back, as King Canute found out.[3]

Writing Action

So, how do we go about writing action or improving our approach to this? Let's imagine a scene. I am going to get the ball rolling by coming up with a setting so I can share with you my process for writing a scene and how I begin to evolve the action. It just so happens that I first mapped out these ideas on a train travelling to London on a Sunday morning in early autumn, so what better place to set this hypothetical scene than on that train?

```
INT. TRAIN - DAY
```

So far so good. Except that it isn't. There are already questions that will be asked – should be asked – by us as a consequence of the lack of specificity in the setting TRAIN. Where we locate the action of the scene should be integral to that action, have a direct effect on it, and potentially be affected, in turn, by it. Specifically, where on the train are we setting the action of this particular scene?

```
INT. PASSENGER COMPARTMENT, TRAIN - DAY
INT. CORRIDOR, TRAIN - DAY
INT. CAFE AREA, TRAIN — DAY
INT. DINING CAR, TRAIN — DAY
INT. GALLEY KITCHEN, TRAIN - DAY
INT. TOILET, TRAIN — DAY
INT. LUGGAGE CAR, TRAIN - DAY
INT. GUARD'S AREA, TRAIN - DAY
INT. DRIVER'S CAB, TRAIN - DAY
```

Or even the beloved location of numerous action thrillers:

```
EXT. ROOF, TRAIN - DAY
```

My decision about the setting and where I choose to place the action of the scene will be heavily influenced by key factors, like the type of story I'm

---

3 According to Henry of Huntingdon's 12th-century account, King Canute the Great (1016–35) set his throne by the sea and ordered the incoming tide to halt and not to wet his feet and robes. Yet *"continuing to rise as usual [the tide] dashed over his feet and legs without respect to his royal person. Then the king leapt backwards, saying: 'Let all men know how empty and worthless is the power of kings'"*.

writing, its genre, the character(s) in that story and what they're doing, and – admittedly, this may be some way down the line when we are first working on a new idea – the level of the production and its budget that might be available to my script.

It is one thing for, say, the *Mission Impossible* franchise to locate a full sequence of action on the roof of the Orient Express[4] as it sweeps through Europe. It is quite another for a no-budget 'weekend' short we might be making with our friends even to get near a static train to shoot a scene, let alone a moving one. From the get-go in the life of a screen idea, we, as writers, need to understand the consequences that a wide range of external and internal factors inevitably have on the scope, scale, and ambition of the action we are hoping to portray in a scene and react accordingly.

Let's go with the setting I was actually in when I began writing this section:

INT. PASSENGER COMPARTMENT, TRAIN - DAY

Now some of you may already be looking at the words PASSENGER COMPARTMENT and asking: is it a second-class compartment or a first-class one? If so – good. You may also be asking when is this scene set – in what period specifically – and where, specifically? Again, good. The more questions like this that we ask ourselves or the writers we are working with from the outset of the development process, and continue asking them throughout it, the better. Look at the number of questions we are already starting to ask and we haven't even got to the action in the scene yet.

The First Line of Action

A professional reader – that is, someone who reads scripts for a living or as part of their job – will often say that they know from the very first line of action description whether the script they're reading is by an experienced screenwriter or at least by someone who has some kind of understanding of the mechanisms of writing for the screen and what it takes to do this. I have heard professional readers all around the world say that they know as soon as they open a new script and start reading whether the writer has any talent as a dramatic storyteller at all.

So, no pressure . . .

Here's an example of what I mean, using a scene on our train and its opening action descriptor. The content and style are based on numerous opening lines of scenes I've read over the years. For the purposes of this exercise, it's

4 In *Mission: Impossible – Dead Reckoning* (2023), a full-scale replica of the Orient Express was built in a UK film studio.

not the opening scene of a script, and it doesn't describe the first time we see the character in the story, so we are coming to this *in media res*:

```
INT. PASSENGER COMPARTMENT, TRAIN - DAY

The compartment has seen better days. The faded red seats and
cream-coloured tables are littered with rubbish. On one table,
there are a dozen empty beer cans, the sort of German Pils-
ner that you can buy from Aldi or Lidl. There are also lots
of empty crisps packets. These beer drinkers obviously like
the nation's favourite crisps - cheese and onion - and who
doesn't! On another table there is an empty bottle of cheap
fizz. It rolls about on the table as the train goes around a
corner, colliding with some empty plastic flutes. Above it
floats a sparkly "Bride to Be" balloon, still attached to the
back of the seat with gold ribbon. And under the balloon sits
Charlie. All alone. Weeping.
```

It's not the worst scene ever written. It paints a picture of where the scene is located. Many of us will have been in a train compartment just after the football fans or the hen party have got off so we can imagine the situation and how we might go about sharing this with the reader. The elements highlighted in the descriptions help create atmosphere and tone. This could be a comedy. Alternatively, it could be a tragedy. Given that comedy can be defined as "comedy equals tragedy plus time",[5] the writing potentially offers subtext as well as context.

However, this paragraph is much less effective when it comes to its key functions, which are to

1. reveal the proposed on-screen action in the scene
2. show this action to us
3. push forward the arc of the character and their journey through the plot in a relevant meaningful involving way

It is predominately an example of 'narrative' storytelling – the style of writing one might find in a novel or short story – rather than 'dramatic' storytelling – the style of writing that is required to tell – to show to us – a

---

5 'Comedy = Tragedy + Time' has been attributed to a number of people. In her 1986 interview with TV host Larry King, the performer Carol Burnett explained that she had heard the saying from a friend and it resonated with her own experiences as a performer. It certainly resonates with mine as a screenwriter and teacher.

screen story. And for the most part, screenwriters are in the business of dramatic storytelling.

Let's deconstruct this opening paragraph in more detail:

```
INT. PASSENGER COMPARTMENT, TRAIN - DAY

(1) The compartment (2) has seen better days. The faded red
seats and cream-coloured tables are littered with rubbish. (3)
On one table there are a dozen empty beer cans, the sort of Ger-
man Pilsner that you can buy from Aldi or Lidl. There are also
lots of empty crisps packets. These beer drinkers obviously
like the nation's favourite crisps - cheese and onion - and
who doesn't! (4) On another table, there is an empty bottle of
cheap fizz. It rolls about on the table as the train goes around
a corner, colliding with some empty plastic flutes(5). Above it
floats a sparkly "Bride to Be" balloon, still attached to the
back of the seat with gold ribbon. And under the balloon sits
Charlie (6). All alone. Weeping.
```

If I was working with the writer of an action paragraph like this, I would be asking the following questions and pointing out the following issues to address in it:

1. The 12-line unbroken action description is too long. A paragraph of action should be 1–5 lines MAX – the shorter the better to focus and locate the action, clarify the narrative for the reader, and speed up the read.
2. Avoid the repetition of the word "compartment". We already know where we are, the scene heading tells us this. Likewise, try and avoid the repetitions of "table", "beer", "empty", "crisps". One way of doing this is to leave them out altogether. After all, what do they actually add? They also potentially limit the universality of the story and its ability to travel.
3. Avoid a long list of descriptions, sometimes called 'the laundry list'. This level of narrative detail is unnecessary and obstructs the main purpose of the scene and its core function in the story. It also doesn't contain any action as such. In your mind, how do you imagine it being filmed? What would we be looking at on screen? Would we understand the details?
4. Why are you breaking the fourth wall like this by inserting yourself in the action, telling us your favourite crisp flavour and installing yourself so overtly and subjectively in the scene? You're the writer, not a friend of the reader.
5. A director could spend an hour working out how to shoot an empty bottle rolling about on a table, but to what purpose as far as the story and its

character is concerned? In its current context, how does this further the character arc, story, plot, or action and our understanding of these?

6. As a result of all these examples, it takes a long time to get to the character, the actual focus of the scene.

Let's have another go at the same scene, preserving the essence of and the essential information in the original as the writer may now see these. You will hopefully have your own ideas and suggestions about how this action descriptor could be shortened, rewritten, polished to improve the sense of action in it, and I encourage you to try these out. Here's my attempt:

```
INT. PASSENGER COMPARTMENT, TRAIN - DAY

Abandoned seats and tables littered with rubbish. Floating
above, a "Bride to Be" balloon. Below this: Charlie. Weeping.
```

My rewrite

1. Sharpens our focus on the opening image in the scene and what we may be intending for this.
2. Locates the character front and centre in it, reflecting my deep interest as a screenwriter on character and my desire always to frame action, incite action, and provoke action by involving and featuring character wherever possible.
3. Brings the setting, story world, and character together in potentially one image (shot).

At a more basic, instrumental level, my revision brings the word count in the paragraph down from 124 to 18. It's not perfect – nothing in screenwriting ever is – and it may even be too short now – but it's an improvement overall because it gets the action of the scene underway in a faster, more dynamic, and more eye-catching way, and it draws our eye and our attention to Charlie. It also means that a busy professional reader has 106 fewer words to read for pretty much the same effect. Multiply that through a 100-page / 200-scene feature screenplay and that's potentially a lot of words and a lot of time saved. And they will thank you for that.

The Three Hierarchies of Knowledge in Scene-Writing

The creation of engaging and involving dramatic action in a scene depends on the knowledge state of the audience through the hierarchies of knowledge. Effective use of the three knowledge positions that are available to the screenwriter influences and affects much of the way that we go about writing a particular scene, what we want to happen in that scene, and how we want the audience to interpret and understand what they are watching.

Our understanding of the meaning of the action that we are reading or watching in a film or TV scene depends on our position of knowledge as compared to that of the character or characters in that scene:

1. We know less than the character / characters (A<C).[6]
2. We know the same as the character / characters (A=C).
3. We know more than the character / characters (A>C).

1. We Know Less Than the Character(s)

```
EXT. DOCKS — NIGHT

The taxi pulls up across from a deserted warehouse.

INT. TAXI, DOCKS — NIGHT

DANA eyes the dark building. Takes a deep breath. Pays the
driver. Gets out.

EXT. DOCKS — NIGHT

The taxi pulls away. Dana is all alone. She keeps to the shad-
ows as she makes her way towards the warehouse entrance.

EXT. WAREHOUSE — NIGHT

At the entrance Dana stops. Listens. Silence. She takes out
her gun. Checks it. Slips inside the building.
```

As written and presented, the predominant knowledge state for the audience through the scenes is that we know less than the character in the scene. For writers, the 'mystery for the viewer' we can create via the action in scenes like these provides us with a means of hooking the audience into the story.

We are watching a character who is clearly up to something or on some kind of mission. The name DANA is in capitals, which often indicates that this is the first time we've met her in the story. Dana is nervous but not enough to be deflected from her objective. She is knowingly going into danger of some sort – so much so that she has brought a gun that she seems prepared to use and knows how to use.

6 A means Audience, C means Character.

Hopefully, by now, the audience is curious about Dana and wants to see how their mission into the warehouse is going to turn out. We have sparked their interest and used action to hook them into the story. So far, so good.

But it is worth bearing in mind that in and of itself, 'mystery for the viewer' – that is, the audience knows less than the character(s) – is the least involving and engaging of the three hierarchies of knowledge at play in scene-writing. Pretty soon the audience members want to know as much as the character they are watching and being asked to invest in knows. Indeed, the audience often wants – and needs – to know more.

2. We Know the Same as the Character(s)

New scenes / action added are indicated in bold:

INT. BRIEFING ROOM, POLICE STATION – NIGHT

The Officers file out. Dana sits there on her own. Thinking. She goes over to the evidence board. Stares at the address beneath the mugshot of Baines. Goes back to her desk. Unlocks a drawer. Takes out her gun. Holsters it. Heads to the door.

EXT. DOCKS – NIGHT

The taxi pulls up across from the deserted warehouse.

INT. TAXI, DOCKS – NIGHT

Dana eyes the dark building. Pays the driver. Gets out.

EXT. DOCKS – NIGHT

The taxi pulls away. Dana is all alone. She keeps to the shadows as she makes her way towards the warehouse entrance.

EXT. WAREHOUSE – NIGHT

At the entrance Dana stops. Listens. Silence. She checks her gun. Cocks it. Slips inside the building.

As you can see, the addition of the first scene significantly changes our knowledge position in relation to Dana in the other four scenes. We now know what she knows. You may notice, too, that it initiates changes to the way the original four scenes are now written and presented. As we often say, the art of writing is rewriting.

For example, the venue is no longer introduced in the first action line as
"a warehouse" but "<u>the</u> warehouse", (i.e., it's the place at the address that,
like Dana, we have seen on the evidence board). This may seem like a small
change, but it affects how the audience interprets and understands the action
in the scene. Likewise, we know Dana is a cop in this version so her character no longer needs to take a deep breath in the taxi. Being a cop is her
job; it's evidently a dirty business and we suspect she is very good at it. And
we already know from the added scene she has a gun, so she confirms to us
that she is ready, willing, and prepared to use it before she heads inside the
building.

The fact that the audience knows what Dana knows via the action creates
a shared knowledge position. We know what Dana knows and are in step
with her, and this state of shared 'mystery' or 'dramatic tension' motivates
and sustains the essential partnership between the audience, characters, and
writer. It can also help create investment in the character and story. Mystery
or dramatic tension is integral to the action depicted in many of the scenes
we will ever write.

3. We Know More Than the Character(s)

New scenes / action added are indicated in bold:

INT. BRIEFING ROOM, POLICE STATION — NIGHT

The Officers file out. Dana sits there on her own. Thinking. She
goes over to the evidence board. Stares at the address beneath
the mugshot of Baines. Goes back to her desk. Unlocks a drawer.
Takes out her gun. Holsters it. Heads to the door.

UNSEEN BY DANA

Captain O'Leary is watching. He makes a call on his cell.

EXT. DOCKS — NIGHT

The taxi pulls up across from the deserted warehouse.

INT. TAXI, DOCKS — NIGHT

Dana eyes the dark building. Pays the driver. Gets out.

EXT. DOCKS — NIGHT

The taxi pulls away. Dana is all alone. She keeps to the shadows as she makes her way towards the warehouse entrance.

```
EXT. WAREHOUSE — NIGHT
```

```
At the entrance Dana stops. Listens. Silence. She checks her
gun. Cocks it. Slips inside the building.
```

INT. 4ᵗʰ FLOOR WINDOW, BUILDING OPPOSITE – NIGHT

Above, A FIGURE watches Dana disappear into the warehouse.

The addition of the two short scenes opens up the action of the story in a
good way and once again fundamentally changes our knowledge position.
The revelation to us that the Captain has been watching Dana all along and
makes a call when she leaves immediately puts us ahead of Dana. We now
know more than she does: we know she has been observed; we know the
Captain knows where she is going; and we know he knows she has a gun.

Our superior knowledge position to Dana creates 'suspense', or 'dramatic
irony', for us and increases further our potential involvement in the story. If
the writing has enabled us to engage with the character of Dana and her situation and put us, to some degree, in her shoes, then our hopes and fears for
her are going to be activated by the action as she heads into danger.

Bear in mind, too, that this has been done in all three versions without the need
for any dialogue, voiceover, or sound to explain the plot or provide exposition.
The characters and their story are being shown to us, not told. Our investment,
such as it is, comes entirely from the dramatic action as it unfolds in front of us.

And yet there is even more at work here – and even more for us to exploit so
that the action in our scenes can further the creation of core drama elements
such as character, plot, tension, engagement, empathy, hopes, and fears.

My division of the scene-writing hierarchies of knowledge into their three
different states could suggest that they operate most effectively singularly. But
this is not the case. Let's look again at the third example presented:

```
INT. BRIEFING ROOM, POLICE STATION — NIGHT
```

```
The Officers file out. Dana sits there on her own. Thinking. She
goes over to the evidence board. Stares at the address beneath
the mugshot of Baines. Goes back to her desk. Unlocks a drawer.
Takes out her gun. Holsters it. Heads to the door.
```

SvdB: 'Mystery' in the scene: we know what Dana knows.

UNSEEN BY DANA

Captain O'Leary is watching. He makes a call on his cell.

*SvdB: The revelation to the audience that O'Leary has seen
all this and makes a call puts us ahead of Dana, creating*

'suspense'. But it also puts us behind O'Leary. Because his call immediately creates another new 'mystery for the viewer'. Who has he called? And why?

EXT. DOCKS — NIGHT

The taxi pulls up across from the deserted warehouse.

INT. TAXI, DOCKS — NIGHT

Dana eyes the dark building. Pays the driver. Gets out.

EXT. DOCKS — NIGHT

The taxi pulls away. Dana is all alone. She keeps to the shadows as she makes her way towards the warehouse entrance.

EXT. WAREHOUSE — NIGHT

At the entrance Dana stops. Listens. Silence. She checks her gun. Cocks it. Slips inside the building.

SvdB: More 'mystery' runs through the short sequence of connected scenes. Again, we know what Dana knows. Plus, we now also know more so we are ahead of her, creating tension and fears for her in us.

INT. 4th FLOOR WINDOW, BUILDING OPPOSITE — NIGHT

Above, A FIGURE watches Dana disappear into the warehouse.

SvdB: 'Mystery' partners with 'suspense' when it is revealed to us that someone is watching Dana. So we now know even more than her. But new 'mystery for the viewer' is also created for us here because we don't know who the FIGURE is. The revelation in the action compels the audience to ask: Who is the Figure? Was this the person O'Leary called? And are they going to be a foe or a friend for Dana?

As this example shows, action can satisfyingly involve all three of the scene-writing hierarchies of knowledge for the audience as information is hidden from us, revealed to us, or recognised, in turn, by another character. In one scene, we can know less than one character (mystery for the viewer), the same as another character (mystery), and more than another character (suspense), deepening the level of tension at work in the scene and adding welcome complexity and layers of this tension to the narrative.

Run these knowledge states alongside one another through the actions of your characters and interweave them in your scenes and you have at hand the vital building blocks to enable you to create tension, drama, comedy, investment, and engagement for the audience in the actions of your characters.

Making Action Happen

Action has to happen. Regardless of the story type, medium, genre, plot, content, character type, setting, period, location, theme, tone, point of view, budget, and audience – action has to happen.

Take a script you may be working on of any length as a writer, developer, director, producer, actor and ask yourself:

- What actions are happening in the scenes in your script?
- Who is making the decisions in the current draft?
- What are the consequences of each of those decisions?
- What effect do these decisions have on the story?
- How do they advance the plot scene by scene in some way?
- Why are we, the readers, still engaged and interested?

The portrayal of action can be immense and world-changing or it can be seemingly minimal and barely noticed. For example, the film *The Diving Bell and the Butterfly* (2007)[7] tells the true story of *Elle* magazine editor Jean-Dominique Bauby who suffers a stroke and is paralyzed. He lies in hospital in a catatonic state, a kind of living death until a nurse caring for him realises he can use his left eye. She notices him blinking this eye and realises each blink means something. Through blinking his eye, he is able to dictate letters of the alphabet to her, and they so begin to communicate, with life-changing consequences for them both.

There are no car chases, or explosions, or parachute jumps, or fights on moving trains. But each blink provides involving, powerful, memorable action, creating a gripping, emotional human story through the most delicate and subtle action of all.

So we have such a broad palette available to us in terms of how we understand, interpret, and use action. The only proviso is: it has to be in your story. It has to happen.

To help us elicit the response that we intend from the audience to the action in a particular scene, there are a number of active questions for us to refer to in the foreground or background throughout the scene-writing process:

- What happens in the scene?
- How does it happen?

---

7 *The Diving Bell and the Butterfly* (Julian Schnabel, 2007), screenplay written by Ronald Harwood based on Jean-Dominique Bauby's 1997 memoir of the same name.

- Who does it happen to?
- Who is in the scene and why?
- What is in the scene and why?
- What are we going to choose to show in the scene?
- Why are we choosing to show this specifically?
- Why does the action happen where it happens?

Let's interrogate one of the scenes from the earlier short sequence to test these questions against to give you an idea of how one might do this to examine the potential of the action in the scene.

```
INT. BRIEFING ROOM, POLICE STATION — NIGHT


The Officers file out. Dana sits there on her own. Thinking. She
goes over to the evidence board. Stares at the address beneath
the mugshot of Baines. Goes back to her desk. Unlocks a drawer.
Takes out her gun. Holsters it. Heads to the door.


UNSEEN BY DANA


Captain O'Leary is watching. He makes a call on his cell.
```

- What happens in the scene?
  Dana stays behind in the briefing room to assess the evidence. She decides to go visit the address on the evidence board. She finds her gun and leaves. All this has been observed by Captain O'Leary.
- How does it happen?
  The scene attempts to externalise for the audience Dana's internal thought processes as a cop to reflect her process of investigation: thought, analysis, assessment, decision-making, action.
- Who does it happen to?
  It happens to Dana. She is the subject of the scene. It is her scene, and she has the objective that creates the action of the scene.
- Who is in the scene and why?
  Dana is in the scene because she a cop, is curious about the case, and wants to solve it. It is revealed to us (but not to Dana) that O'Leary is also in the scene, in that he is watching her.
- What is in the scene and why?
  Despite the brevity of the scene, a lot is situated in it to provide the action, reinforce the police precinct world, and progress the plot, such as evidence boards, evidence, a photo, the address of the warehouse, Dana's desk, and her gun. There is also an area of the room where O'Leary can conceal himself.

- What are we going to choose to show in the scene?
  As the writer, I chose to show: a) Dana's doggedness, b) key objects associated with the investigation, c) Dana's moment of decision to take action, d) that she has a gun, and e) that all this is observed by O'Leary.
- Why are we choosing to show this specifically?
  I want to show the pivotal moment when Dana decides to take action and infer that her impulsiveness and her desire to operate outside the rules of the precinct may – will – put her in danger. This is reinforced by the presence of her boss Captain O'Leary which is revealed to us but not to her.
- Why does the action happen where it happens?
  Because this is the moment when Dana decides that she has to act and she can't put this off anymore. Setting this in the middle of the police precinct reinforces the difficulty of taking action on her own.

Ask Yourself

Look at the scene you may be writing or working on and ask yourself: What actions happen in it? What actual tangible physical actions take place? What new information, element, character, idea does the scene introduce?

Don't censor yourself as you reflect on this. *The Diving Bell and the Butterfly* confirms that we can count a seemingly small thing – the discovery of the ability to blink an eye – as action in a scene so long as it delivers for the characters and plot. Action doesn't have to be big, generic, physical, obvious. Each scene will be different, and the action in the particular scene will be influenced by the moment in time that you have chosen to write about to inform the audience about your story, genre, characters, and world.

A good place to start is to reflect on who is making the decisions in the scene. Ask yourself: Whose decisions are creating the story? Whose decisions from scene to scene are creating the action of the film or TV show?

You'll think it's the person you have identified as your main character. But when you look at it objectively, you may begin to realise that your protagonist is supposed to be doing this but there's this other character over there that is actually doing everything and making the key decisions scene by scene. Now, it is, of course, possible to have a passive protagonist in scenes, sequences, even an act. But it is important for writers to look at this open-mindedly to make sure that this type of passive character offers us the greatest potential for the action of our story and its plot.

We often encounter a protagonist in the Act 1 scenes of a film or TV story whose instinct is to be evasive and avoid everything – conflict, other people, moving on, decisions, life itself. They want to avoid taking action, so they avoid action *per se*. There is often an overt or covert reason they are behaving like this and hiding in the shadows, and this comes out as the story unfolds. And as the story unfolds, they are increasingly required to make decisions in scenes and so become more and more active. Their passivity is often indicative of that person's problem or flaw. And they will be required, at some point, to draw a line in the sand, rebel, fight, change, stand up to people, step out of the shadows into the light.

In short – to take some sort of action.

Troubleshooting

The writing of action in scenes also has pitfalls. Well-meaning caveats and advice for writers abound when it comes to writing action, such as "Don't tell – show!", "Less is more", "Don't use flashbacks", and "How do we know?"

A good place to start when mapping out the action in a scene to try and avoid pitfalls like these from the get-go is to ask yourself the following questions:

- What's your scene about? What happens in it?
- What are you trying to achieve with the action in the scene?
- How do you want the audience to feel as it watches this action?
- What new knowledge are we going to learn about your characters and the plot in the scene because of the action?
- How does the content in the scene contribute to and support all of these questions?
- What's your scene really about?

Three distinctive and essential elements make up a scene's content:

1. Plot – If the screenwriter views plot as the dramatic events we choose in order to tell our story in the most logical, entertaining, and satisfying way for the audience, then the action in a scene should generally revolve around and depict one of these events. The nature of that action, its tone, and how it reflects the overall story and genre all depend on where we are in the story.
2. Setting – the setting of the scene is where the particular plot event is located and plays out. It also confirms the intended world of the story as the writer envisages it, along with its tone, atmosphere, and genre.
3. Character – Screen characters who are in a scene and involved in the action are not usual, typical people. They are heightened versions of usual, typical people with recognisable human qualities that are intended to be represented and portrayed by actors. The actions of screen characters in scenes reflect the verb to *do* rather than the verb to *be*.

This chapter has offered examples of how we can write and rewrite the action in a scene to ensure that less on the page is more and that, where possible, we are showing the action of the story to the audience rather than telling it to them.

However, by far, the most common mistake I see by first-time, emerging, and even experienced screenwriters is the writing of action that makes the reader keep asking, "How do we know?"

How Do We Know . . .?

When I was developing and writing my screenplay *Boney and Betsy* at the Maurits Binger Film Institute (MBFI),[8] my excellent screenwriting teacher on that project David Howard joked that he had to write, "How do we know?" so many times on the grad screenwriting scripts at USC that his students clubbed together to buy him a stamp with red ink that he could use to put "HOW DO WE KNOW?" on the scripts to save him having to write it each time.

Having worked with writers of all levels and abilities, taught screenwriting for more than 20 years, and read millions of words of action, I know how he used to feel.

Here's a heightened example of what I mean using one of the scenarios from earlier in this chapter. As you read it, keep in mind that in screen storytelling, we can only know what we see or hear on the screen in some way. Ask yourself: How do we know . . .?

```
INT. BRIEFING ROOM, POLICE STATION — NIGHT

The Officers file out. Dana sits there on her own as usual. She
is thinking about what she saw the night before, trying to make
sense of it. She goes over to the evidence board. Stares at
the address beneath the mugshot of Baines, the man who served
her in the gas station and made the cryptic remark when he saw
her police badge. Goes back to her desk. Unlocks a drawer.
Takes out her gun. Thanks her lucky stars she did her shooter
training the month before and got 5/5 bull's eyes. Holsters
it. Heads to the door.

UNSEEN BY DANA

Captain O'Leary is watching. He is certain that Dana is on to
him. He makes a call to Baines' friend on his cell.
```

---

8 I was the first British screenwriter to be accepted on the 5-month screenplay development programme at the Maurits Binger Film Institute (MBFI), Amsterdam 1996–97, with my project *Boney and Betsy*.

How do we know . . .

- Dana usually sits on her own and is potentially a loner?
- she is thinking about what she saw the night before?
- she is trying to make sense of what she saw?
- Baines served her in the gas station and made the cryptic remark?
- she did her shooter training the month before?
- she got 5 / 5 bull's eyes doing this training?
- O'Leary is certain Dana is on to him?
- O'Leary is calling Baines' friend?

Most of the description in this version of the scene relates to action and events that we haven't seen on the screen. The internalised nature of the delivery of information is effectively narrative storytelling (i.e., like the storytelling in a novel or short story) in which we are often told what characters are thinking, seeing, remembering, dreaming.

In dramatic storytelling (i.e., like a film or TV show), the job of the screenwriter is to portray information like this in the ongoing dramatic action in the scenes using the appropriate mechanisms and systems of screen storytelling available to us.

Conclusion

Ten Things to Remember About Writing Action in a Scene

1. Action is everything that we are looking at via the screen.
2. Action happens in the present tense, in real time, as we are watching it.
3. Lines of action involve a subject, a verb, and an object of some sort.
4. Avoid using too many descriptive words or a 'laundry list' in your action.
5. How do we know . . . what you are telling us in your action?
6. Don't tell us something – show it to us!
7. Action is a consequence of Cause + Effect scene by scene.
8. How does the action support the story world, tone, genre?
9. Whose scene is it? Who is making the decisions and taking action?
10. How does your action make use of a scene's hierarchies of knowledge? In your scene, who is there? And who knows what, when, where, how, and why?

Let's refer back to the core dramatic story notions of external physical character Want and internal emotional character Need.

Action shows us the story. In that respect, it is visible, on screen, seen, external, physical. It provides context for the audience and reflects the objective and goal of your characters scene by scene.

In many ways, action represents what your scene, your film, is about.

As a counterpoint to action, dialogue can tell us the story. At its most effective, dialogue is mercurial, unseen, overheard, subjective, inferred, subtextual.

As we shall see in the next chapter, dialogue represents what our scene, our film, is *really* about.

Action – Scene-Writing Exercise

"Creating Action" Exercise

As we've discussed, action provides us with the means of showing the story to the reader. Use this non-dialogue scene-writing exercise to explore some of the ideas in the chapter.

Step 1 – *Write a paragraph of prose, for example, a paragraph in a novel or short story describing a series of things that your character is thinking about internally. Take a character, situation, and scene you're working on or come up with a new character and a situation and scene they might be in. Locate them in the story world.*

Here is an example. Please use this if it helps you get going on the exercise.

Malek took his coffee and sat down. As he sipped it, oblivious to the other customers in the diner, he thought back to what happened when he visited his father. He remembered the row he'd had afterwards with his sister. He wondered when she'd notice the $500 was missing. He was so wrapped up in his thoughts that he failed to see one of the customers remove a sawn-off shot gun from a holdall and stride towards the counter. Malek only realised what was going on when he heard the gunshot.

Step 2 – *Adapt the paragraph of prose into a scene or connected scenes of action, with a slug line / scene heading and action lines. Avoid using dialogue if possible.*

As you read the prose, ask yourself:

- Where is the setting for the main scene?
- What's the time of day? Tone? Atmosphere? Main genre?
- What is the specific objective / goal of the character in the scene?
- What are the subject / verb / object in each action line in the scene(s) you're writing?
- How do we know what the character is thinking?
- How are you going to show this to the reader / audience?

Step 3 – *Once you've written the scene(s), compare the action in them to the original prose. Ask yourself:*

- What did you keep the same?
- What did you have to change / decide to change and why?
- What's working in your scene(s), what's better?
- What's not so effective? How could you improve this?
- Would dialogue improve the scene / scenes? How? Why?
- How could you adapt this paragraph without using any flashbacks?

Notes:

- Remember: action in scenes happens in the present tense, in real time, as we are watching it.
- Don't tell – show, wherever possible.
- Less is more – keep it brief and try not to use dialogue.

4

DIALOGUE

What Are Your Characters Trying to Say?

Introduction

Billy Wilder's succinct and vivid commandment *"Always write dialogue you can see"*[1] verbalizes the fundamental challenge facing the screenwriter when it comes to writing dialogue. At its most basic level, dialogue is what our characters are saying in our scripts. It's meant to be brought to life and spoken by actors for an audience to hear, enjoy, laugh at, be moved by, and shocked by.

We may 'see' it because we can envisage a particular character saying it. Or because it is vibrant and colourful. Or because it paints pictures in our mind – images that are not the ones we are seeing on the screen. Or because it gives us insight and understanding about the characters and the story we're watching.

However, for most of its life in a script, dialogue is read, not heard. If it reputedly takes on average seven years for a produced script to get made, then that script's dialogue exists passively as words on a page for 80% of that time – 5+ years of it being potentially static and inanimate when it is written to be active and alive.

Indeed, the first time a screenwriter may actually hear the dialogue they've written in a script is when they watch the produced film on the screen. The paradox of this is that for many screenwriters, writing dialogue is the most

---

1 This saying is beloved of screenwriting teachers and is attributed to writer, director, and producer Billy Wilder (1906–2002). However, I am yet to find the source for this quote, and so whether Wilder actually said it. Regardless of this Wilder and his co-writer IAL Diamond (1920–88) wrote some of the greatest movie dialogue.

DOI: 10.4324/9781003293927-5

personal, distinctive, and enjoyable part of the entire writing process – the bit we look forward to the most because we feel we can make it our own.

We undergo the lonely hard yards of finding an idea, developing its characters and story, organising these into a TV or film plot via prescriptive prose-type text documents such as outlines, synopses, and treatments for the opportunity of getting these characters and this story up on their feet via its dialogue. Writing the dialogue and setting it free through our characters is generally the apex of our freedom, our anarchy, even.

Unique to the scene-writing element of a script's development, writing dialogue is where the screenwriter most often feels that they and their work have a chance to shine – to reveal their own voice and create the subtext that reflects what their work is *really* about.

In Billy Wilder's films, there is a wonderful patina and texture to the dialogue, a human quality to it that brings the characters to life on screen. The dialogue has a distinctive pattern, rhythm, colour, and texture that maximise the emotional content of what is often very dark comedy.

For the screenwriter, the ability to write effective dialogue scene by scene is high stakes. Because great dialogue is the hallmark of great TV and movies. And great TV and movies gain critical acclaim and win the recognition and awards that can change screenwriters' lives.

So once again – no pressure.

Verbal Action

I started my career in the theatre as a university student, worked backstage as a flyman and stagehand, then went to drama school[2] before working professionally as a director and sometime actor. Throughout this journey, the Soviet Russian theatre practitioner Konstantin Stanislavski (1863–1938) was a significant figure in my theatre training and development, largely because of his seminal text *An Actor Prepares* (1936),[3] which was a key manual for actors and directors of my generation.

Among his advice and instruction, Stanislavski refers to the notions of 'verbal' and 'physical' action.[4] Correct training in the use of the voice and speech was as important to Stanislavski in creating a system – a method – of acting as an actor's physical training of their body – their 'action' if you like. By applying Stanislavski's approach to ours as screenwriters, we can see how

2 Bristol Old Vic Theatre School, 1983–84.
3 Stanislavski's subsequent texts *Building a Character* (1948) and *Creating a Role* (1957), published posthumously, also offer insight for writers as well as actors and directors.
4 Benedetti, J. (1998) *Stanislavski and the actor.* Taylor & Francis Group.

FIGURE 4.1   Simon (sitting, left) as Sir Andrew Aguecheek in *Twelfth Night* by William Shakespeare, Warwick University Arts Centre, 1980 (dir. Alison Sutcliffe).

the idea that the dialogue is 'verbal' action chimes with Billy Wilder's advice about writing dialogue we can see.

Ultimately, dialogue in theatre, in TV, in film, is written to be heard, not read – which only serves to reinforce the challenge that confronts us as screenwriters.

Dialogue as Verbal Action

Go out to a public space. Listen to the people around you and what they're saying – and how they're saying it. On the bus, in a café, in a museum. I go to art exhibitions as much to listen to the people there talking about stuff as to see the exhibits on the walls. Observe how, to some degree, what they are saying begins to paint a picture in your imagination and the extent to which this makes you see an aspect of the person or story they're talking about in a different way. Insight? Understanding? Empathy? Revulsion? How you respond is up to you and depends on how the particular picture being painted in your imagination works on you.

Here is a real-life example of what I mean.

Some years ago, I was travelling south on a train from London that went via Gatwick Airport, minding my own business, reading a newspaper. I just wanted to get home. I became aware of a strident domineering MALE VOICE booming out from the next bay of seats. I took a quick peek – and saw an

ELDERLY COUPLE sitting side by side in silence, listening to a large MAN (40s) sitting opposite them, sounding off. He was in the middle of an impossibly long list . . .

```
                    MAN
        I've been all over the world, I have.
        Travelled everywhere. South America,
        up the Amazon, down it, Africa,
        Indonesia, Papua New Guinea, Australia.
        And I've eaten all kinds of food. I've
        eaten dog, cat, spider, scorpion. I've
        had snake and camel. Beetle. And
        kangaroo's testicles. Sheep's eye. Twice.
        I've eaten everything. And there's only
        two types of food I can't stand.
```

He paused. For dramatic effect. Like me, everyone in the compartment was waiting for it . . .

```
                    MAN
        Raw fish.
            (with a flourish)
        And monkey's brains!
```

In my dramatic reconstruction of this scene, the Elderly Lady smiles at the Man – and promptly vomits all over his lap. A small act of revenge. But, in reality, she didn't. The Couple just sat there in silence, as did the rest of us. Imagining, perhaps? Ticking off how many things we'd eaten from his list? (I'd eaten four of them if you're asking). Until the train stopped at Gatwick Airport and our monstrous gastronome got off with his luggage, to fly off to who knows where. Or to find a new victim to tell his story to. The relief when he shut the train door was palpable.

I've remembered his monologue pretty much word for word for 30+ years because of the picture it painted in my head. It remains for me, to this day, as a vivid example of verbal action.

It works on two levels. It provides context, making me think of the places and things on his impossible list. But it also provides subtext. It transports me straight back 30 years into that train carriage. Back to that younger version of myself. That person half my lifetime ago, with his hopes, dreams, and aspirations. It opens a window of opportunity for me to look at my life and weigh up what I have done since: my successes and my failures; how my hopes, dreams, and aspirations turned out; and how I feel about that.

That is the power of dialogue.

Five Different Types of Dialogue

When I am working on a script on my own and I'm writing the dialogue, I will often read the lines out loud. Sometimes I'll even get up and act them out. My dog, Muriel,[5] is an excellent audience. When you read stuff aloud to yourself and hear your own words, you often begin to think: "That doesn't sound quite as good as it could." Long before I let anyone else read the script, I'm reading the scenes out to myself, playing the parts, hearing the dialogue. And revising, rewriting, polishing it. Because as we know, dialogue is written to be heard.

The term 'dialogue' is often used as a generic, one-size-fits-all, all-encompassing word for what are, in reality, different means and modes of verbal communication that are available to us as writers to enable our characters in scenes in screen (and stage) stories to communicate with one another and with the audience.

For the purposes of our work in this area, there are five primary distinctive types of dialogue, and each of these has a particular approach and function:

1. Conversation
2. Monologue
3. Soliloquy
4. Talking to camera
5. Voiceover

1. Conversation

When we think of dialogue in film and TV, the two-way conversation in a scene between two or more characters is the mode of dialogue that most often comes to mind. We're most familiar with it; it's a staple of dramatic writing, and it will feature in many scenes in pretty much any script we ever write.

Let us return to our train carriage and our elderly couple:

```
INT. TRAIN CARRIAGE — DAY

The train comes to a halt at the station. DIANA (70s) and NICK
(70s) look out the window.

                    DIANA
          East Croydon.

                    NICK
          It usually is.
```

---

5 Muriel is named after the eponymous character in *Muriel's Wedding* (1994, P. J. Hogan), partly because I wanted to be able to exclaim "You're terrible, Muriel!" whenever she did something naughty.

```
The train door by them RATTLES. Someone on the platform is
having trouble opening it.

Nick leans across and obliges.

The door swings open and STEW (40s) clambers in. PUFFING.
Pulling a very large suitcase after him.

                    STEW
          Thanks...

He sits down opposite them. Diana eyes his case. Then him.

                    DIANA
          Going somewhere nice?

                    STEW
          Tashkent. Uzbekistan.

Pause.

                    DIANA
          I think this train only goes as far
          as Eastbourne.
```

Many of our favourite scenes in the movies, TV dramas, sit-coms, and soaps that we've watched will feature a verbal exchange between the characters in those scenes, and this lives long in our memory.

Countless times, writers and filmmakers I've taught, been taught by, met with, or worked with will start our own conversation by saying: "Have you seen [insert as applicable]? I loved that scene [that line, that speech, that moment] when . . ." This invitation to try and identify a shared experience provides a touchstone that is integral to building meaningful, productive, collaborative professional relationships.

Of course, describing conversation in scenes as a 'verbal exchange' falls way short of identifying what's actually going on between the characters in this type of dialogue – the intellectual emotional battle, sparring, jousting, gymnastics, one-upmanship, bullying, cruelty, kindness, love, hate, dismissal, inclusion, declaration, truth, lie – we are creating between them that may enable them, their stories, and their situation to live long in the memory of the reader or audience.

2. Monologue

Monologues also feature in scenes between two or more characters, but this dialogue is not a conversation. The character speaking is not interested in the other character(s) verbal responses – and, indeed, in many scenes where monologue is predominant, there is no verbal response from the other character, no verbal exchange.

As the scene unfolds, it is no longer about the speaker conversing with or talking to the other character(s). It becomes a kind of extemporisation, almost an out-of-body experience in which the speaker is potentially revealing their inner feelings or beliefs, or deeper fears or truth, about themselves and / or the other character(s).

The scene I shared earlier featuring the well-travelled – and well-dined – man on the train is, therefore, an example of monologue rather than conversation. There may be two other characters in the scene, but the speaker is not interested in them or their views. There is no conversation between them as such, there is only his monologue.

> MAN
> I've been all over the world, I have.
> Travelled everywhere. South America,
> up the Amazon, down it, Africa,
> Indonesia, Papua New Guinea, Australia.
> And I've eaten all kinds of food. I've
> eaten dog, cat, spider, scorpion. I've
> had snake and camel. Beetle. And
> kangaroo's testicles. Sheep's eye. Twice.
> I've eaten everything. And there's only
> two types of food I can't stand.
>   (Pause)
> Raw fish.
>   (with a flourish)
> And monkey's brains!

Depending on how this is presented in the scene by the writer, this monologue will either reveal information about him, about one or both of the characters he is talking at, about someone else in the carriage who overhears this, or about all of them in some way.

3. Soliloquy

Those of us who have studied a Shakespeare[6] play at school – in particular, one of the Tragedies such as *Hamlet* or *Othello*[7] – will be familiar with the notion of the soliloquy, that key moment when the character privately articulates their deepest secret, fear, truth, lie – for example, the scene[8] in *Hamlet*

---

6 William Shakespeare, English dramatist (1564–1616).
7 *Hamlet* was written sometime between 1599–1601, *Othello* in around 1603.
8 Act 3 scene III, *Hamlet*.

when newly crowned King Claudius admits he murdered Hamlet's father the former king, Claudius's brother.

During a soliloquy, other characters that may be in the scene effectively disappear from the drama. They count for nothing. Often, they hear nothing, too. Only the audience can hear the speaker and her thoughts, spoken aloud and articulated by her for her own reasons. A soliloquy is often used by writers to provide exposition – key information the audience needs to know to understand the story – that in some way answers the ever-present question: "How do we know?"

As with our action writing, the ongoing fluctuating hierarchies of knowledge[9] that exist between the audience (A) and character(s) (C) in every scene are also available to the screenwriter when we write any mode of dialogue:

- A < C (mystery for the viewer)
- A = C (mystery, dramatic tension)
- A > C (suspense, dramatic irony / comic irony)

A soliloquy can often take the form of a confession that is effectively overheard by the audience. At the start of the particular scene, we may know less than the person who is about to deliver the soliloquy (A < C: mystery for the viewer). However, the confession and the sharing of an innermost thought or feeling by the speaker in the soliloquy make the audience complicit in the storytelling. As a result of this, we now know what the speaker knows (A = C: mystery / dramatic tension). And we very likely now know more than what other key characters in the story know (A > C: suspense / dramatic or comic irony).

Let us return to Diana, Nick, and Stew:

```
INT. TRAIN CARRIAGE — DAY

Diana (70s) eyes Stew (40s) opposite her. He is asleep.

Next to Diana: Nick (70s), fast asleep too.

The daylight disappears as the train THUNDERS into a tun-
nel. A light illuminates Diana. She continues to stare at the
sleeping Stew.

                    DIANA
          In my experience, young man, it is a
          mistake to underestimate little old
          ladies. Trying to shock us with
```

9 See the previous chapter on action for a fuller explanation of the three hierarchies of knowledge in a scene.

```
        your silly list of food. I mean, who
        hasn't eaten dog. Or snake. And you
        left my favourite food off your list.
           (eyeing Stew's chubby neck)
        Flesh.
```

```
Nick opens an eye. Shocked. He has heard everything.
```

There is a further twist that can be exploited by the screenwriter. If it is revealed to us that the soliloquy is overheard by another character and they are now aware of what the secret that speaker is confessing, then the hierarchy of knowledge for the audience is further extended. We now know more than the speaker of the soliloquy because we know that they have been overheard and we know who overheard them. We know that their secret is out.

4. Talking to Camera

Talking to the camera, in which a character suddenly addresses the audience directly down the lens by looking into the camera and taking us into their confidence, is, by its nature, an extension of the soliloquy that has been made available to us and enhanced by moving image technology.

It is a mode of dialogue that is beloved by certain filmmakers and is associated with certain actors and certain types and styles of film and TV stories, such as mock-doc or mockumentary, in which the techniques of documentary filmmaking are knowingly incorporated in movies and sit-coms to create a sense of vérité[10] or fly-on-the-wall[11] in the storytelling.

The film or TV character becomes aware of the presence of the audience, looks into the camera, and addresses us, sharing with us directly, one-to-one, personally their deepest secret, fear, truth, lie. This breaking of the so-called fourth wall,[12] initiated in the theatre and adopted by film and TV, can create powerful, involving, personal moments of drama and comedy as we are taken into the confidence of the character during their crisis.

Back to Diana, Nick, and Stew:

```
INT. TRAIN CARRIAGE — DAY

Diana (70s) eyes Stew (40s) opposite her. He is asleep.

Next to Diana: Nick (70s), fast asleep too.
```

---

10 The art or technique of filming something such as a movie so as to convey candid realism.
11 Filming people as they do things they do in their typical daily lives.
12 A performance convention in which an invisible imaginary wall separates actors from the audience.

The daylight disappears as the train THUNDERS into a tunnel.
A single overhead light illuminates Diana.

She turns slowly. Looks into the camera. Right at us.

                            DIANA
                    (conspiratorial)
                Look at him.
                    (indicates Stew)
                Sleeping like a baby. Child-like. Trusting.
                Little does he know what he's got himself into.
                    (back into the camera)
                But you know, don't you. My friends. The
                keepers of my little secret. Oh, and
                don't forget. If any of you blab, I know
                where you live.

A GULP next to Diana. She turns to Nick. He has heard it all.

Like the soliloquy, the potential of talking to the camera as a mode of dialogue is enhanced if the hierarchies of knowledge available to the writer in a scene are used in some way to maximise the opportunities for tension, conflict, and comedy.

5. Voiceover

Voiceover is, potentially, the most contentious of the modes of dialogue that are available to us. Screenwriting approaches and teachers are often prescriptive and adamant about voiceover – the use of the voice of a character on the soundtrack only of a film or TV drama – and recommend we should avoid its use wherever and whenever possible.

However, like most of the rules in screenwriting, the 'do not use voiceover' rule is one that is regularly broken – and broken successfully and to great dramatic effect. Many iconic and memorable movie and TV drama scenes feature voiceover, addressing the audience directly via the soundtrack and making them privy to some kind of key story or character information. Voiceovers can take many forms and represent different stages of a character's life – before they are born, at the start of their life, at the end of their life, after their life, or anywhere in between.

There may be a snobbery about the use of voiceover in some screenwriting areas but not in this book. The correct use of voiceover can set the whole story up, get the story going with a bang, supply vital information quickly and efficiently, and compliment or contrast with the images, characters, or story on the screen.

Why expend precious time and energy writing ten pages (ten pages = ten minutes of screen time) of intricate character action and dialogue across several scenes to avoid voiceover just for the sake of it when you can impart the same information in two pages (two minutes of screen time) using voiceover, cut to the chase and get the story and its characters moving?

With imaginative and efficient use of voiceover, your audience can quickly and concisely know what you want them to know, such as who these characters are, where they are, the story world they exist in, and their situation in that world when their story starts or at a particular stage of it.

Let's return to Diana, Nick, and Stew one last time:

```
INT. TRAIN CARRIAGE — DAY

The train has stopped. The carriage is empty. Apart from
Diana (70s). Standing there, TAPPING her foot. Waiting.

                    DIANA
            Get a move on, Nick.

Nick (70s) appears around from behind the seats. Pulling a
very large suitcase. Stew's suitcase.

                    DIANA
            Is it heavy?

                    NICK
            What do you think.

He wheels the suitcase towards the train door.

                    NICK (V.O.)
            I only caught the train on a whim. I
            wanted to see the sea. And have proper
            fish and chips.
                (a beat)
            Who knew I'd meet Diana.

As Nick passes Diana he stops. Gazes at her. Gives her a peck
on the cheek.

                    NICK (V.O.)
            Fate. Kismet. Luck. You decide.

She SHOOS him away. He smiles at her. Besotted. Then lugs
the heavy case out through the train door.
```

```
Diana scans the carriage. Checks the seat where Stew sat.
Carefully. Smiles.

                        NICK (V.O.)
              Isn't she amazing.

Diana follows Nick out onto the platform. The train door
shuts firmly.

IN THE TRAIN TOILET

The contents of Stew's suitcase. Piled high. Abandoned.
```

These different modes of dialogue are all available for you to adopt and use as you see fit. There are few hard and fast rules about this. The only 'rule', such as it is, is for you to choose the right method of dialogue and the right approach to that dialogue in order to make your characters, your story, and your script come alive on the page in the best way – and the way that you want it to.

What Is Good Dialogue?

Here is a summary of what effective dialogue is intended to do scene by scene:

- **Define your characters** – their class, cultural background, educational level, beliefs, worldview, philosophy, politics, and so on.
- **Characterize the speaker** and the person being addressed.
- **Reveal the speaker's motivation** or attempt to hide their motivation.
- **Reflect the speaker's status** in the scene and their relationship to other characters.
- **Define the period and the setting** of your film or TV show.
- **Advance the action** of the story and the plot – what your story is about.
- **Be connective** as good dialogue grows out of the preceding speech / action and leads to another speech / action.
- **Impart information and exposition** (the information the audience needs to understand the story) as required.
- **Sound credible and believable** and don't stand out or jar – unless we want it to do that for a very good reason.
- **Foreshadow** what is yet to come.
- **Be idiomatic** and signify the script's intended style, tone, genre, atmosphere.
- **Convey mood, emotion, and inner life.**
- **Suggest subtext** – what your story is *really* about.
- **Help attract, engage,** manipulate, and seduce an audience.
- **Be clear and comprehensible** to its audience.

So, no challenge then . . .

I'm being ironic. This is a huge list, a daunting list, and if you were to go through it as you are writing a scene and try and observe all the ideas in it faithfully line by line, this would very likely take all the fun out of writing that dialogue.

Like so many of the skills and tools that I am trying to share in this book, these concepts are best used as editing and rewriting tools rather than prescribing that you sit there with a blank page as you start on your dialogue for your scene thinking, "Have I got point one, point two, point three?" and trying to use them as a checklist from the get-go.

Write your scene. Commit your ideas to paper / to screen. Get the characters talking.

Who cares if the dialogue is a bit too vague or too 'on the nose' at first? Who cares if the dialogue is too long or too short?

After all, at this stage, you are the audience. So write your scene – write your scenes – fast. Get through them. Get to the end. Then go back later and apply the skills and tools suggested here to make sure that the scene and its dialogue and action are the best that they can be – and the best that you can make them. Because the art of writing is . . . rewriting.

Ask yourself:

- Does this scene have a unique, dramatic question?
- What is that question, the goal / objective of the character in the scene?
- How does the dialogue reflect, test, challenge this goal?
- What strategies do the characters use in their dialogue to achieve that goal?
- What strategies do the characters use in their dialogue to avoid it?
- What are you planting in the dialogue or paying off?
- Is the character mostly lying or being evasive?
- Or are they actually telling the truth but no one believes them?

There are a number of ways that you can advance your writing and improve your dialogue. But I suggest that you get it down first, then go back and rewrite and sculpt and review and read out aloud and then go back and write and sculpt, and so on.

We set ourselves a very high bar when it comes to developing and writing dialogue. Some writers have a natural affinity with dialogue, some writers don't, but it is possible to improve your dialogue by writing and rewriting. Only rarely do you need to put more dialogue in. It's usually a case of cutting it down or out.

In the first place, decide on your scenes and think about the content and key components of each, what happens in them, who is in them, and so on.

Then write these scenes fast. Get them down on paper without editing yourself too much. Take a break – and then go back through these scenes.

Read them closely. Objectively. Test the dialogue and action you've written against the ideas in this and other chapters. Ask yourself and your scene the questions you suspect I or a script developer would ask. To what degree is your dialogue answering this?

If the dialogue in the scene feels like it is there primarily as filler or decoration, is there just for the sake of it or because you think the character should be saying something, cut it. If the dialogue is really just repeating what we are also watching on the screen – again, cut it. Because in scene-writing, less is generally more.

Remember, what people actually say is not as interesting, involving, or exciting as what people aren't saying – the subtext. In the final Diana and Nick scene, the subtext reinforces the idea of the power of love. Love can suddenly occur in the most unlikely place – on a train going to the seaside for the day – make you do the most unexpected thing – murder someone – and change you and your life forever.

One of our greatest challenges in this process is that if the audience notices what you are doing or becomes aware of the dialogue in a way that is not intended, then it is not working and the whole illusion is destroyed.

How Can You Learn to Write Better Dialogue?

I am sometimes asked, "How can I learn to write dialogue?" A more pertinent version of this question might be: "How can I learn to write better dialogue?" One of my screenwriting teachers used to say that screenwriting is like a muscle, you have to keep exercising it. This notion of exercise – practice – repetition – is common to many creative endeavours, and it's particularly true when it comes to writing dialogue.

I've already shared with you my now not-so-secret habit of overhearing people and their dialogue – not because I'm interested in what they're saying *per se* but in *how* they're saying it. Listening to people and beginning to discern the different rhythms, notes, tunes, cadences, dialects, sentence lengths, words, and vocabulary at work in how each of us speaks is a first step on the journey of writing better dialogue. As Aaron Sorkin said,

All dialogue is inherently musical. Any time a person speaks for the sake of performance as opposed to "please pass the butter" it has all of the properties of music – tone, rhythm, pitch, timbre, intervals, it is music.[13]

---

13 Aaron Sorkin (*A Few Good Men* (1992), *The West Wing* (1999–2006), *The Social Network* (2010), *The Trial of the Chicago 7* (2020)), *This Cultural Life*, BBC Radio 4, 2 April 2022.

We have to train our ear. Be nosy. Listen to the dialogue – on the bus, in shops, cafes, restaurants, sports events, pubs, in waiting rooms, schools – all around us to find out how people really speak. On a walk the morning when I wrote this, I heard compelling snatches of dialogue from a man walking past on the street, the woman who served me in a café, the person telling their friend a story loudly in that café, and the traffic warden and householder arguing in a street about a parking ticket. Different people. Different characters. Different dialogue. Everywhere.

I regularly read short film scripts, TV dramas, feature films in which every single character speaks in exactly the same way – the same sentence structures, same vocabulary, same number of words per sentence – because they speak like the writer. On the page, they sound the same – so much so that if we cover the name of the character up on the page, we are unable to tell which character was actually speaking. And yet, as we know, in real life, no two of us speak exactly the same:

- How do people really speak?
- How do screen characters really speak?

If our screen characters are recognisable, accentuated, or heightened versions of real people, then so is their dialogue. How does that dialogue define:

1. Their vocation, job, or hobby?
2. Their location?
3. Their culture?
4. Their historical period?

1. Vocation, Job, or Hobby

Let's imagine we are creating a new TV series set in a busy hospital somewhere. Full of staff and patients, insiders and outsiders, comings and goings, tragedy and comedy for its characters situations and stories, little wonder it is a perennially popular precinct that writers and producers regularly return to for TV dramas, soaps, and sit-coms. In our large fictional hospital 'St. Somewhere', there are

- consultants, doctors, professors, surgeons, and clinicians
- managers, administrators, scientists, IT, and business people
- nurses, students, medical staff, ancillary staff, and mortuary staff
- support staff, contractors, and white-collar and blue-collar workers
- people working their first day, last day, on work experience, or job interviews
- patients from a rich variety of backgrounds, types, social classes

We can already see the potential the plethora of different jobs and vocations in this precinct offers us. Which makes it all the more frustrating for the reader when: a) all the characters in St. Somewhere sound the same and b) none of them sound like real people who spend their lives in and around a hospital.

Often, this lack of care and depth in the dialogue the characters use is reinforced by a glaring lack of care in the research into the characters and their jobs. For example, I regularly read scenes located in a generalised medical world with dialogue like this:

```
INT. HOSPITAL - DAY

The Doctor stares at the Patient.

                    DOCTOR
               (to the Nurse)
          Go and get a tube and stick it into
          them. Quick!

The Nurse runs off...
```

If we were the patient and we heard a doctor speaking like that, we'd be heading for the door if we could. Most likely because that's how we would express it – and we know we're not medically trained either! However, if we heard them say –

```
INT. CUBICLE, ACCIDENT & EMERGENCY, ST. SOMEWHERE - DAY

                    DOCTOR
          Nurse, we need a cannula and line here,
          and prep 50 mils of vancomycin...

The Nurse nods. Heads towards the medical supplies.
```

– we might decide to stay put. For now. Because the term "Doctor" coupled with the dialogue is still vague. What type of doctor are they? Consultant? Surgeon? General Practitioner? Dentist? Doctor of philosophy (i.e., an academic)? And what type of 'Nurse'?

I am always surprised by how little thought some writers give to the jobs or vocations of their characters. It's as if they think 'my character's a doctor' or 'my character's a nurse' and that's it. Think about it. If they are a doctor or a nurse, then they have a certain way of talking, and it is incumbent on us as writers to have researched this and understand it. I read many scenes in which there's a nurse or a doctor talking and it doesn't sound like any nurse or doctor I've ever met or ever known.

These are medical professionals, and we will have seen them on TV documentaries and in real life over the years. They have a particular way of speaking and behaving because of the things they are dealing with – the life-and-death situations they may be confronted by every day. This means they speak and behave in a certain way – and our characters based on them need to talk and behave in that certain way, too.

How do screen characters really speak: vocation, job, hobby

- doctor? junior consultant? professor? surgeon?
- brain surgeon? military field hospital surgeon?
- nurse? senior nurse? student nurse?
- maternity nurse? emergency theatre nurse?
- patient?
- child patient? child patient's parent? parents?
- geriatric patient?
- train-spotting patient?
- porter? porter working to pay their way through drama school?
- cleaner? 'after hours' cleaner?
- 'after hours' cleaner studying for a phd?
- and so on . . .

All of the listed examples will speak and behave differently. The screenwriter's job is to understand why and how – and then implement this in / through the dialogue.

2. Location

The way we speak is also determined by our location, where we are living, and where we are from. Born in London, I have lived and worked in diverse places including the south of England, Bristol, Los Angeles, Australia, and York in the north of England. And whilst I may not have demonstrably changed my mode of speaking from place to place, the people living in those places – the native speakers from those places if you like – have noticeably all spoken in a different way. So, why not our characters?

Once again, when you're out and about, listen for dialogue that defines the location and origins of the people around you. Depending on where you are, people in that community will sound largely the same or there will be significant diversity in the speakers and their dialogue. Both are equally valid and revealing.

Now apply this to your own characters and their actual situation. Where are your characters from? Which location? Where were they born? Where do they live? Is it the same place? Why did they move? What age? The UK is a London-centric country, but we know there are so many different regions. When we talk about a character living in the north, where in the north? Do we mean the northeast? Northwest? Far north? Scotland? Or are we talking about the northwest of Scotland?

Are they from this country? Are they from a different country? Which country? What's their status in their world? Do they work in an office? Where do they work in that office? In reception, in the boardroom, or in the canteen? Do they work on the shop floor, on the trading floor, carpeting floors, and so on?

Each of these locations, where your character might spend upwards of a third of their adult life, is going to affect the way they speak, the particular dialect of the language they use, and the type of character potentially that they are. And sometimes, we are going to discover how this can be subverted and much more complicated or nuanced than it first seemed.

INT. MINI-CAB, LONDON - NIGHT

Some years ago, I was travelling late at night in a mini-cab across London with my family. They were asleep in the back. I sat up front next to our driver. We started chatting. At first, he was the mini-cab driver and I was his fare. But as we got talking, I found out he was a professor of anesthesia in his country of origin. He'd had to flee that country for political reasons and had come to England. His family were in Liverpool, but he couldn't work in the UK as an anesthetist, so every weekend he would leave them and come to London to drive a mini-cab to make ends meet.

It was one of the most revealing, memorable, life-changing conversations I've ever had. Job, vocation, location, origin, and culture were at the forefront in helping me to begin to understand him, his character and situation, and he mine.

For writers, listening, asking questions, and making discoveries like these are the essence of truthful characterisation and dialogue development.

How do screen characters really speak: locations

- the south of your country of origin or residence?
- the east or west of your country of origin or residence?
- the north your country of origin or residence?
- its northeast? southwest? centre?
- Scotland? Wales? Northern Ireland? Ireland?
- London? South London? North London? The East End?
- New York? Chicago? Atlanta? Key West? El Paso?
- Goa? Kerala? Mumbai? New Delhi? Shimla?

- office? boardroom? canteen? washroom?
- restaurant? café? greasy-spoon? street food stall?
- hospital? ic unit? funeral parlour? church?
- and so on . . .

3. Culture

As the anecdote about my late-night encounter with the mini-cab driver reveals, the culture of our characters is also key to who they are and how they really speak. In the same way, who our fictional characters in our made-up hospital St. Somewhere really are and the cultural background they are from will inevitably influence how they speak and what they say.

Ask yourself: What's the culture and the cultural background of your characters? Are they indigenous to your own country of origin or residence? Are they indigenous to another country? What's their origin? If they're from an island, what kind of island? People on islands often speak in distinct ways because islands can be isolated or remote.

How would the characters in our fictional hospital speak if St. Somewhere were located in the centre of a huge city or on a distant island? In the US mid-west or in Asia? In a rich neighbourhood like Beverly Hills or down the road in less wealthy Compton? What if our hospital had two campuses, one in each neighbourhood? Or, if it were a community hospital or a private one?

Is your character an only child? One of five? Eldest of five (like me)? If they have siblings, where are they in the age order? Eldest? Youngest? In the middle? A twin, perhaps? If so, do they speak in the same way as their identical twin? Do they stop and start sentences intuitively because they know what each other is going to say and when they're going to say it?

Are your characters wealthy? Poor? Or is your repertoire of characters a mix of the two? What is their background? For example, are they 'posh but poor' or 'posh and rich'? Despite their blue blood and their noble births, some of the British upper class live in relative poverty. But regardless, they talk in a certain way. They're still going to sound 'posh' even if they're living in a rented flat in the wrong part of town.

On the other hand, a person born in relative poverty can retain their accent even if they work hard, become a multimillionaire, and climb the social strata. They may, indeed, look upon their accent, mode of speaking, and vocabulary as badges of honour – evidence of their authenticity at the country club, in the Ritz hotel, or on their super-yacht on the Côte d'Azur.

How do screen characters really speak: culture

- indigenous? incomer? migrant? new arrival?
- ethnic? mixed race? pure-blood? royal?

- island? big island? small island? remote?
- Detroit? New York? Arkansas?
- twins? identical? non-identical?
- upper class? lower class? working class? middle class?
- poor upper class? wealthy lower class?
- city? rural? 'street'? suburban?
- social media? BBC? pirate? underground? revolutionary?
- Silent Generation? Boomer? Gen X? Millennial? Gen Z? Gen Alpha?
- A.I.? alien? extra-terrestrial? feral?
- and so on . . .

4. Historical Period

Movies, TV dramas, and sit-coms set in a different historical period to our own are perennially popular. But this setting provides specific challenges for us when it comes to the dialogue and the way characters can speak.

How does the period sound in your version of the character and their dialogue of that time? How do you want it to sound? Is the most important thing for you that it is authentic for the characters and the period?

Or is the dialogue knowingly and deliberately contemporary sounding, pointing up the contrast with the actual period in which the story is set?

Or is the dialogue intended to act as a bridge between the two – between the world of your story and our world?

One of my favourite anecdotes about dialogue and period concerns the movie *Amadeus* (1984), Milos Forman's multi–Academy Award[14]–winning film about rival composers Antonio Salieri and Wolfgang Amadeus Mozart. A British audience member complained sniffily that the actor[15] playing Mozart spoke in American rather than English. It was pointed out to him that if the actor had spoken the dialogue in Mozart's authentic 18th-century German, he would have understood even less of the film.

If you are going to set your film back in the past, avoid making the dialogue sound jarring, parodic. It has to have elements of that past and give us a hint that it is set 100 years ago, 50 years ago, or whenever your story is set, but it also has to resonate with your contemporary audience.

Even 50 years ago, key elements of the world then were very different in terms of the way that people spoke and their language and dialogue. A lot of the words and idioms that we use today habitually in and about our digital age didn't exist 50 years ago. For example, in the story world of 1974, birds

14 Nominated for 11 Academy Awards (Oscars), *Amadeus* won 8 in 1985, including Best Picture, Director, Lead Actor, and Adapted Screenplay.
15 Tom Hulce.

tweet, football pools coupons are marked with an X, messages are posted via telegram, and clocks go "tik-tok".

Ask yourself: Is the vocabulary your characters are using appropriate for the time your story is set in? Again, this comes down to our research. There are a lot of words that weren't in the vernacular 50, 100, 200, 500 years ago.

The same applies when it comes to the stories and characters we locate in the future. In your future world 50, 100, 200, 500 years from now, how are the characters going to speak? Indeed, will they speak? Will they need to speak? Will they be allowed to speak?

There are no hard and fast rules about the approach to dialogue when it comes to the historical period or future you are setting your film or TV scenes in. The important thing is whatever you decide has to be logical within your chosen story world, genre, and tone and be coherent and consistent for all the characters in that world.

How different would the dialogue for the characters in our fictional hospital TV drama St. Somewhere have to be if the series was set 50 years ago? 100 years ago? 500 years ago? Or 200 years in the future? 1,000 years in the future?

How do screen characters really speak: historical period?

- present day?
- 1960s?
- 1960s 'Swinging' London? 1960s 'Cold War' Soviet Union?
- Post-war? Pre-war? Which war?
- 19th century? 16th century? 10th century?
- 19th-century Australia? 16th-century India? 10th-century China?
- pre-historic?
- late 21st century? 25th century?
- 5,000 years into the future?
- and so on . . .

One of the ways of understanding how people spoke in the recent past or distant past is to check out diaries, novels, theatre plays, newspapers, and journals written in the particular time in which your story is set – in other words, do your research!

Bringing It All Together in Scenes

As you begin to work on the dialogue in your script and scenes, ask yourself the following questions to bring it all together.

- What is each character's agenda in the scene?

What is their agenda in each scene – and how is this articulated because of their specific goal in that scene? Allied to this goal, what are they trying to achieve – or avoid – using their dialogue? How do they go about doing this through the way they speak, what they say, how they say it, who they say it to, what words and vocabulary they use?

How is this also evident not just in the scene itself but in the scene preceding it and in the scene that is about to come? Scenes don't exist in isolation. They are part of a narrative thread, intersecting, working together, providing contrast, conflict, and tension to create what Orson Welles called the "ribbon of dreams".[16] Dialogue in scenes provides us with opportunities to plant things about the characters and plot, remind the audience about these, and pay them off sequentially through the story.

The dialogue of a character in each scene has a distinctive part to play in this process of unfolding narrative storytelling, reflecting that character's specific agenda, a unique agenda in that scene – often for that scene only.

- Do my characters speak like people really speak?

In our daily lives, we use our own version of dialogue. People use a verbal shorthand. They tend to often cut in and across one another when they're speaking. Does the dialogue your screen characters use reflect this? Our actual dialogue is rarely as well-composed as the dialogue we spend a long time putting down on the page and then honing and polishing.

- Who is in control in the scene (really)?

Throughout every screen story, there is a continual ebb and flow in the character's status, reflecting the arc and development of that character. Through my work on scene-writing, I came to realise that it is the dialogue of characters rather than their actions that reflects their status and, so, who is in control in the scene versus who is *really* in control.

The dialogue a character uses in conversation can, by turns, suggest, confirm, or reveal the perceived, assumed, and actual status[17] of those characters. And this is true in our own lives. Depending on your status in any given

---

16 "A film is a ribbon of dreams." *A ribbon of dreams* by Orson Welles (1915–85), pub. 1958 International Film Annual #2.

17 See Chapter 2 for more on the notion of perceived / assumed / actual status of characters in scenes.

situation, you will be able – or not able – to say to the person you are with what you really want to say to them, what you really think of them, and so on.

- How does the dialogue reflect the evolving status of the characters?

Status affects everything that we do and, in particular, in the way we talk to other people, what we say to them, and what they can / do say to us:

Perceived status: external, contextual – usually equates to character Want
Assumed status: external and internal, contextual and subtextual – usually equates to character Want, hints at character Need
Achieved status: internal, subtextual – usually equates to character Need

Troubleshooting

Here is a list of issues that are regularly identified in discussions and round-tables when we're working with writers on their dialogue:

- The dialogue feels flat.
- The dialogue is too literal, too 'on the nose'.
- It's too expositional.
- It's telling us what we're seeing on the screen.
- There's no difference between the characters when they're talking.
- There's no distinctive individuality or 'voice'.
- There's no space in the dialogue for the meaning beneath it – the subtext.
- It's too complicated.
- It's too long.

Sometimes we read our dialogue and we realise – and we can barely admit it – it feels kind of . . . boring.

And if it's boring to us, the chances are it's going to be boring to other people.

Ask yourself: <u>Why is it boring?</u> Is it too 'on the nose'? Too literal? Too expositional? Is it telling us the story instead of showing it to us? Is it dialogue we can't 'see'? Is it telling us what we're also seeing on the screen? Are the action and the dialogue doing the same thing? Do you need to add subtext to it? Take stuff out? Leave stuff out?

What if the dialogue was opposed to the action? Or notably different from it in some way? Said something different to the action? Created a deliberate gap[18] between the action and the dialogue?

As with the gap Robert McKee describes between what a character wants and what a character needs, in the gap between action and dialogue, there

---

18 In his *Story* workshops (e.g., Sydney, Australia, 2012), Robert McKee refers to the gap between a character's Want and their Need.

lurks opportunities for drama and comedy. It also encourages the audience to participate: we enjoy the gap between what the action is showing us and what the dialogue is telling us, and this creates an emotional response in us. It can create identification, interest, empathy, and engagement in our characters and our writing.

Is there a lack of distinctive individuality or voice? Is there also no space for meaning underneath – the subtext – that is so vital in screen storytelling?

Context is usually all around us on screen, but subtext also should be everywhere. Subtle, hidden, subterranean, secretive, intrusive.

Is the dialogue too complicated, too long, is there too much of it?

As a general rule, put in literally only what the audience needs to know or hear to understand the story.

Checklist

Ask yourself:

If each character represents a musical instrument, which instrument does each of them speak like?

If each character represents a colour, what colour does a particular character speak? Do they speak big, bold, prime colours – reds and yellows and blues? Or is their dialogue more subtle? Are they characters that speak in pastels, a light pink, or soft red until, one day, they turn into prime colour red?

Regardless of genre, film and TV scripts are usually 65% action, 35% dialogue – there is twice as much action on the page as dialogue in most scenes we write. This is more a guide than a rule of thumb: many of our favourite film and TV scenes will be memorable precisely because of the predominant dialogue in them. But these scenes stand out because the dialogue when it comes is featured, notable, distinctive rather than being 50 / 50 in every scene all the way through.

The *Final Draft* screenwriting software has a handy reporting facility that allows you to see the percentage of key elements such as action, dialogue, character in your script. The following table gives you these percentages for some of my screenplays and TV dramas in the order they were written and also indicates the different genres.

Once we add together all the elements we see on the screen – for example, scene heading (location), action, character, parentheses, and transition – this average totals 68%.

The TV drama pilots / specs I've written have a similar average percentage of action to dialogue (71% / 26%) as do my short film scripts (69% / 26%). Only in my sit-com pilots / specs does the dialogue percentage equate (49% / 46%) to the action percentage, confirming the dialogue-driven nature of that particular medium, similar to the early draft rom-com example (*Brilliant, Weber & van der Borgh, 2004*) in the table.

TABLE 4.1 Percentages (%) of Action and Dialogue Elements in Feature Film Screenplays and TV Drama Scripts Written by Simon van der Borgh (2000–2024)

% of Action and Dialogue Elements in Screenplays and TV Scripts by SvdB (2000–2024)

TITLE / FEATURE FILM	SCENE HEADING %	ACTION %	CHAR- ACTER %	PAREN- THESIS %	DIA- LOGUE %	TRANS- ITION %	SHOT %	TOTAL %	GENRE
STRANGE HEROES 2000 spec	4	60	3	2	29	0	0	98	COMEDY CRIME
BONEY and BETSY v2001 optioned	4	60	3	1	29	0	0	97	PERIOD ACTION
THE ALLENS HAVE LANDED spec	5	60	4	1	27	0	0	97	COMEDY FAMILY
BRILLIANT v2004 spec US/ UK	4	41	6	3	44	0	0	98	ROM-COM
BRILLIANT v2008 spec US/ UK	4	45	5	3	39	0	1	97	ROM-COM
IN TRANZIT v2006 produced	3	63	3	1	26	0	0	96	PERIOD DRAMA
RIDING THE FIRE v2007 comm.	8	57	4	0	28	0	0	97	PERIOD BIO-PIC

SHADOW OF THE WITCH v2009 comm.	7	64	3	0	20	0	3	97	SUPERNATURAL HORROR
BLOOD OATH v2007 spec	5	67	3	1	22	0	0	97	SUPERNATURAL THRILLER
BLOOD OATH v2009 optioned US	6	65	3	0	21	0	3	98	SUPERNATURAL THRILLER
BLOOD HUNTERS v2014 spec	6	60	4	0	27	0	0	97	HORROR
FORGOTTEN MEN v2014 spec	7	56	4	0	30	0	0	97	COMEDY DRAMA
FORGOTTEN MEN v2020dr optioned UK	6	55	4	0	32	0	0	97	COMEDY DRAMA
THE WONDER KID v2024 spec	6	49	4	1	38	0	0	98	COMEDY SPORTS
AVERAGE	5.5	57.5	4	1	29.5	0	0	97.5	VARIOUS

As you write your dialogue, keep the following in mind:

- Dialogue is more like poetry than prose.
- Sentences of dialogue are 6–8 words long on average.
- Speeches in dialogue build.
- The best stuff comes at the end of the speech.

I often describe written dialogue as being more like poetry – reinforcing the sense that we should be writing dialogue we can see – than prose, with every sentence sequentially imparting exposition and information to us, its 'subject, verb, object' approach and structure commonly used to write action.

I encountered this short exchange while I was working on this chapter the other Sunday when I went to buy a newspaper:

```
INT. NEWSPAPER SHOP, YORK — DAY

SIMON approaches the counter with his newspaper.

                SIMON
        When are you closing?

                SHOPKEEPER
        Today, or forever?

Silence. Simon thinks about this.

                SIMON
        Today.

                SHOPKEEPER
        Seven o'clock. Or maybe earlier
        if it's forever.
```

Sentences in movie script dialogue are generally 6–8 words long – short, sharp, clipped, with longer sentences as and when they're needed. This creates difference and texture, colour, and subtext. Hold back longer sentences of dialogue for when you want them to be noticed and make an impact.

Speeches also build. Planting or paying off vital story information, playing with character status, contrasting Want with Need, establishing confrontation and conflict, providing revelation, confirming tone and theme, context and subtext, are some of the writing elements we can employ to help us escalate and elevate a speech. In a longer speech, the best stuff generally comes at the end because that's the bit the audience and the other characters are going to remember. When I overheard that overbearing man on that train all those years ago, the part that stayed in my mind ever since was the final four sentences:

```
            MAN
I've been all over the world, I have.
Travelled everywhere. South America,
up the Amazon, down it, Africa,
Indonesia, Papua New Guinea, Australia.
And I've eaten all kinds of food. I've
eaten dog, cat, spider, scorpion. I've
had snake and camel. Beetle. And
kangaroo's testicles. Sheep's eye. Twice.
```
I've eaten everything. And there's only
two types of food I can't stand. Raw fish.
And monkey's brains!

In recreating that scene for this book, everything in the speech leading up to the last four sentences (in bold) was carefully constructed to create the maximum impact and effect of those final lines – the punchline – on the reader and audience to try and replicate the effect that it had on me.

Conclusion

Regardless of your character's job, location, culture, and period, the dialogue we create for them needs to be effective within the terms of that character and world as you establish them.

For me, effective dialogue is

- dialogue that a character needs to say or use
- at that particular moment in the scene and story
- to achieve a particular goal or objective.

Avoid over-using dialogue. We should, ideally, use the minimum amount of dialogue that is required for that particular event in the plot, for the particular moment in the scene or story to achieve the particular goal or objective for the characters and story that you want – whether that objective is character development, story development, moving the action forward, planting something or paying it off, giving the audience exposition, or creating comedy, drama, and conflict.

Dialogue doesn't happen to fill space. It doesn't happen randomly. Its purpose is not to use up a couple of minutes until we get to a more interesting scene.

And it is almost always strongly and directly motivated.

As Konstantin Stanislavski (1863–1938) said to his actors:

> If you know your character's thoughts, the proper vocal and bodily expressions will naturally follow.[19]

I happen to think it is also very helpful advice to writers. Because if we know our character or characters, if we understand them, if we have a real sense of who they are, then it's inevitable that we'll start to write them on the page so that they will move, behave, and speak in the way that is the appropriate and unique for them, who they are, and the story world that they inhabit.

During my *Writing Dialogue* masterclass at the Australian Film Television and Radio School – Sydney (AFTRS),[20] I proposed the following:

> We try and make our dialogue neat and smart-looking. But actually, in many respects, the opposite is true. If Action is organized, structured, neat, clear, then Dialogue is often anarchic, chaotic, messy. If Action represents the external and physical in a story – the Want, if you like – then Dialogue represents the internal and emotional – its Need. The two meet in pretty much every scene you will ever write. Where they meet, how they meet, and the gap between them, is what makes the scene – and your writing – fresh, new, interesting.

Dialogue – Scene-Writing Exercise

"Job / Location / Culture / Period" Exercise

As we've discussed, dialogue – verbal action – provides us with the means of bringing our characters and their stories vividly to life in the story. Use this dialogue scene-writing exercise to explore some of the ideas explored in this chapter.

Step 1a – *Choose two characters from this list:*
Doctor
Junior consultant
Professor
Surgeon
Brain surgeon
Nurse

---

19 *An Actor Prepares* (1936).
20 August 2012, Australian Film Television and Radio School, Sydney, Australia.

Senior nurse
Student nurse
Maternity nurse
Emergency theatre nurse
Patient
Child patient
Geriatric patient
Mortuary attendant
Porter
Cleaner
Another character type you're interested in

Step 1b – *Choose a location (i.e. where each comes from) for these two characters.*
Step 1c – *Choose a culture for these two characters.*
Step 1d – *Choose a historical period for these two characters.*

Step 2 – *Write three short scenes showing us these two characters:*

1. At their place of work during working hours
2. Getting their lunch in a local café outside the hospital
3. Taking part in an evening class of their hobby after work

Step 3 – *Once you've written the scenes, compare them. Ask yourself:*

- Read the scenes out to yourself. How do they sound?
- What parts of the dialogue can you see?
- What modes of dialogue are you using: Conversation? Monologue? Soliloquy? Talking to camera? Voiceover?
- What do these modes add / take away?
- Read the scenes out to someone else. What did they understand?
- Is their status to one another the same in each scenario?
- How does the dialogue reinforce the different statuses of the characters?
- How does the dialogue play with the status of the characters?
- What is the ratio of action to dialogue in the scenes?
- Would less or more dialogue improve the scene / scenes?

5

THE SETTING

The Arena Where and When the Action Is Located at a Particular Point in the Story

Introduction

```
INT. LIBRARY, KING'S MANOR, YORK — DAY¹
```

The scene heading, or slug line, is the first element we encounter at the start of every scene we read or write.

The term 'slug line' is derived from the newspaper industry. Reputedly, the first screenwriter was a newspaper reporter who wanted to use industrial terms he was familiar with to describe the formatting and layout of screenplays:

> In newspaper lingo, "slugs" are sticks of lead produced by Linotype machines: they are also type lines used to identify blocks of type that have already been set. So a reporter's story or copy would be given a slug line at the editor's desk – such as "Fire", "Governor", "Parade". The slug line then would be used by the headline writer to identify the headline that went with the story. The Linotype operator, who set the story in type, would "slug" the work for identification. The makeup editor would use the slug line to identify the placement of the story and how much space it

---

1 This scene heading denotes where I spent a lot of time writing this book. Part of the University of York, The King's Manor was originally the Abbot's House of St Mary's Abbey. It served the Tudors and Stuarts as a seat of government, becoming residences in the 18th century and a school in the 19th.

DOI: 10.4324/9781003293927-6

would take on his "dummy" page of the paper. All these elements came together in the composing room where the slug lines and their particular components "made up" the Newspaper.[2]

An essential element in the formatting and dramatic action of your screen story, the slug line or scene heading comes at the top of each scene and introduces it, effectively also acting as the scene's title.

It is worth bearing in mind that the scene heading *per se* often only comes into being some way into the development process of a film or TV script. Early on, you may spend useful time working up your idea via a series of short documents, such as a synopsis, outline, or treatment before you feel ready to embark on the script stage and the highly formatted process of writing the screenplay. And it may only be when you expand your idea from a treatment into a scene-by-scene breakdown of it that you include a specific slug line for each scene.

For example, an early synopsis or outline may contain the lines:

```
Safara waits. When she is sure the house is deserted she uses
the stolen key to get in. She begins to look around, searching
the place carefully from room to room.
```

It is only when you begin to expand the action in a longer treatment or step outline and place Safara in specific locations that are relevant to her, to her goals, to the plot, and to the world of the story that you will identify specific scenes and slug line for those scenes:

```
EXT. STREET — DAY
EXT. HOUSE — DAY
INT. HOUSE — DAY
```

And so on.

Components of the Scene Heading

The following slug lines are typical of those used every day in scripts worldwide to locate our scenes and their action:

```
INT. HOUSE - DAY
EXT. OFFICE - NIGHT
I/E. CAR - CONTINUOUS
```

2 *Elements of Style for Screenwriters* by Paul Argentini (Lone Eagle Publishing, 1998).

As we can see, three distinct physical elements [1. 2–3] are being defined for the reader in the scene's heading:

1. Whether the action in the scene takes place somewhere inside (INT. = interior), somewhere outside (EXT. = exterior), or somewhere that's a combination of the two (I/E)
2. Where the scene is located – for example, inside a house, outside an office, or a combination of inside and outside a car.
3. The time of day in which the unit of action in the scene happens, predominately DAY or NIGHT.

The numerous screenwriting software versions that are available create some variance in the physical presentation of the heading for your scene.[3] For example, some automatically put the scene heading INT. HOUSE – DAY in bold type as **INT. HOUSE - DAY**; some underline it as <u>INT. HOUSE - DAY</u>; others put it in bold type and also underline it as <u>**INT. HOUSE - DAY**</u>.

Regardless of the software you're using or the type of script – feature, TV drama, soap, short, sit-com, etc. – you're writing, the three core elements of the scene heading and their principles are common to each scene in order to fulfil its primary purpose of locating that specific unit of contained dramatic action in the plot of the story for the reader and, ultimately, for the team responsible for bringing that scene to life on the screen.

The scene heading provides an overarching unifying framework for the events and characters in the particular scene, establishing as concisely as possible where and when the new scene is taking place. It introduces the general or specific setting of the particular scene while also indicating to the reader that a new scene, and a new unit of dramatic action, is beginning.

In this respect, a scene heading provides an automatic cut from the previous scene, resetting the location, time, action, characters, and events for us. Imagine a scene set INT. HOUSE – DAY followed by a scene set EXT. OFFICE – NIGHT followed by a sequence of scenes set I/E. CAR – CONTINUOUS.

Now add a genre – for example, horror – to these scene types and imagine the cuts in place and time when moving from a house scene in a horror film, to a horror story office scene, to a sequence of horror story car scenes. Contrast this in your mind with another genre, such as romantic comedy. The movement and cuts this relocation create – the tempo of your writing – are even different depending on which act of your script they are in.

---

3 I generally refer to *Final Draft*'s software to illustrate the formatting and layout I advocate. But as my students keep reminding me each year, many other screenwriting software programmes that format and lay out your scenes and scripts to industry standards are available!

The movement created by the previous scene headings in Act 1 – the act of set up and character introduction – of our imaginary horror or romantic comedy will generally be very different to a sequence of the same scenes in Act 3 – the act of climax and resolution – as the stakes and conflict for your characters reach their climax and the tension in the dramatic action of your story and its plot intensifies.

You can begin to see how this relocation from scene to scene can help install the idea of movement – action – in your story and your writing – and even more importantly, instill this in the mind of your reader.

An agent at William Morris[4] in Los Angeles once told me that you can't read a script until you've read a thousand scripts. The trouble is, reading all those scripts and their scenes is inherently passive – the opposite of seeing the same scenes play out on the screen. So anything we can do to enhance the sense of flow and progression in time and place from scene to scene, page by page and, thereby, enable our reader to begin to see the film in their head makes them more likely to engage with the dramatic action of the story they are reading – and engage with us and our writing.

Our goal is to seduce the reader through our writing into becoming a participant in our stories, activating their hopes and fears in the characters they are reading about and the story worlds those characters inhabit. The scene heading is the signpost into this, scene by scene. Yet, for most writers – me included – the scene heading is the element that we are least interested in and we spend the least time thinking about.

We'll often bung anything down – INT. HOUSE – DAY, EXT. OFFICE – NIGHT, I/E. CAR – CONTINUOUS – because we want to get on with the fun stuff: the scene itself. If we enjoy writing action, we want to get on with that. If dialogue is our thing, we want to get on with that. We want to spend our time with the characters we're creating, the situations we've put them in, and the consequences of those situations. After all, who thinks about the signpost once we've reached our destination?

We may very well be missing a trick.

Let's examine the slug line and its components in more detail.

1. **Where we are:** INT. EXT. or I/E

These (INT. EXT. or I/E) are the accepted descriptors generated by all screenwriting software. The three options available to us are pre-set; they are the historic and accepted terms used in the industry, a generic part of screenplay formatting and layout, their use reinforced in style guides and manuals.

---

4 Currently called WME Agency (2024).

They give us a straightforward location for the unit of action we're about to write or read, which is going to take place inside, outside, or inside and outside the intended location. Writers tend to accept this and apply these contractions without demur – even if they don't actually understand what they mean. Every year I get students guessing that INT. means "INTERNAL" and EXT. "EXTERNAL", which can potentially convey a rather different meaning to the one intended.

Where the use of INT. EXT. or I/E becomes more interesting, complex, and potentially uncertain is when it is used in relation to certain types of locations.

Here's an example of my train of thought when I'm working on a slug line for a scene I'm writing:

Say I want to set a key scene on a river:

EXT. RIVER - DAY

My character is on the run and has managed to find a rowing boat which they are escaping in – note the word "in" – on this river:

EXT. ROWING BOAT, RIVER - DAY

Now it happens that this is set during the monsoon season. It's raining. So the rowing boat has a fixed canvas canopy and my character is sitting under this while they row:

EXT. CANOPY, ROWING BOAT, RIVER - DAY.

In my mind's eye, my character is effectively under – inside – this structure. So is it actually EXT.? Maybe it's:

INT. CANOPY, ROWING BOAT, RIVER - DAY?

A debate now ensues in my mind. Is this scene INT. or EXT.? What are the ramifications of this decision? What is the right / best / correct thing to do?

After much deliberation, I decide that the easiest thing is to change the rowing boat to a small motorboat with a wheelhouse cabin!

INT. CABIN, MOTOR BOAT, RIVER – DAY

This is a backward step dramatically speaking. After all, the rowing boat requires my character to row. It means they have to engage in a physical action – and one that isn't their skill set – to keep one step ahead of their pursuer. They have to power their escape. This is active and reveals character.

Added to this, maybe they've been injured while getting away, which hampers their ability to row even more, escalating the potential for drama, stakes, tension, conflict, increasing the reader's hopes and fears in them, and creating more even engagement in my character and their story – and in my scene.

So I decide to lose the canopy and go back to:

```
EXT. ROWING BOAT, RIVER - DAY
```

While crossing the river – in a monsoon – the rowing boat capsizes. After all, we know by now that my character is not a very good rower – and my character gets thrown into the water.

They start to sink . . .

I want to show this in a new scene:
```
EXT. WATER - DAY
```
But my character is in / inside / under / the water. So maybe it's:
```
INT. WATER - DAY
```

Out of curiosity, when writing and thinking about these, I put the following into an internet search engine: "When a character is in the water in a script, is that INT or EXT?"

Many pages of well-intentioned but often conflicting and subjective advice came up, some of it helpful, a lot of it not. Beware the Internet.

In trying to work out this kind of scene issue logically and objectively so that it conforms, keep in mind the industrial factors that come into play and can help us determine whether the particular scene is INT. EXT. or I/E, such as

- where we (the writer / reader) are in the scene
- what our intended point of view is, as we envisage it as the writer, in relation to the action and events in the scene
- where and / or what the light source is in the scene
- where the camera is in our imagined version of our scene – but remember, we're the writer, not the director of photography or the director!

Some of the responses that came up online in answer to my question advised writers to put UNDERWATER in the slug line, thereby avoiding the other scene heading elements – INT. / EXT. / I/E. and DAY / NIGHT – altogether:

```
UNDERWATER

The Rower begins to sink...
```

In other words, let someone else worry about this down the line!

2. **Where the scene / unit of action is located:** HOUSE / OFFICE / CAR

The second component in the scene heading – the locale in which the unit of
   action you're writing is to be placed or situated – gives us opportunities to
   specify and customise our slug lines and make them integral and unique
   to our screen story.
Let us look at one of the most common and generic settings we will ever use
   in our scene-writing:

EXT. HOUSE — DAY

Imagine a house. Your character is outside it. What does it look like? Is it on
a city street? Up a long drive? On its own in the middle of nowhere?
   Is the house you're imagining detached? Semi-detached? A terraced house?
End of terrace? Mid terrace? Brick? Wood? Glass? Pitched roof? Thatched
roof? Flat roof? Corrugated iron? Where is the entrance to it? At the front?
Round the side? Round the back? Up some steps? Down some steps below
street level?
   Now think about how you would describe your HOUSE in the slug line.
   Here's an example of the type of location description one can sometimes
get from new or inexperienced writers:

EXT. 18th-CENTURY DETACHED COTTAGE WITH THATCHED ROOF - RED
SQUIRREL LANE - MIDDLE OF NOWHERE - NORTH YORKSHIRE - DAY

My first observation is that as a rule of thumb, I always try and format the
content of a scene heading on a single line. A slug line is primarily a summary – a signpost or title for the unit of action that's to follow – so the shorter
and clearer the better.
   My next observation is: How do we know all this stuff in the description
provided? Given that we can only know what we see or hear on the screen
as part of the action or dialogue at a particular moment in the plot, how do
we know that we're in:

RED SQUIRREL LANE — the MIDDLE OF NOWHERE — NORTH YORKSHIRE?

More to the point, what's the relevance of this level of detail to the characters
and the plot? How relevant to the plot is it that the cottage is:

18th-CENTURY — DETACHED — THATCHED?

Bear in mind that it is not the job of the screenwriter to intrude into the work
or roles of other people such as the production designer or art director and
impose unnecessary details.

In my experience, human nature being what it is, talented creative people have plenty of their own ideas and may do the opposite of something that we've described on the page if they don't see the point of it or it's not integral to the story or plot in some way.

Thus, the poetic, atmospheric:

```
EXT. 18th-CENTURY DETACHED COTTAGE, WINDING LANE, MOORS — DAY
```

in the original script becomes the somewhat different:

```
EXT. GLASS-FRONTED MODERN APARTMENT, CLIFFTOP, OCEAN — DAY
```

when the writer finally gets to see it on the screen.

The level of location detail in the 2-line scene heading example I provided also slows down the read. Less is generally more when it comes to scene-writing. Giving your work clarity and making it a fast and enjoyable read helps engage the reader and make them feel positive towards your story. This starts with the slug line.

It may well be that you are imagining details like those in the example in your head when you write the scene. This level of detail is important to some writers because it helps give the characters and their world context and bring them to life for you while you are developing ideas and writing. But in the draft itself, we generally only specify or include key information that is relevant to the story and feature in the plot – for example, if the thatched roof of the house you're envisaging is going to be set alight in some way while your character is locked up inside.

But as a dramatic writer, you would still want to make sure that the nature of the roof and its flammable potential is brought to the attention of the reader, planted in the plot, and incorporated in the action and dialogue in some way. This is a key part of the job of a screenwriter, and it is incumbent on us to think about this and solve it in the script.

Simply stating details like the roof is thatched in the scene heading alone relies on the director and other members of the team subsequently working out how to show this in the film, establishing it for the audience, and making its existence clear somehow in the plot if it is to feature.

This slug line may give us all we need to know plot-wise:

```
EXT. THATCHED COTTAGE, MOORS - DAY
```

More Than One Scene

Greater complications and bigger issues tend to arise once your character and the action relocate inside the house. Take a look at this example, based on similar ones I've read in student scripts over the years. What are the problems with it and with the action description that follows it?

```
INT. HOUSE - DAY
```

```
A cloudy mild day in Cornwall. DIANA (70s) is in her kitchen
looking anxious. She can't think about anything except the let-
ter she's just read. Up in her bedroom, she searches through
every cupboard looking for her diary. That night, she looks
for it in the bathroom. Then she remembers last time she saw
her diary was in the living room. She finds it on the table by
the TV.
```

Note that this an extreme example and there are a variety of issues in it. Too many elements in the action description make us ask: "How do we know?" We can't know that Diana is in Cornwall or what the weather / temperature outside is like if we are inside with her, and we don't establish this or see characters interact with this in some way. Likewise, we can't know that Diana is thinking about the letter, or the diary, or about where she remembers last seeing this if we don't see or hear these essential elements as an integral part of the plot in some way.

However, the overriding issue – and the one that affects every subsequent aspect of the ensuing scene-writing of this connected series of events – is embodied in the scene heading. The action being described is taking place in more than one location. The stated scene heading INT. HOUSE – DAY fails to specify the actual locations in which the events of the plot are specifically taking place. As if by magic, Diana moves from the kitchen to her bedroom in the day, and then at night to the bathroom and finally into the living room in search of her diary, without a shift of time or place being indicated through the sole slug line.

In this excerpt:

```
INT. HOUSE - DAY
```

is in reality 6 different scenes in 5 different locations:

```
EXT. DIANA'S HOUSE, CORNWALL — DAY
INT. KITCHEN, DIANA'S HOUSE - DAY
INT. BEDROOM - DAY
INT. BATHROOM — NIGHT
INT. KITCHEN - NIGHT
INT. LIVING ROOM — NIGHT
```

The following is an indication of how this could be laid out more effectively and more clearly using scene headings to indicate the locations and the time of day that are actually indicated in the original action description.

I haven't fixed the other issues – the "How do we knows" – but I've put notes in the text so that I can remind the writer – and myself – that these have to be fixed:

```
EXT. DIANA'S HOUSE, CORNWALL — DAY
```

It's a cloudy mild day in Cornwall. *(SvdB: We still need to establish this in some way)*

```
INT. KITCHEN, DIANA'S HOUSE - CONTINUOUS
```

DIANA (70s), looking anxious. She can't think about anything except the letter she's just read. *(SvdB: We still need to show / make it clear that Diana is thinking about this in some way)*

```
INT. BEDROOM — DAY
```

She searches through every cupboard looking for her diary.

```
INT. BATHROOM - NIGHT
```

She looks for it [her diary] in the bathroom.

```
INT. KITCHEN - NIGHT
```

She remembers that last time she saw her diary was in the living room. *(SvdB: We still need to show this process of realisation by Diana in some way)*

```
INT. LIVING ROOM — NIGHT
```

She finds it [her diary] on the table by the TV.

Our writing imposes consequential temporal and location factors which have a physical effect on events and the way we depict them. These factors, in turn, have an effect on the reader's understanding and interpretation of what we are intending in our screenwriting.

Writing Is a Code

Writing is a code. The words we choose to use as writers form the code that enables us to send out to the reader the meaning and the message of our screen story that we want them to decipher. This is particularly true when it comes to the choice we make of words in slug lines to describe where we are locating our scenes.

When I was developing and writing my movie project *Boney and Betsy* at the MBFI, we had regular visits from industry professionals to talk about various aspects of the process of screenwriting and screen storytelling.

The Hungarian director István Szabó (*Mephisto,* 1981)[5] spent time rehearsing a scene from an early draft of my screenplay with actors, which was an invaluable experience for a new screenwriter to observe. In a masterclass, he also played the following game with us:

> I want you to imagine a simple line: through the window of my grandmother I see some flowers. Is that understandable? Then start with the word *flower.* Will you please close your eyes, and think about the flower. What can you see? Can you tell me what kind of flower you have seen?

He got various contributions from participants. Inevitably, amongst a group of individual filmmakers from across Europe, every flower mentioned was different.

> The second word is *window.* Close your eyes? So, what kind of window do you have, please? What does your window look like?

Again, István got a different window from each participant.

> And now the most difficult thing of all. Will you close your eyes? I will give you the word grandmother. I don't want to ask you what your grandmother looks like, but I am very sure that everyone's image or vision of their grandmother is different.[6]

Based on our own personal experiences, words like "flower", "window", and "grandmother" will inevitably create individual and emotive meanings in each of us.

In the same way, familiar words such as house, office, car, street, wood, church that we may use regularly in a slug line to locate the particular unit of dramatic action allow the reader to interpret that word in the way they want to, or are conditioned to, or have personal experience of rather than the specific way that the writer is envisaging or intending.

A screen story's intended medium (e.g., film or TV) and its genre or story type add another layer to this ongoing process of interpretation and understanding.

The intended atmosphere, tone, look and feel of, say, a CHURCH, and the way that this type of location may be presented to us and then used in a

---

5 *Mephisto* (1981) won István Szabó the 1982 Academy Award for *Best Foreign-Language Film.*
6 István Szabó; *Sources of Inspiration Lecture 4, 1994.*

scene will be markedly different in a horror film, a romantic-comedy, a crime story, a soap, or a sit-com. There may also be a consequential effect on how the particular scene is viewed depending on the reader's residual feelings and views about churches or other religious buildings. The fact is, every word we choose and write can affect the reader in some way.

```
EXT. CHURCH — DAY
EXT. CHURCH — NIGHT
INT. CHURCH — DAY
INT. CHURCH — NIGHT
```

are the entry points and signposts for scenes that contain a world of possibilities for our characters and their stories which are only limited by our imaginations – and our budgets.

There is a much-used saying in the film industry: if you don't have the budget, you have to make a creative decision. Nowhere are the imaginative ramifications of making this kind of creative decision more active and impactful – and carry more potential and be more consequential – than where we decide to locate our scenes.

The Order of Things

It is inevitable in a subject as broad and organic as scene-writing that customisation takes place depending on factors like where you are writing, what you're writing, who you're writing it for, and what software you are writing it on.

Imagine that I want to set a scene in a bathroom in a character's house at night. I have identified the three key elements that define the specific location for the unit of action:

1. INT.
2. BATHROOM, SAFARA'S HOUSE
3. NIGHT

My habit and my experience encourage me to write this in a slug line as follows:

```
INT. BATHROOM, SAFARA'S HOUSE — NIGHT
```

However, some writers and teachers I've worked with, and some of the scripts I read, present the order of the key words that indicate where the scene is set in a different order, for example as:

```
INT. SAFARA'S HOUSE — BATHROOM — NIGHT
```

Students ask me, which comes first? What is the right order of things in the scene heading? And why?

INT. BATHROOM, SAFARA'S HOUSE — NIGHT

or

INT. SAFARA'S HOUSE — BATHROOM — NIGHT

As a screenwriter, I always use the former:

INT. BATHROOM, SAFARA'S HOUSE — NIGHT

It may be because I started out as a director in theatre and film before I became a screenwriter and teacher, but I favour identifying and situating the precise location in the slug line – BATHROOM – over the more general one – SAFARA'S HOUSE – in my mind and in the mind of the reader.

After all, the specific unit of action is taking place in the bathroom, not the house *per se* which may have several levels, rooms, and bathrooms. It is also taking place in the bathroom for a reason:

a. as an integral part of the ongoing real-time action in the scene itself;
b. as a consequence of something that's happened in a previous scene or scenes that preceded this scene;
c. or as the set up of something that is then going to happen and be germane to the action and the scene(s) to come.

Added to this, depending on factors like a) the type / budget level of the production, b) the importance of the scene in the story, and c) the action contained within it, the bathroom identified for the shoot may be a practical one in an actual house – and not necessarily in the house that's being used to represent the location SAFARA'S HOUSE in the script – or it may be a bathroom set built in a studio for the production.

Indeed, if I'm writing a sequence or series of scenes set in the same overarching location like SAFARA'S HOUSE, I will often drop SAFARA'S HOUSE from the scene heading in early / selling drafts once this main location is established to speed up the read for the reader and avoid repetition. Rather than the reader thinking, "Yeah, I get it, we're in a house – the same house – Safara's house", we want to encourage them to think, "We're in a hallway, now we're going up the stairs, now we're in the bathroom, now we're going into the attic – Uh, oh, that's not a good idea" and so on.

In practical and industrial terms, too, my experience suggests that the order of the locating words I use in slug lines – SPECIFIC LOCATION, MAIN /

OVERALL LOCATION – is understood by the major filmmaking and production software when it comes to using the scenes and slug lines as the basis
for generating pre-production, shooting, and post-production reports and
documents such as location sheets, schedules, call sheets, logs, and so on.

And this, ultimately, is the main factor, over and above any reason or habit
you may have, for ordering locations in a particular way.

Whether you write:

```
INT. BATHROOM, SAFARA'S HOUSE — NIGHT
INT. BATHROOM — SAFARA'S HOUSE — NIGHT
INT. SAFARA'S HOUSE, BATHROOM — NIGHT
INT. SAFARA'S HOUSE — BATHROOM — NIGHT
```

the key thing is that your intentions on the page are clear for the reader,
the team, and the technology that may one day be required to work on the
scene, process and analyse it and its components, and bring these to life on
the screen.

Whatever aesthetic, cultural, habitual, or industrial influences that we may
bring into our screenwriting or bring to bear on it when we compose a slug
line, the key thing is that it – and our intentions – are clearly understood.

As the influential screenwriting teacher Frank Daniel[7] reputedly used to
say to his U.S. screenwriting students: "Beware the fear of being understood".

That deceptively simple advice continues to influence my thought processes in many aspects of my work as a writer, script consultant, and teacher
of writers since it was first introduced to me. It is as relevant in the context
of the scene heading or slug line we may be proposing as it is to any other
aspect of screenwriting.

3. **The time of day in which the scene happens:** DAY or NIGHT

Convention has it that there are two fundamental times of day for us to consider in the slug line: DAY or NIGHT. However, screenwriting software like
Final Draft offers us more options than these, such as:

```
AFTERNOON
EVENING
LATER
MOMENTS LATER
MORNING
THE NEXT DAY
```

7 František 'Frank' Daniel (1926–96), screenwriter, film director, and teacher.

And other software can additionally offer:

```
DAWN
DUSK
```

Indeed, there is nothing to stop you writing what you want in the 'time of day' part of the slug line, and over the years, I have read a number of logical and exotic indications of this. I know from my own experience that when you're working on a spec script, the constant use of DAY or NIGHT can become repetitive. Adding in the occasional MORNING or AFTERNOON provides a welcome sense of variety to the process.

However, I learnt a big lesson about the consequences of this when I was working on turning the production draft into the shooting script of *In Tranzit* (Tom Roberts, 2008) in St. Petersburg, Russia, in the days leading up to the first day of principal photography.

My work on the script in the preceding months had helped bring stars like Vera Farmiga, John Malkovich, and Thomas Kretschmann onto the project and move the project into production. So I was proud of my work. I continued lovingly and carefully to polish the script, for instance, going through it scene by scene doing a 'colour' pass, adding DAWN, MORNING, AFTER-NOON, DUSK to the slug lines to enhance – as I saw it – the context and the atmosphere of the scenes for the talent. The majority of the film was set in a Soviet women's transit camp at the end of WWII, so I thought that a bit of 'poetry' like this would help add difference to scenes.

However, in a production meeting with Andrew Warren, the movie's line producer, I was told in no uncertain terms to remove these descriptions – my poetry! When I asked why, he asked me how we knew it was, say, MORN-ING? What was it in the specific action or element in the scene that told us this? As far as he was concerned, when it came to the proposed time of day of a scene we could only ever know what we could see or hear in the script. That's why films and TV scenes feature clocks on walls and bedside tables, people sipping afternoon tea, drinking morning coffee, eating lunch, going on dawn runs, etc. to varying degrees of logic and success.

As far as Warren was concerned, from a production management point of view there were – are – only two times of day: DAY and NIGHT. He explained to me that this was to help him and his team schedule the shoot. Depending on the time of day of the scene, this would generally determine the process and the order of the way that the shooting of the script would be scheduled for the crew, talent, extras, and all the associated support and services involved in it. My so-called 'poetry' was replaced by industrial practice.

Once again, beware the Internet, which offers directly contradictory advice here. Typing the question "What time of day can you put in scene headings?" into a search engine elicits the following examples:

- There are just two acceptable times of day: 'DAY' and 'NIGHT'. Unacceptable times include 'THE NEXT DAY', 'LATER THAT MORNING', and 'THAT SAME MOMENT'. No matter when one scene takes place relative to another, all that's evident on screen is whether it's day or night.[8]
- As for the time of day, you can be as specific as is relevant to the story, so feel free to use day, night, dawn, dusk, morning, afternoon, etc.[9]

The reality lies somewhere between these two opposing views and, ultimately, depends on where you and your script are in the writing, development, and pre-production process.

For example, when you're working on an early draft of your 'spec' script under your own initiative and your main goal is to gain potential producer, talent, or financing interest in it and you, a little bit of 'poetry' here and there in elements like the time of day and the action and character descriptions is acceptable if it enhances the read and brings the work to life off the page – that is, if it helps sell you and your work.

However, once you and your project are advancing along the more formal script development road and every single element in the script has a consequence or an implication and begins to convey a meaning to the industry reader and to carry an attendant cost, then adhering to the specificity of DAY or NIGHT in the proposed time of day indicates that you have thought about and understand the ramifications and implications of what you are writing.

Favouring the precise and the pragmatic in this way over the poetic confirms to experienced readers that you understand what it really takes to bring ideas to life. It can also suggest that you're going to be a good partner and collaborator.

The Use of CONTINUOUS

As well as DAY or NIGHT, there is a third option that is widely available and can indicate time of day: CONTINUOUS. For example:

```
EXT. CAR — DAY

Jo opens the car door and gets in.

INT. CAR — CONTINUOUS

She slides into the driver's seat and checks the rear-view mirror.
```

8 https://www.storysense.com/format/headings.htm#
9 https://www.socreate.it/en/blogs/screenwriting/are-day-and-night-the-only-descriptions-you-can-use-in-a-slug-line

The use of CONTINUOUS here indicates to the reader that the action between the scenes is unbroken. There is no ellipsis in time and the dramatic action continues from scene to scene in real time.

There may be times in a script when you want to give the reader a sense of connection and unity of action from scene to scene to heighten the drama in a short sequence of scenes and unify the dramatic action.

For example, the tension in chase scenes and the clearly established predicament of the character being pursued can be unified and heightened if the reader gets the sense that events are happening moment by moment in real time. This can raise the visceral nature of the writing and the sense of stakes, increasing our hopes and fears in the character and sustaining our emotional engagement and investment in them:

```
EXT. CAR — DAY

Jo opens the car door and gets in.

INT. CAR — CONTINUOUS

She slides into the driver's seat and checks the rear-view mirror.

IN THE REAR-VIEW MIRROR — CONTINUOUS

He lunges for her. Jo evades him, diving to her side...

EXT. CAR — CONTINUOUS

Jo falls back out through the car door. Gets to her feet.
Starts running.

BEHIND HER

Dirk clambers out the passenger door. Starts running after her.

EXT. STREET — CONTINUOUS

Jo pounds along the pavement. Past the bins. Through the entry
door. Back into the block of flats.

INT. STAIRWAY, FLATS — CONTINUOUS

She races up the stairs two at a time.

BEHIND HER

Dirk bursts through the doors. He takes the stairs three at a
time. Closing on her...
```

```
And so on.
```

However, I regularly read examples of the use of CONTINUOUS that are erroneous, for example:

```
INT. OFFICE — NIGHT

Absa stares out at the city skyline. Sees the Festive lights.
Makes a decision. Moves towards the exit.¹⁰

INT. LIFT — CONTINUOUS

As the lift descends Absa zips up his reflective jacket.

INT. FOYER, OFFICE — CONTINUOUS

The lift door PINGS and Absa steps out.

INT. BIKE COMPOUND, OFFICE — CONTINUOUS

Absa unlocks his bike. Finds his helmet. Puts it on. Wheels his
bike out of the compound. The gate CLANGS behind him.

EXT. HIGH STREET — CONTINUOUS

Absa speeds along, overtaking a bus — just missing A REVELLER
in the road who yells at him.

EXT. SUBURBAN HOUSE — CONTINUOUS

The sun is rising when Absa pulls up outside the front gate.
He stares at the front window. All the lights are off.
```

This may seem an extreme example, but it is based on actual script samples. The ellipsis between the supposedly CONTINUOUS is plain to see, involving significant changes in location, point of view, action, and time of day.

For the most part, I recommend avoiding the use of CONTINUOUS except for the most clear-cut and obvious examples in which its correct use significantly adds to the overall experience of the read and the drama of the plot.

Bear in mind, too, that ultimately, in the production and shooting drafts of your script, the industrial process of scheduling the production is still going to be determined by whether the time of day in your scene is DAY or NIGHT.

---

10 NB. Readers should be asking "How do we know?" he makes a decision!

Setting Scenes in Unexpected or Contrasting Locations

`INT. MORTUARY — DAY`

When the director Richard Loncraine came to talk to us at the MBFI, he had recently completed a movie version of William Shakespeare's much produced 'history' play *Richard III*, starring Ian McKellen as the eponymous main character. This version of *Richard III* (1995) was re-imagined by Loncraine and McKellen into a 1930s England that was increasingly gripped by Richard's desire to seize the throne and install his version of fascism.

Loncraine made it clear that the limited budget[11] meant that creative decisions were always to the fore – and always had to be to the fore. As he explained to us in a workshop with his producer Stephen Bayley, one of the ways of freshening up a story and its characters or presenting them in a new and thought-provoking way is to set scenes in unexpected or contrasting locations. By way of example, Loncraine talked us through their decision to set the notorious seduction scene by Richard of the recently widowed Lady Anne (Kristin Scott Thomas) in a mortuary in the vicinity of the body of her dead husband Edward.

The obvious thing to do when thinking about where to set a scene of seduction is to situate it in a location that reinforces the sense of romance, such as a fancy restaurant, on a bridge in Paris, or on a gondola in Venice. Throw in rose petals, champagne, and a ring, and the job is done.

But what if you deliberately set it somewhere that worked against the reader's expectations and conventions like the mortuary setting in *Richard III*? What would this add to the scene? What additional difficulty does it create for the character(s) and their situation? What additional conflict and tension might a different setting introduce? How might it raise the stakes for the characters in the scene? What might it add to the subtext and content of the unit of action that's to come?

The relocation of archetypal scenes to settings that may offer a contrast or a challenge to more stereotypical ones that merely reinforce the audience's genre expectations can work for a number of genres and story types, and we'll explore these and other ideas more in the scene-writing exercise at the end of this chapter.

Conclusion

As this chapter has revealed, there is more to composing an effective scene heading than simply writing `INT. HOUSE — DAY` and charging into the scene.

---

11 The film's budget was £6M (Estimated; imdb.com).

Of course, momentum is important in writing. Early versions of your slug lines will often act as bookmarks, reminiscent of the newspaper industry origins of the 'slug line' term. But, as is so often the case in our field, the art of writing is rewriting:

```
INT. HOUSE — DAY in today's first draft evolves into
INT. BATHROOM, HOUSE — DAY in tomorrow's second draft and
on into
INT. SAFARA'S BATHROOM, THATCHED COTTAGE — CONTINUOUS in next
month's sixth draft.
```

When they are thought about and constructed at the requisite level, your scene headings can act as contextual and subtextual signposts for the units of action to come. Well-designed and written slug lines can complement and resonate the thematic, genre, tonal, and atmospheric intentions of your work.

They give the stated arena for your scene its own distinct title, and they are the first element of the scene that we encounter, every scene.

With your slug line composed, you are now ready to begin to involve the reader in the action and dialogue in the scene to come.

As we have seen, central to that action and dialogue are your characters.

In the next chapter, we will look at how you bring all the elements we've discussed so far together on the page and into one entity: your script.

The Setting – Scene-Writing Exercise

"Setting the Scene" Exercise

As we've discussed in this chapter, the scene heading or 'slug line' acts as the signpost for the scene, the character(s), and the unit of action to come. Use this short non-dialogue scene-writing exercise to explore some of these ideas.

Take a character, situation, and scene you're working on or come up with a new character and a situation and scene they might be in. Locate them in the story world.

Step 1 – *Imagine your character is arriving somewhere to meet someone who is not present in the scene yet:*

- Where are they arriving?
- When are they arriving?
- EXT. or INT.? DAY or NIGHT? Why?

Step 2 – *What slug line / scene heading best describes your initial intentions for the character, situation, scene, location, genre, tone, atmosphere, etc. before you write the action?*

Step 3 – *Write a short paragraph under the slug line describing the action in your scene:*

   a. Write this action first in a way that suggests horror
   b. Rewrite it so that it suggests comedy
   c. Rewrite it again so that it suggests romance, drama, detective, or another genre you're working in / interested in.

Step 4 – *Review your scene heading each time you do Step 3:*

   • How does the slug line reinforce the genre, story world, character, or situation?
   • What do you have to change in the slug line for it to better reinforce the genre, story world, character, or situation?

Step 5 – *Finally, relocate the scene to an unexpected location that contrasts with action and the character in some way:*

   • What does this change of setting add to the scene?
   • What does it take away from it?

Notes:

   • Using this non-dialogue task to try out characters from a film or TV idea you may have is a useful way of bringing them to life in the early stage of character development.
   • Write your scene action in one paragraph (as you would in a treatment, step outline, or scene breakdown).
   • Less is more – keep it brief and don't use any dialogue.
   • Use one scene heading as you're writing a single unit of dramatic action.
   • Think about the location of the scene in your slug line.
   • What happens to the slug line if you change the genre, atmosphere, or tone?

6

FORMATTING AND LAYOUT

What Should a Scene Look Like on the Page?

Introduction

You've done the hard bit. You've found a great idea for a film or TV story. You're excited about it. You've spent every waking hour – and many sleeping hours – thinking about it, living it, dreaming it. You've worked on the characters and plot, the story type, genre, tone. You've identified the audience for it, the broadcaster, the producer. You've grabbed time here and there, away from family, friends, and life, to write the first draft. As I say, you've done the hard bit. And then you screw up the easiest bit of all: your presentation of it. How it looks. Its formatting and layout. Its one chance to make a first impression. <u>Your</u> one chance.

You may be lucky. An agent, producer, or developer might take time to read it no matter what it looks like. But it's a big risk. I know this because it's my own story.

In the early 1990s, I was a director on a documentary film project. We were filming on 35 mm all around the world, and I was due to go to Kenya for a 3-week shoot over Christmas and New Year's. Then the producer pulled rank. He told me he'd decided to direct the shoot and take his family. To lessen my disappointment, he gave me three weeks off on full pay. When you're a freelancer, these things matter; they don't happen very often. So I decided to make the most of the time I suddenly had. I sat down to write my first-ever film script, *Thank You, Pavarotti!*

I didn't know it at the time, but it turns out that being bumped off the Kenya gig by my boss and having the unexpected opportunity to write *Thank You, Pavarotti!* set in motion a chain of events that literally changed my life.

DOI: 10.4324/9781003293927-7

IMAGE 6.1   Directing on location in Germany, 1992 ©IPCA

However, looking at the script and its formatting and layout today in the light of everything that I know now and I'm sharing with you in this book, it could so nearly not have. It would have been all too easy for an industry decision-maker to take one look at the below-par non-industry standard presentation of my script and chuck it in the bin – regardless of its intrinsic merits or the potential talent in its pages.

I was lucky. My then agent felt obliged to read the script and loved it. Her response encouraged me to believe that I could be a screenwriter. So I used the script to apply to the screenwriting programme at the UK's National Film and Television School and was short-listed for an interview. On the interview panel was the movie producer Sandy Lieberson.[1] He had read the script, and despite its many presentation errors, he responded warmly to it. I was accepted on the 2-year screenwriting programme. The rest, as they say, is history. Yet it could so easily not have been. All because I didn't know – or more accurately, didn't bother to find out – how to format and lay out a movie script correctly.

1 Sandy Lieberson, U.S. film producer. Films include *Performance* (1970), *That'll Be the Day* (1973), *Jabberwocky* (1977).

1.

BLACK

MUSIC. THE OPENING TITLE MIXES UP:

" THANK YOU, PAVAROTTI ! "

WHICH DISSOLVES TO

SCENE 1. EXTERIOR, DAWN. A BACK STREET IN ROTHERHITHE.

A TYPICAL, TRADITIONAL DOCKLANDS STREET, NOT NEW, SHINY, GLASS. THIS STREET HUGS THE RIVER THAMES, AND IT'S NARROW, DIRTY, LINED WITH BRICK WAREHOUSES.

A CAR PASSES THE CAMERA, HEADLIGHTS ON.
IT'S A WINTER MORNING, NOT YET LIGHT.

THE STREETS SEEM DESERTED.

SUDDENLY...

A FIGURE FLITS OUT FROM THE SHADOWS, AND DARTS BACK IN.

CUT TO

THE FIGURE, PRESSED TIGHT AGAINST A BRICK WALL.
HE'S UNRECOGNISABLE, BECAUSE HE'S WEARING A BLACK BALACLAVA.

LOOKING DOWN THE STREET, HE FREEZES.

CUT TO

A WIDER SHOT. A POLICEMAN ON A BICYCLE EASES PAST. THE FIGURE IS HIDDEN FROM THE CYCLIST'S VIEW, WHICH IS CLEARLY THE WAY HE WANTS IT...

CUT TO

THE SINISTER-LOOKING FIGURE AGAIN, BREATHLESSLY WATCHING THE POLICEMAN GO BY. THE ATMOSPHERE, COUPLED WITH THE OPERA MUSIC, IS STRANGELY TENSE.

IMAGE 6.2 Page 1, *Thank You, Pavarotti!* by Simon van der Borgh (3rd draft), 1994.

My ignorance meant I unwittingly took a big risk – a needless one that we can quickly and easily mitigate by using industry-standard formatting and layout. Ideas are difficult. They are the hard bit. The correct presentation of those ideas is, by comparison, the easy bit.

If you've read the earlier chapters of this book, I'm sure – I'm hoping – that you looked at the first page of *Thank You, Pavarotti!* in disbelief. How could I make so many basic errors in one scene?! Take heart from this. Because you're not now going to make the same mistake, are you?

The Key Elements of Formatting and Layout

As we've discussed in the previous four chapters, the fundamental components of a scene are

Character – who is on screen
Action – what we see happening on screen
Dialogue and Sound – what we hear on screen
Setting – where the core elements above are located

A combination of these core elements is at play, to varying degrees, in every scene we will ever write, and their importance in the scene-writing process and the on-screen storytelling process is, by now, clear to see.

We are watching and listening to the actions and sounds created by screen characters in identifiable locations scene by scene. These elements also constitute the core formatting and layout elements around which most scenes are structured:

```
SETTING...

ACTION...
                            CHARACTER...
            DIALOGUE...

SOUND...
```

However, there are additional formatting and layout elements that feature regularly in scenes in film and TV scripts even if their functions and the rules for their use are, at times, opaque.

Parentheses

Parentheses, also known as parentheticals, are the brief comments or directions within brackets that relate to the specific speaker in the scene and are commonly situated in the body of that speaker's dialogue. They relate either to

- that speaker's / character's action – what they are doing / how they are doing it
- that speaker's / character's dialogue –what they are saying / how they are saying it

```
EXT. FRONT PORCH, HOMESTEAD, FARM, PRAIRIE — DAY

                        INGRID
                  (angry)
            What you doing here?
                  (raising her rifle,
                  pointing it at Jeff's
                  heart)
            Get off my land.
                  (beat)²
            Now.
                  (adept)

She COCKS the rifle.
```

However, in my experience as a writer and reader, story information like this is better expressed in an action line wherever possible, for example:

```
EXT. FRONT PORCH, HOMESTEAD, FARM, PRAIRIE — DAY

Ingrid eyes Jeff. Cold fury.

                        INGRID
                  What you doing here?

She raises the rifle. Points it straight at Jeff's heart.

                        INGRID (CONT'D)
                  Get off my land.

She COCKS the rifle. Adept.

                        INGRID (CONT'D)
            Now.
```

The second version (my preferred version) takes up 15% more space on the page, comprising 16/52 lines of the scene compared to the 14/52 lines of the

---

2 NB. The term 'beat' has a different usage and meaning here to, say, one of the 6 Key Story Beats that we've previously referred to. Used in this context, it suggests to the reader that there should be a brief pause within the dialogue or the action to create emphasis or dramatic effect. Note that a beat is shorter than a pause.

first version. But its more precise and effective use of parentheses *vis-à-vis* action means the resulting layout and the meaning of the words on the page are clearer.

At just over 2/8 of a page, it also equates more accurately to the actual, real time that the exchange is likely to take on screen. If a properly formatted and laid out page of a script equates to 60 seconds of screen time (i.e., 1 page = 1 minute), this exchange covers approximately 15 seconds of screen time at 2/8 of a page.

A film script page is traditionally divided into eighths for budgeting and scheduling purposes, and scenes in screenplays are commonly described as lasting for 2 and 3/8 pages, 7/8 of a page, 1 and 4/8 pages, and so on.

Crucially, too, more space on the page makes the script easier to read and visualise. Ironically, a longer but better spaced, better composed scene is quicker and more enjoyable to read than a seemingly shorter, tighter one.

There are other benefits, too. As Nick Whitfield, a writer-director I've worked with a few times over the years, said in an interview in *The Guardian* newspaper:

> Because this game is so strange and complex, you're constantly learning. Sometimes it's the littlest thing. I once worked with a great script editor called Simon van der Borgh, who insisted that I press return on the keyboard more often. And pressing return more often made me think in terms of shots.[3]

The chances are that if effective spacing, formatting, and layout mean we are beginning to think subliminally in terms of shots as we write our scenes, the reader may, too.

Parentheses Issues

Here are some of the risks and potential pitfalls that we should be aware of when we use parentheses in place of action:

1. Overuse

By their nature, the overuse in scenes of short directions and actions in brackets throughout the script can spoil the presentation of the work and begin to affect how we are reading it. For the busy industry reader, it is easy to skim through a scene and miss or ignore the parentheses, thereby missing potentially important actions and plot information.

2. Telling the Director / Actor / Other Crew Their Job

It's the director's job to direct your script. Too many short instructions and directions in brackets risk intruding into the work of key people like this.

---

3 Nick Whitfield, writer and director, *Skeletons* (2010), Winner of the Michael Powell Award, Edinburgh Film Festival, interview in *The Guardian*, 24 September 2010.

This is especially true if we are indicating the feeling state of the character – (e.g., they are (angry) (confused) (amused) (scared)). There is a cautionary tale of a first reading of a script where the new writer watched as the leading actor went through the draft scene by scene putting a line through the parentheses and exclaiming noisily: "I know when I'm supposed to be 'angry'". Although he should have handled this situation more tactfully, the actor did have a point. It should be clear from the dialogue and / or action how the reader – in this case, the actor playing the role – is meant to interpret the feeling state of the character at the particular point in the scene, story, and script.

3. Favour the Action Line and / or Dialogue Over Parentheses

As my earlier example involving Ingrid and Jeff illustrates, parentheses can be used to convey an action instead of putting the information in the action line itself. Likewise, parentheses are often used to support or replace the intention of the dialogue. Parentheses can be a shorthand, at times, for example, when a clearly established activity is being repeated in a scene, but it shouldn't be used to replace action or dialogue. Let's return to Ingrid and Jeff:

```
INT. HOMESTEAD, PRAIRIE - NIGHT

Jeff is watching Ingrid in the candlelight as she measures and
cuts the cloth to make her dress. Skillful.

                    INGRID
          Well, I'm going whether you like it
          or not.
               (measures)
          It's the first invitation we've had
          since we arrived in this hellhole.

She marks the cloth. Picks up the scissors. Lines them up.

                    INGRID (CONT'D)
          Of course, it's up to you what you do.
               (cuts)
          But I am going.

The scissors SLICE through the velvet material.
```

4. Action Versus Activity

One of the areas where parentheses can be helpful and earn their place is when it comes to activity.

Action encompasses the specific events that take place in the scene and, as described, are intended to affect and involve the characters and create the plot.

Activity refers to the allied actions, the secondary repetitive actions in which a character might be engaged in and around a scene.

For example, a character is smoking a cigarette throughout a scene in which they are about to face a firing squad. Smoking a cigarette in this context may be viewed as an activity. The character has got to do something. They could equally be chewing their nails, playing with rosary beads, or trying to eat their final meal.

However, if our character uses that lit cigarette to light a trail of fuel that causes an explosion that creates a diversion that enables them to escape that firing squad, then the act of smoking that cigarette becomes an action. It has a specific developing purpose and function within the dramatic action of the scene that influences, affects, and creates the plot and its characters.

Sound

Sound cues are written in capitals and tabulated on the left-hand side of the page, most usually as part of the action. Sometimes a cue is given its own line if it describes a key sound in the plot that needs to be brought to the reader's attention.

Given the importance of sound in the telling of any screen story, I am always surprised about how casual writers and directors can be about using this essential tool in our toolkit and their lack of awareness about the importance of sound. Having watched hundreds of shorts and micro-budget films from all over the world, I can confirm that these are usually let down more by their mediocre sound than their camerawork. The audience will accept a bump in a track or a missed focus, but poorly recorded dialogue and badly mixed sound stick out like a sore thumb.

This tendency to fixate on the image and what we are seeing on screen at the expense of the sound and what we are hearing starts with screenwriting. Every year, I set a variety of non-dialogue and dialogue scene-writing exercises for my student writers. In their scenes, they carefully describe the characters, setting, action, dialogue. But most of them forget the sound. They imaginatively locate their scenes in the city, countryside, a deserted island, underground, in space, houses, offices, cafes, pubs, hotel rooms, train stations, gas stations, space stations, bathrooms, kitchens, caves . . . But how do we know this from the sound in the scene? The fact is, we wouldn't know from the soundless vacuum that the dramatic action of the particular scene all too often takes place in. No traffic, dawn chorus, distant alarm, tick-tock of a clock, hum of machinery, clank, clang, bell, engine, helicopter, plane, drip of water. Not even a hint of the world of the location and beyond.

Please stop reading for a minute. Listen to the space you're in, wherever you are. Really listen. What can you hear around you? What sound or sound cues can you discern? Is there a general sound state or one dominant sound? Different sounds, intruding? Are they regular or irregular? How would you write what you can hear – the diegetic sound all around you – as sound cues in the scene you are currently living in?

Here's my scene as I write this:

```
INT. STUDY, TERRACED HOUSE, YORK — DAY

Simon stops writing. Reads the screen. Listens:

By his feet — a LOUD SIGH: his dog Muriel.

Across the room — a LOW HUM, and a RATTLE: the wine fridge.

Simon HUMS and RATTLES too. Then SIGHS. And carries on TYPING.
```

Depending on where I might be when writing this – in a café, on a train, in the library – the sound cues around me would inevitably be different. So why aren't they different in our scenes? More to the point – why aren't they in our scenes at all, even when they are being made as a result of some kind of integral action?

What is your scene, in the here and now, where you are? What are the sounds in it that you can hear? Which of those sounds is relevant – vital – to the scene and its action, and which aren't? How would you write this so it is clear to the reader?

Diegetic and Non-Diegetic Sound

Diegetic[4] sound is sound that originates from a source within the story world and is heard by the audience and the characters in the scene. It emanates from action on or off the screen, and its source is either a) visible to us on the screen or b) unseen by us but understood by us to be there, such as

- voices of characters – (e.g., conversation, monologue, soliloquy, talking to camera, voiceover)
- sounds made by objects in the scene
- sounds resulting from character actions in the scene
- music coming from instruments or devices such as radios or TVs in the scene

---

4 Diegetic comes from *diegesis*, Greek for "recounted story". A film or TV drama's *diegesis* is the total world of the story action. Another term for diegetic sound is actual sound.

Non-diegetic sound refers to sound whose source is not present in the scene and is, therefore, coming from a source outside the story world and the scene, such as

- narrator's commentary – (e.g., voiceover)
- sound effects which are added in post-production for dramatic effect
- composed music

The screenwriter is responsible for establishing the diegetic sounds in a scene. Key sound cues need to be represented in the script in a way that confirms that these come from and exist within the story world of the particular scene. Non-diegetic sounds are generally added during post-production on a film or TV drama. For the most part, these come from outside the context of the story world and so are not the responsibility of the screenwriter, apart from, say, voiceover.

Sound cues in scenes tend to be put in capitals to indicate to the sound team that the specific sound needs to be generated. This scene has a lot of sound in it:

```
EXT. WATERLOO STATION, LONDON — DAY

The Steam Train PUFFS along the platform, slowing as it passes
the Military Band PLAYING, the Crowd CLAPPING, Children CHEER-
ING and YELLING excitedly. The Train Driver HOOTS THE WHISTLE.
Brakes SCREECH, wheels LOCK and the train GRINDS to a halt. The
Cannon BOOMS a 'gun salute' and the FIREWORKS start.
```

I'm sure we can agree that there are a lot of diegetic sound cues in this scene. Too many. It gets to the point where the reader begins to tune out specifics in the action – train, driver, band, crowd – and is left with the overriding sense that there is a lot going on, and a lot of noise being made. That could be what we want as the writer – maybe the onus of the scene is on the sense of celebration and community rather than the perspective of individual participants and groups of participants – but this requires thought and then careful presentation to make sure the writer's intentions are clear for the rest of the team.

The addition of non-diegetic sound in this scene – for example, the voice of a narrator – only adds to the complexity, layers, and contextual and sub-textual meaning of the scene.

```
EXT. WATERLOO STATION, LONDON — DAY

The Steam Train PUFFS along the platform, slowing as it passes
the  Military  Band  PLAYING,  the  Crowd  CLAPPING,  Children
```

```
CHEERING and YELLING excitedly. The Train Driver HOOTS THE
WHISTLE. Brakes SCREECH, wheels LOCK and the train GRINDS to a
halt. The Cannon BOOMS a 'gun salute' and the FIREWORKS start.

                    NARRATOR (V.O.)
          People return from war in many different
          ways. To military bands. Weeping mothers.
          Medal ceremonies. Or in a casket. Me? I'm
          in the back of that train.
               (beat)
          In the casket.
```

As screenwriters, we can play with the conventions of diegetic and non-diegetic sound in certain story types and scenes to create irony and ambiguity or play with the expectations of the audience and surprise them. The increasing use of genre hybridity in films and TV series also encourages this mash-up of conventions.

Shots

As the opening page from *Thank You, Pavarotti!* confirms, I was eager to describe the shots and shot types as I envisaged them when I was writing the script:

A WIDER SHOT. A **POLICEMAN** ON A **BICYCLE** EASES PAST. THE **FIGURE** IS HIDDEN FROM THE CYCLIST'S VIEW, WHICH IS CLEARLY THE WAY HE WANTS IT . . .

This is because I was a director back then, not a screenwriter. I envisaged the characters, story, story world, action, plot in my head as a director. The script was one of the stages in what I viewed as the process of making the film – a film I was going to direct. In that respect, the script was a shorthand for me as its director.

I now know differently. Even when working with writer-directors, I encourage them to approach the writing part of the process exactly like a writer does and go through all the stages, elements, and emotions that a writer has to go through when writing a script. And then, when they and their team are happy with the script, hand it over to the director – in this case, to themselves. Read that draft as the director, like a director. Work out how they're going to direct the script, the shots they envisage, the aesthetic of the film, and so on. Add the shots in at this stage.

If we view ourselves as the writer only – as I do myself now – then it is even more incumbent on us not to specify shots, camera moves, frame sizes, close-ups, or how the camera moves in the scene's action descriptions.

When shots are specified in a script, they are written in capitals and tabulated on the left-hand side of the page as part of the action description. However, this is commonly referred to as 'directing on the page' and should be avoided at all costs, not least because doing it risks alienating a writer's most important resource – the director or DoP whose job it actually is to decide on how your script is best shot, what it should look like, and how it might best be brought to life on screen.

If you don't like the terms of this relationship, then by all means position yourself as a writer-director.

In the meantime, let us return once again to Ingrid and Jeff and see what happens to their scene in the hands of an overzealous, shot-driven writer:

```
EXT. FRONT PORCH, HOMESTEAD, FARM, PRAIRIE — DAY

WE CRASH ZOOM IN ON:

Ingrid, eyeing Jeff. Cold fury.

BIG CLOSE UP ON INGRID

                    INGRID
           What you doing here?

WE TRACK AS

She raises the rifle. Points it straight at Jeff's heart.

MEDIUM CLOSE UP — JEFF'S FACE

                    INGRID (CONT'D)
           Get off my land.

MID SHOT

Ingrid COCKS the rifle. Adept.

CLOSE UP ON INGRID

                    INGRID (CONT'D)
           Now.
```

This is obviously exaggerated to make a point. But if it were an actual written scene, who could blame the director if he read it and decided that he was going to cover the whole scene in a single shot using a drone? And how would you feel as the writer if this was what you saw on the screen?

The bottom line is, think about what you would like to see on the screen – what you are imagining in your head – and then work out how to describe this clearly and simply involving the characters, action, dialogue, sound, and story world that you have envisaged for each scene. And do this in such a way that weeks, months, years, even decades later, that vision will be what you see on the screen.

Transitions

Transitions from one scene to another or from one moment in time to another are written in capitals and tabulated on the right-hand side of the page.

Transitions – a device by which we visualise relocating the action or setting from scene to scene or within a scene – have similar pitfalls for the screenwriter as shots. Their use to create dramatic effect in the script, enhance the read, reinforce the tone and atmosphere, or highlight a key moment is one thing. Their intrusion into the roles of the editor and the rest of the post-production team is quite another.

Once again, the first page of *Thank You, Pavarotti!* confirms my own ignorance in this key area:

A FIGURE FLITS OUT FROM THE SHADOWS, AND DARTS BACK IN.

CUT TO

THE FIGURE, PRESSED TIGHT AGAINST A BRICK WALL. HE'S UNRECOGNISABLE, BECAUSE HE'S WEARING A BLACK BALACLAVA. LOOKING DOWN THE STREET, HE FREEZES.

CUT TO

<u>A WIDER SHOT.</u> **A POLICEMAN ON A BICYCLE** EASES PAST. **THE FIGURE** IS HIDDEN FROM THE CYCLIST'S VIEW, WHICH IS CLEARLY THE WAY HE WANTS IT . . .

CUT TO

THE SINISTER-LOOKING FIGURE AGAIN, BREATHLESSLY WATCHING **THE POLICEMAN** GO BY. THE ATMOSPHERE, COUPLED WITH THE OPERA MUSIC IS STRANGELY TENSE.

Looking at this text with the benefit of distance, hindsight, and a greater knowledge of the subject of scene-writing, it is possible to view the CUT TO instructions as replacements for scene headings:

A FIGURE FLITS OUT FROM THE SHADOWS, AND DARTS BACK IN.

EXT. BRICK WALL – DAWN

THE FIGURE, PRESSED TIGHT AGAINST THE BRICKS. HE'S UNRECOGNISABLE, BECAUSE HE'S WEARING A BLACK BALACLAVA. LOOKING DOWN THE STREET, HE FREEZES.

EXT. BACK STREET – CONTINUOUS

A POLICEMAN ON A BICYCLE EASES PAST. THE FIGURE IS HIDDEN FROM THE CYCLIST'S VIEW, WHICH IS CLEARLY THE WAY HE WANTS IT . . .

EXT. BRICK WALL – CONTINUOUS

THE SINISTER-LOOKING FIGURE AGAIN, BREATHLESSLY WATCHING THE POLICEMAN GO BY. THE ATMOSPHERE, COUPLED WITH THE OPERA MUSIC IS STRANGELY TENSE.

CUT TO is also often used mistakenly as a transition device between scenes. Remember Absa and his bicycle journey in the *Setting* chapter? What if we used a series of CUT TOs in order to further point up the extent of his city ride:

```
INT. OFFICE — NIGHT

Absa stares out at the city skyline. Sees the Festive lights.
Makes a decision. Moves towards the exit.⁵

                                               CUT TO:


INT. LIFT — NIGHT

As the lift descends Absa zips up his reflective jacket.

                                               CUT TO:
```

5 As before, readers should be asking "How do we know?" that Absa makes a decision.

INT. FOYER, OFFICE — NIGHT

The lift door PINGS and Absa steps out.

                                        CUT TO:

INT. BIKE COMPOUND, OFFICE — NIGHT

Absa unlocks his bike. Finds his helmet. Puts it on. Wheels his
bike out of the compound. The gate CLANGS behind him.

                                        CUT TO:

EXT. HIGH STREET — NIGHT

Absa speeds along, overtaking a bus — just missing A REVELLER
in the road who yells at him.

                                        CUT TO:

EXT. SUBURBAN HOUSE — DAWN

The sun is rising when Absa pulls up outside the front gate.
He stares at the front window. All the lights are off.

I regularly see the use of CUT TO like this between scenes in scripts, especially by new writers. There is generally no need to write CUT TO between
two scenes because the new scene heading infers a change of location and
thus implies a visual cut.

   The only scenes in this sequence of scenes that might benefit from a CUT
TO are the ones either side of the final transition. The location change allied
to the temporal change – from NIGHT to DAWN – warrants being brought
to the reader's attention:

INT. OFFICE — NIGHT

Absa stares out at the city skyline. Sees the Festive lights.

Makes a decision. Moves towards the exit.

INT. LIFT — NIGHT

As the lift descends Absa zips up his reflective jacket.

INT. FOYER, OFFICE — NIGHT

The lift door PINGS and Absa steps out.

```
INT. BIKE COMPOUND, OFFICE — NIGHT
```

```
Absa unlocks his bike. Finds his helmet. Puts it on. Wheels his
bike out of the compound. The gate CLANGS behind him.
```

```
EXT. HIGH STREET — NIGHT
```

```
Absa speeds along, overtaking a bus — just missing A REVELLER
in the road who yells at him.
```

```
                                                        CUT TO:
```

```
EXT. SUBURBAN HOUSE — DAWN
```

```
The sun is rising when Absa pulls up outside the front gate.
He stares at the front window. All the lights are off.
```

The CUT TO in this instance also helps reinforce the sense of the scene taking place 'Some time later' without us having to write 'Later'.

As in this instance, there are times when it may be appropriate to write CUT TO, or FADE OUT, FADE IN or FADE TO, or DISSOLVE TO or BACK TO, to reinforce or support a sense of the transition in the reader's mind and to position this as some kind of visual effect. But as with the specifying of shots in scenes, decisions like this about the movement between scenes are generally decided on in post-production and so are best left to the editor and director.

Montages

Montages are tabulated on the left-hand side of the page in the same way as action. The start of a montage is usually indicated in capitals at its beginning, the conclusion of the montage is also indicated by capitals at the end.

A montage is a short series of shots or images that are linked in some way plot-wise, thematically, or emotionally. To illustrate this, let's return to Absa:

```
INT. OFFICE — NIGHT
```

```
Absa stares out at the city skyline. Sees the Festive lights.
```

```
Makes a decision. Moves towards the exit.
```

```
START MONTAGE
```

```
A) In the lift, Absa zips up his reflective jacket...
```

```
B) The lift door PINGS and Absa steps out into the foyer...
```

C) Absa unlocks his bike. Finds his helmet. Puts it on.

D) He wheels his bike out of the compound. The gate CLANGS behind him.

E) Absa speeds along the city street...

F) He overtakes a bus — just missing A REVELLER who yells at him...

G) In the zone - Absa, cycling as if his life depends on it

END MONTAGE

EXT. SUBURBAN HOUSE — DAWN

The sun is rising when Absa pulls up outside the front gate. He stares at the front window. All the lights are off.

This particular series of shots features the same character throughout, but montages can often feature disparate elements. Note that I've added an additional, new shot in the montage series (Shot G) because when I was working on it, I felt that it needed a little extra something to heighten the montage and Absa's character.

Some poetry is allowed in elements like montages in a 'spec' or selling script and they can be used in an artful way to create emotion and a sense of culmination. They can also signify the passage of time in the story, leading into the next act or sequence.

I have labelled and ordered my series of shots by letter but there are various ways of presenting them. Numbers are sometimes used, or a dash at the beginning. As ever with screenwriting, the main thing is clarity – of both the storytelling and the writer's intention:

A) In the lift, Absa zips up his reflective jacket...

or

1) In the lift, Absa zips up his reflective jacket...

or

— In the lift, Absa zips up his reflective jacket...

Whichever way you decide to present your montage, bear in mind that once the script is in production each shot will need to be identified in the usual way with a scene heading identifying location, setting, and time of day so that it can be scheduled during the shoot along with everything else.

Flashbacks, Flashforwards, Dreams

Like a montage, narrative devices like these are tabulated on the left-hand side of the page in the same way as action. The start of a flashback or a dream sequence is usually indicated in capitals at its beginning, the conclusion is also indicated by capitals at the end.

Views in screenwriting are as polarised about the use of flashbacks in scenes as they are about the use of voiceover. For my part, there are times when using a flashback can be a useful imaginative narrative tool that saves time and ensures that the audience knows what you want them to know when you want them to know it. Scenes featuring flashbacks and dreams can also add to and heighten the genre, atmosphere, tone, subtext, and meaning of your screen story.

However, if these devices are being used as a lazy way of explaining exposition, a plot event, or a character action to the audience, then flashbacks and dreams should be avoided. We should identify a better integrated, more compelling, more dramatic way in the present of our story's narrative to impart this information.

If you do decide to use flashbacks, flashforwards, or dream sequences, you will also need to think about how you want your story's narrative to transition from the particular scene in its present into the flashback or dream sequence. What causative image, action, prop, or sound cue are you going to incorporate to effect the transition from the present into the past, dream, or future, and why? Likewise, what causative image, action, prop, or sound cue in the past, the dream, or the future that you are showing us are you going to use to initiate or motivate the transition back into the return scene and create the requisite cause and effect in the present in your story?

```
EXT. CITY STREET — NIGHT

In the zone - Absa, cycling as if his life depends on it.

Street lights flash on the wet tarmac as he races along...

BEGIN FLASHBACK

INT. OFFICE — NIGHT

Festive lights flash on the city skyline. Absa stares out at
them. Makes a decision. Moves towards the exit.

INT. LIFT — NIGHT
```

```
As the lift descends Absa zips up his reflective jacket.

INT. FOYER, OFFICE — NIGHT

The lift door PINGS and Absa steps out.

INT. BIKE COMPOUND, OFFICE — NIGHT

Absa unlocks his bike. Finds his helmet. Puts it on. Wheels his
bike out of the compound. The gate CLANGS behind him.

EXT. HIGH STREET — NIGHT

Absa speeds along, overtaking a bus — just missing A REVELLER
in the road who yells at him. The YELL reverberates into...

END FLASHBACK

EXT. SUBURBAN STREET — DAWN

BREATHING...

ABSA — ON THE BIKE

Still cycling. Metronomic.

EXT. SUBURBAN HOUSE — DAWN

The sun is rising when Absa pulls up outside the front gate.
He stares at the front window. All the lights are off.
```

Note that I've used an image – the city lights – as the way into the flashback from the story's present and sound – a yell, evolving into breathing – as the mechanism to return us from the flashback to the action in the present. I admit it's not the best flashback sequence in screenwriting history, but hopefully, it offers guidance and food for thought about how you might approach this narrative device in your own script.

Dual Location Scenes

I often get asked about how to format and layout scenes that involve intersecting action and dialogue situated in two different locations, such as phone calls.

If you are writing a scene involving a phone call or one that requires the characters to be speaking to one another from two different locations, the key thing is not to ignore this or leave it to other people to solve down the line. Keep in mind that where you imagine the camera to be determines the location.

INT. HALLWAY, HOUSE — NIGHT

JULIE approaches the door. Tries the handle. It is locked.

> JULIE
> Safara?

INT. BATHROOM — NIGHT

SAFARA is sitting on the floor. Hugging herself.

> JULIE (O.S.)[6]
> Safara? Are you in there?

INT. HALLWAY — NIGHT

No reply.

> JULIE
> Are you alright?

Silence.

> JULIE (CONT'D)
> Let me in. Please.

> SAFARA (O.S.)
> No.

INT. BATHROOM — NIGHT

Safara, eyeing the door.

> JULIE (O.S.)
> Would you like a nice cup of tea?

> SAFARA
> No.

---

6 (O.S.) is short-hand in a script for "Off Screen" and is used when a character is heard but not seen in a different room or location to another character and/or the Point of View of the camera. (O.C.) is short-hand in a script for "Off Camera" and is used when a character is heard but not seen in the same location as another character and/or the Point of View of the camera.

                         JULIE (O.S.)
                  Coffee, then?

Safara half-smiles

                              SAFARA
                  No.

INT. HALLWAY — NIGHT

                         JULIE
                  Hot chocolate?

                         SAFARA (O.S.)
                  No.

                         JULIE
                  With whipped cream?

                         SAFARA (O.S.)
                  No.

                         JULIE
                  Hot water and a slice of lemon?

INT. BATHROOM — NIGHT

                              SAFARA
                  No.

                         JULIE (O.S.)
                  A slice of lime?

                              SAFARA
                       (smiles)
                  No.

INT. HALLWAY — NIGHT

Julie stares at the locked door.

                         JULIE
                  Do you always say no?

                         SAFARA (O.S.)
                  No.

Julie smiles. SOUND of the bathroom door being UNLOCKED.

This version of the exchange between Safara and Julie is laid out in the conventional way scene to scene with slug lines for each. But once the reader understands that the action and dialogue are taking place in two different but associated locations that are interlinked for the purpose of this exchange – like an on-screen phone call – the key thing is to focus the reader on the conversation rather than the mechanism of switching in locations.

Given the repetitive nature of this conversation to and fro between the two characters, it could be laid out in a more economical way to help accentuate the dialogue and the through-the-door 'ping-pong' element:

```
INT. HALLWAY, HOUSE — NIGHT

JULIE approached the door. Tries the handle. It is locked.

                    JULIE
          Safara?

INT. BATHROOM — NIGHT

SAFARA is sitting on the floor. Hugging herself.

                    JULIE (O.S.)
          Safara? Are you in there?

BACK TO HALLWAY

No reply.

                    JULIE
          Are you alright?

Silence.

                    JULIE (CONT'D)
          Let me in. Please.

                    SAFARA (O.S.)
          No.

BATHROOM

Safara, eyeing the door.

                    JULIE (O.S.)
          Would you like a nice cup of tea?

                    SAFARA
          No.
```

                    JULIE (O.S.)
           Coffee, then?

Safara half-smiles

                    SAFARA
           No.

BACK TO HALLWAY

                    JULIE
           Hot chocolate?

                    SAFARA (O.S.)
           No.

                    JULIE
           With whipped cream?

                    SAFARA
           No.

                    JULIE
           Hot water and a slice of lemon?

BATHROOM

                    SAFARA
           No.

                    JULIE (O.S.)
           A slice of lime?

                    SAFARA
                (makes a face, smiles)
           No.

BACK TO HALLWAY

Julie stares at the locked door.

                    JULIE
           Do you always say no?

                    SAFARA (O.S.)
           No.

Julie smiles. SOUND of the bathroom door being UNLOCKED.

Scene Numbers

I read a lot of early-stage short film scripts, TV pilots, and movie scripts that include scene numbers from the first draft. This is frowned upon by the industry. The general rule is that scene numbers are only added once the script's development has happened, the project enters pre-production, and the draft that forms the basis of this stage has been 'locked off' by the producer. This mean that all heads of departments (HoDs) and crew will be working to the same scene numbers.

The reason for this is that in development, scripts change. Scenes are added and cut. Thus, scene numbers change, and having these numbers too early can cause confusion. The scene that is numbered Sc.26 in an early draft can become Sc.17 in a later draft, then Sc.48, before being cut altogether by the time we get to the production draft.

When I'm teaching, I am not always so absolute or adamant about this rule. When it comes to the development of student scripts and you're working with writers in the classroom, it can be helpful to be able to refer to "Scene 26" and discuss this.

When the time comes to add scene numbers, the software you're using should be able to do this for you. But make sure you proofread the draft afterwards. It is not uncommon even in the best-formatted scripts, using the best screenwriting software, to discover that a scene number has been randomly missed from one of the slug lines or wrongly ascribed to a random line of action.

Draft Numbers

According to the title page of *Thank You, Pavarotti!*, that draft was labelled the '3rd draft' by me. Again, this confirms my lack of knowledge and newness to the screenwriting game. The script wasn't formally optioned and never went into production. So, for all intents and purposes, it remained – it remains – the first draft even if it was the third draft as far as I was concerned as the writer.

In reality, until you share a script externally and industrially, to an agent, developer, screen agency, producer, director, etc., it is always the first draft no matter how many versions you may have done of that draft up to that point.

I often get first draft scripts from students labelled '15th Draft', which certainly lets me know how much work they've put into it! Bear in mind that Michael Arndt reputedly did 110 drafts of his Academy Award–winning script *Little Miss Sunshine* (2006).

To help me keep track of my own draft when I'm working on it at the earliest stage and before I've shown it to anyone in the industry, I usually label / date the version "Draft 1 v26.10.2023" in the file name itself and on the title page to help me keep track. When it's ready to send out (and depending on who it's going to) I label it as follows on the title page:

```
1st DRAFT

v.2.11.23
```

Conclusion

There are industrial differences in the formatting and layout of scenes depending on whether you are writing a feature film, TV drama, sit-com, or soap. The one element that is immutable is the fact that all scripts are written in Courier 12. A throwback to the days when the keys on typewriters were preset in Courier 12, this became the standard for all screenplays and, subsequently, all screenwriting software. A page of Courier 12 script was found to equate to a minute of screen time, allowing the reader to estimate the approximate running time of the proposed film.

Today, screenwriting software like *Final Draft* includes structure, script, TV, graphic novel, and text document templates to enable you to present your work in the expected way depending on the medium you are writing for. But it is also incumbent on a screenwriter to do our own research in this area. U.S. dramas format and layout scripts and scenes differently from U.K. broadcasters (e.g., the BBC, ITV, and Channel 4), German broadcasters, French, Australian, Chinese, and so on.

If you're writing a 'spec' (as in specimen) script for a particular existing TV series or show you love and want to write for, that drama may have nuances in its formatting and layout that are different to another long-running series or sit-com. Bear in mind that 'spec' can also mean 'speculative', referring in this context to a script for an original film or TV idea that has not been commissioned. Usually the writer's own idea, it is written speculatively to sell or option to a producer in due course.

There are many resources and websites accessible online to help us avoid what this chapter might classify as the *Thank You, Pavarotti!* mistake when it comes to formatting, layout, and presentation. After all, we only ever get one chance to make a first impression.

Formatting & Layout – Scene-Writing Exercise

"Formatting & Layout" Scene Exercise

As we've discussed, formatting and layout is integral to our work being presented properly and taken seriously. This can make the difference between getting our work read or not. Use this scene-writing exercise to explore some of the ideas explored in this chapter.

Step 1 – *Take a look at the first page of my script* Thank You, Pavarotti! in Image 6.2.

Step 2 – *Identify the formatting & layout errors (there are 17+)*

Step 3 – *Rewrite this scene (or better still, one of your own scenes) thinking about how you would fix these errors to present the work to industrial standard*

1.

BLACK

MUSIC. THE OPENING TITLE MIXES UP:

" THANK YOU, PAVAROTTI ! "

WHICH DISSOLVES TO

SCENE 1. EXTERIOR, DAWN. A BACK STREET IN ROTHERHITHE.

A TYPICAL, TRADITIONAL DOCKLANDS STREET, NOT NEW, SHINY, GLASS. THIS STREET HUGS THE RIVER THAMES, AND IT'S NARROW, DIRTY, LINED WITH BRICK WAREHOUSES.

A CAR PASSES THE CAMERA, HEADLIGHTS ON. IT'S A WINTER MORNING, NOT YET LIGHT.

THE STREETS SEEM DESERTED.

SUDDENLY...

A FIGURE FLITS OUT FROM THE SHADOWS, AND DARTS BACK IN.

CUT TO

THE FIGURE, PRESSED TIGHT AGAINST A BRICK WALL. HE'S UNRECOGNISABLE, BECAUSE HE'S WEARING A BLACK BALACLAVA.

LOOKING DOWN THE STREET, HE FREEZES.

CUT TO

A WIDER SHOT. A POLICEMAN ON A BICYCLE EASES PAST. THE FIGURE IS HIDDEN FROM THE CYCLIST'S VIEW, WHICH IS CLEARLY THE WAY HE WANTS IT...

CUT TO

THE SINISTER-LOOKING FIGURE AGAIN, BREATHLESSLY WATCHING THE POLICEMAN GO BY. THE ATMOSPHERE, COUPLED WITH THE OPERA MUSIC, IS STRANGELY TENSE.

IMAGE 6.2   *(repeated): Page 1, Thank You, Pavarotti! by Simon van der Borgh (3rd draft), 1994.*

1.

BLACK

MUSIC. THE OPENING TITLE MIXES UP:

"THANK YOU, PAVAROTTI!"

WHICH DISSOLVES TO

SCENE 1. EXTERIOR. DAWN. A BACK STREET IN ROTHERHITHE

A TYPICAL, TRADITIONAL DOCKLANDS STREET, NOT NEW SHINY,
GLASS, THIS STREET HUGS THE RIVER THAMES, AND IT'S NARROW, DIRTY, LINED WITH BRICK WAREHOUSES.

A CAR PASSES THE CAMERA, HEADLIGHTS ON.
IT'S A WINTER MORNING, NOT YET LIGHT.

THE STREETS SEEM DESERTED.

SUDDENLY . . .

A FIGURE FLITS OUT FROM THE SHADOWS, AND DARTS BACK IN.

CUT TO

THE FIGURE, PRESSED TIGHT AGAINST A BRICK WALL.
HE'S UNRECOGNISABLE, BECAUSE HE'S WEARING A BLACK BALACLAVA. LOOKING DOWN THE STREET, HE FREEZES.

CUT TO

A WIDER SHOT. **A POLICEMAN ON A BICYCLE** EASES
PAST. **THE FIGURE** IS HIDDEN FROM THE CYCLIST'S
VIEW, WHICH IS CLEARLY THE WAY HE WANTS IT . . .

CUT TO

THE SINISTER-LOOKING FIGURE AGAIN, BREATHLESSLY
WATCHING **THE POLICEMAN** GO BY. THE ATMOSPHERE,
COUPLED WITH THE OPERA MUSIC IS STRANGELY TENSE.

1. *i) Wrong format for page numbers*

BLACK *ii) Transitions are tabulated to the right*

MUSIC. THE OPENING TITLE MIXES UP: *iii) Formatting: wrong font / type face throughout*

"THANK YOU, PAVAROTTI!" *iv) TITLES: THANK YOU, PAVAROTTI!*

WHICH DISSOLVES TO *v) Transitions are tabulate to the right*
SCENE 1. *vi)* EXTERIOR. DAWN. A BACK STREET IN
ROTHERHITHE. *(vii)*
vi) No scene numbers in a 'spec' (speculative) script
vii) Order of information in slug lines + How do we know we are in Rotherhithe?

A TYPICAL, TRADITIONAL DOCKLANDS STREET, NOT
NEW SHINY, GLASS, THIS STREET HUGS THE RIVER THAMES,
AND IT'S NARROW, DIRTY, LINED WITH BRICK WAREHOUSES.
viii) Action is not formatted in CAPITALS + How do we know it's the River Thames?

A CAR PASSES THE CAMERA, HEADLIGHTS ON. *ix) Avoid drawing attention to the camera and directing on the page*
IT'S A WINTER MORNING, NOT YET LIGHT. *x) incorrect formatting & layout + How do we know it's a winter morning specifically?*

THE STREETS SEEM DESERTED.

SUDDENLY . . .

A FIGURE *xi)* FLITS OUT FROM THE SHADOWS, AND DARTS
BACK IN.

xi) Use CAPS but not **BOLD** *the first time we see a character in the story only*

CUT TO *xii) Avoid using CUT TO like this. Don't direct on the page.*

THE FIGURE *xiii),* PRESSED TIGHT AGAINST A BRICK WALL. HE'S UNRECOGNISABLE, BECAUSE HE'S WEARING A BLACK BALACLAVA. LOOKING DOWN THE STREET, HE FREEZES.
xiii) Use CAPS the first time we see a character in the story <u>only.</u>

CUT TO

A WIDER SHOT. *xiv)* **A POLICEMAN ON A BICYCLE** EASES PAST. **THE FIGURE** IS HIDDEN FROM THE CYCLIST'S VIEW, WHICH IS CLEARLY THE WAY HE WANTS IT . . .
xiv) Avoid shots, don't direct on the page.

CUT TO

THE SINISTER-LOOKING FIGURE AGAIN, BREATHLESSLY WATCHING **THE POLICEMAN** GO BY. THE ATMOSPHERE, COUPLED WITH THE OPERA MUSIC IS STRANGELY TENSE.

xv) Is this more than one scene, set in more than one physical location?
xvi) Unclear use of diegetic sound and sound cues
xvii) Proper formatting & layout puts more action and dialogue on the page

On the next page, this first script page has been formatted and laid out using screenwriting software:

   BLACK

OPERA MUSIC PLAYS

OPENING TITLES: *THANK YOU, PAVAROTTI!*

EXT. RIVER THAMES, LONDON DOCKLANDS — DAWN

Mid-winter. The sun is rising. Reluctant.

EXT. BACK STREET, ROTHERHITHE, LONDON — DAWN

Traditional Docklands brick warehouses hugging the river. Not
yet shiny new 'Yuppie' developments.

A car passes by, headlights on.

A DISTANT BOAT HORN. The streets seem deserted...

SUDDENLY

A FIGURE in a black balaclava flits out from the shadows. Then
darts back in.

IN THE SHADOWS

Flat against the brick wall, the Figure looks down the street.
And freezes as:

A POLICEMAN ON A BICYCLE eases past.

Hidden from view, the sinister-looking Figure watches the
Policeman go by. Not daring to breathe.

The atmosphere — coupled with the OPERA MUSIC — is tense.

When the coast is clear and the ARIA is building towards its
climax, the Figure looks to the ground.

                         THE FIGURE
                   That was close...
                      (talking to someone)
                   We'd better get home, Pavarotti.

The ARIA reaches its climax as BRIAN (the figure in the balaclava) steps out from the shadow pulling a dog lead.

Attached to the end of the lead — nervous, reluctant to follow
its master — is an unmuzzled Pit-Bull Terrier.

THIS IS 'PAVAROTTI'

7

STYLE

What Does the Scene Look, Feel, Sound Like?

Introduction

In March 2009, I was in Australia developing my movie project *Blood Oath*. I was also attached to direct the film, and the film's then producer and I were location scouting in the Pilbara, the vast ancient land in the north of Western Australia.

It was an exciting time. The movie was in 'go' mode. My producer had flown in from the US, we'd had positive meetings with potential co-producers and financiers in Perth, and we'd identified our ideal cast for the lead roles.

IMAGE 7.1   The Pilbara at sunset, Western Australia ©Simon van der Borgh

DOI: 10.4324/9781003293927-8

Finding locations for the shoot was the next step. I went into the Pilbara with a clear plan: making my film.

Searching for suitable locations for *Blood Oath* – a remote campsite, a ghostly-looking town, a gorge, an outback property – took time and involved spending many hours bumping along on dirt roads in a 4x4. Our guide Kevin Danks and I bonded. One afternoon, he asked me if I'd like to visit a site few people knew about or had visited before. It was an unplanned offer I felt I couldn't refuse. As it turned out, it changed my life.

Several hours later, way off the beaten track, many miles from any settlement, we stopped. As we walked through the bush towards an outcrop of

IMAGE 7.2 Figure with tail on rock, Pilbara, Western Australia ©Simon van der Borgh

rocks, Danks told me the story of what I was about to see. According to the local indigenous people and archaeologists, somewhere between 10,000 and 20,000 years before, an aboriginal group had stopped by these rocks for a period of time and made their home here. It might have been a riverbank, so they may have settled there to fish.

While they were there fishing and hunting, the women of the group began to create images on the rocks – the characters in their stories, their myths.

Looking at these images, created by our ancestors at a time that predates our recorded history by thousands of years, remains for me a humbling

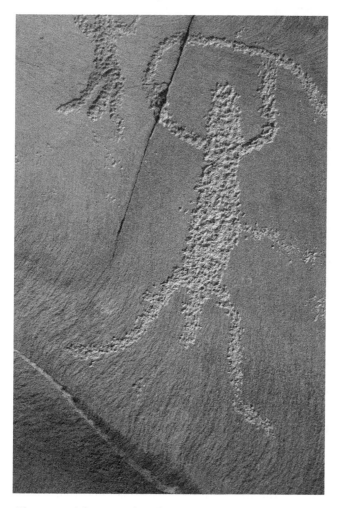

IMAGE 7.3 Close-up of figure with tail, Pilbara, Western Australia ©Simon van der Borgh

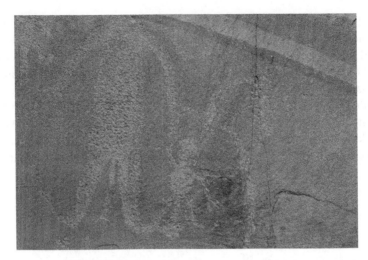

IMAGE 7.4   Child holding hands, Pilbara, Western Australia ©Simon van der Borgh

life-changing experience to this day. I will let you decide what these figures are, who they are, what they represent, what they may mean. According to Danks, what makes them even more unusual and mysterious is the method by which they were applied to the rockface. They weren't painted on or carved on. They were etched.

We returned to Perth with energy and purpose. But as is the way of these things, gradually, the project's momentum slowed and the producer gave up his option on it. *Blood Oath* remains unproduced. But the figures I met on those remote rocks in the Pilbara that afternoon started, little by little, to influence me and my approach to stories and teaching. As my plans changed, the images came with me and became an integral part of my new plan, my new life as a teacher. They will remain with me for the rest of my life.

Revisiting my encounter in the Pilbara for this book encouraged me to think about how I would write the scenes of that story. There'd be an EXT. scene establishing the 4x4s in the red landscape and the INT. scene in one of those 4x4s in which Kevin Danks first mentions the ancient site to me and asks whether I'd like to take a detour and visit it.

There'd probably be a few I/E. scenes accentuating the time that journey took, taking us further and further off the beaten track. There'd be the I/E. scene of our arrival at the site and the EXT. scene of us walking through the bush towards the rocks with Danks explaining what we are about to see. Then there would be the EXT. scene when I first set eyes on the images on the rocks. As I explore these, maybe there would be a flashback EXT.

scene by the river, imagining those same images being punched into the rock 10,000+ years before by our ancestors.

As usual, there would be plenty of content for me to get my teeth into as a writer. But as important in the writing of these scenes, and often harder and more elusive to achieve, is the desired effect that we want that content to have on the reader.

Up until now, we have predominately focused on the <u>content</u> in a scene – what happens in it and what it's about and the key components that are required to explain this. But equally important is how these foundation elements are used to create the <u>effect</u> of that scene – what we want the scene to do to the reader or audience.

Put another way, if the content in a scene provides its architecture and its context, the effect of the scene provides its subtext and its emotional core. If a scene's content is predominately external and physical, then the effect is internal, emotional.

So how do we go about applying the key components in a scene's content and incorporating these with other facets of dramatic writing so that they combine to create the effect we intend for the reader, our industry colleagues, and, ultimately, for the audience?

Content and Effect

Early in my teaching career, I became aware of the importance of content and effect and the relationship between the two in helping to establish a film or TV script's story world and genre. The more I taught script development and scene-writing, the more scripts I read, the more I realised that this notion could be hard-wired into the development of every scene within that film or TV script.

Content refers to all the elements we've discussed so far in a scene – the action in it, the characters, their dialogue, its setting, the ongoing plot, and the theme or themes being explored. Content is what we see and hear in the scene. It reflects what the scene is about.

Effect refers to the impact that the content in the scene is intended to make on the reader and the emotional response we want to elicit from them – laughter, tension, unease, fear, happiness, and so on. Effective scenes make readers feel, think, react in some way to what they're reading and imagining in their heads. It reflects what the scene is *really* about.

The combination of content and effect in a scene increases the likelihood of reader (and, ultimately, audience) engagement with characters and their stories because we begin to care about them and what happens to them. We cross an invisible line emotionally and intellectually as they begin to come alive for us on the page.

A beneficiary of getting this right is the genre of our story. Get the genre working effectively in each scene and ensure that each scene reflects the intended genre in some way, and it stands to reason that this will improve, clarify, and deepen the genre (or genres) of the script as a whole.

In development, we tend to refer to the genre of the script we may be working on as if it were an entity, a single overarching amorphous thing – a horror film, a psychological drama, a thriller, a situation comedy. We spend much less time considering that script's intended genre in the light of each scene. Yet, if a script's genre seems unclear, uncertain, inconsistent overall, this is often because that genre is unclear, uncertain, inconsistent in how it is applied <u>scene to scene</u>.

Content: What Happens in the Scene (i.e. What the Scene is About)

Four key elements to consider when it comes to identifying and establishing the content of a scene and what happens in it are plot, theme, setting, and character.

1. Plot – what is happening in the scene and how it happens, for example:

   - a chase in a thriller
   - a car chase in an action film
   - the first meeting[1] of the lovers in a rom-com
   - stealing the diamond in a TV drama
   - the shoot-out in a western or crime story

2. Theme – the implicit or recurring idea that the writer aspires to bring out in the story and is reinforced in some way in each scene, for example:

   - 'vigilance' in a thriller
   - 'self-reliance' in a crime drama
   - 'pride' in a comedy
   - 'resilience' in a horror
   - 'family' in a social drama

3. Setting – when the scene happens and where the plot and characters are physically located, confirming the intended story world, for example:

   - urban and futuristic in a sci-fi
   - magical and imagined in a fantasy

---

1 Often referred to as the 'cute meet'.

- realistic, recognisable, domestic in a drama
- a graveyard at night in a horror
- a city apartment in a rom-com or sit-com

4. Character (external characteristics) – often equating to the external physical goal or objective of the character(s) in the scene, the external characteristics of the main character, antagonists, and other characters can include

- who the characters are in society
- their social and economic status
- where they are from
- their work and domestic lives
- their age, appearance, gender

Effect: What the Writer Wants the Scene to Do to the Reader / Audience (i.e. What the scene is really about)

Four key elements to consider when it comes to identifying and establishing the effect of a scene and how we want the reader to feel are tone, point of view, stylistic devices, and character.

1. Tone – the writer's attitude towards their subject and its audience as implied in the scene, for example:

- 'fantastical' or 'epic' in a musical
- 'gritty' or 'unsettling' in a crime drama
- 'realistic' or 'serious' in a war story
- 'involving' or 'scary' in a thriller
- 'dark' or 'heightened' in a fantasy

2. Point of view – the perspective of the narrative in the scene from a viewpoint chosen by the writer, for example:

- 'subjective' in a domestic drama
- 'omniscient' in a thriller
- 'close-up' in a horror
- 'objective' in a true-life drama
- 'wide' in an action-adventure

3. Stylistic devices – the requisite narrative elements and techniques the writer uses to reveal the story scene by scene in a way that engages the audience, for example:

- the shoot-out in a western
- blood and gore in an attack in a horror

- the mysterious death in a detective story
- the ticking clock in a thriller
- the dream or flashback in a domestic drama

4. Character (internal characteristics) – Often equating to the internal emotional need of the character(s) in the scene, the internal characteristics of the main character, antagonist(s), and other characters reflect the good and bad qualities in well-drawn characters that bring the audience to the point where they are willing and able to identify with them. These can include

- The characters' hopes and fears
- their dreams and desires
- their secrets and wishes
- their flaws and wounds
- their 'shadow'[2]

TABLE 7.1 Content and Effect Grid with Their Key Elements

Content and Effect Grid

Content:	*What Happens . . .*	*Effect:*	*How We the Reader / Audience Feel . . .*
PLOT:	Can be told in a sentence	TONE:	How the writer wants the reader to interpret their attitude to the story
THEME:	The implicit recurring idea conveyed scene by scene	POINT OF VIEW:	The viewpoint chosen by the writer for the story
SETTING:	Where the story happens	STYLISTIC DEVICES:	The narrative elements and techniques the writer uses to reveal the story
CHARACTER (EXTERNAL):	Can equate to the character's external physical Want (i.e., their goals, objectives)	CHARACTER (INTERNAL):	Can equate to the internal emotional Need (i.e., their desire, shadow, flaw, wound)

2 Swiss psychiatrist and psychoanalyst Carl G. Jung (1875–1961) advanced the concept of the 'shadow', the embodiment of the suppressed unconscious within each of us (*Psychology and Religion*, 1938). His idea that enlightenment comes from "making the darkness conscious" is central to the internal emotional Need of a screen character and their recognition and resolution of this.

By way of illustrating what I mean, here is a sample of films and TV shows that I've used over the years to illustrate how the concepts of content and effect can be used to define the particular story and its world as a whole.

TABLE 7.2 Content and Effect Grid for Feature Film: *Die Hard (1988)*

Feature Film – Die Hard (1988)

Content:	What Happens . . .	Effect:	How We the Reader / Audience Feel . . .
PLOT:	Terrorists take over a building with McClane's wife inside	**TONE:**	Heightened realism: our world, but . . .
THEME:	Good v. Evil, the Family	**POINT OF VIEW:**	Objective, omniscient, favouring the hero
SETTING:	Los Angeles: a tower block and its surrounds	**STYLISTIC DEVICES:**	Stunts, special effects, explosions, guns, gear
CHARACTER (EXTERNAL):	Maverick, heroic, resourceful, moral, 'never say die'	**CHARACTER (INTERNAL):**	Alone, estranged, *in extremis,* desperate

TABLE 7.3 Content and Effect Grid for TV sit-com: *The Office (2001–3, BBC TV)*

TV Sit-Com – The Office (2001-3, BBC TV)

Content:	What Happens . . .	Effect:	How We the Reader / Audience Feel . . .
PLOT:	A documentary series charting the efforts of an office to beat closure	**TONE:**	Realistic, recognisable, our world
THEME:	"Paper People"	**POINT OF VIEW:**	Semi-omniscient, favouring its main character
SETTING:	Office and allied locations: pub, car park, etc.	**STYLISTIC DEVICES:**	Documentary, handheld, single camera, fly-on-the-wall
CHARACTER (EXTERNAL):	Ordinary, workers, existing, going through motions	**CHARACTER (INTERNAL):**	Unfulfilled, lonely, unhappy, misunderstood

TABLE 7.4 Content and Effect Grid for 1-Hour TV Drama Episode: *Mad Men (2007, AMC)*

1-Hour TV Drama Episode – Mad Men (1.01, 'Smoke gets in Your Eyes', 2007, AMC)

Content:	What Happens . . .	Effect:	How We the Reader / Audience Feel . . .
PLOT:	A top advertising exec struggles to come up with an idea that will win over his tobacco clients	TONE:	Heightened, ironic, we know more than the characters, the past is out there & will find them
THEME:	The 'family', secrets & lies, who are we really?	POINT OF VIEW:	Omniscient, favours Don Draper, also shows us other characters and subplots
SETTING:	Work & play in Manhattan, family & home out in the suburbs	STYLISTIC DEVICES:	Story of the week, the three 'Unities', 1960s attitudes & events viewed from 21st C
CHARACTER (EXTERNAL):	Urbane, selfish, sales people, ruthless, wannabe	CHARACTER (INTERNAL):	Trapped, despairing, big secrets, unhappy, alone

TABLE 7.5 Content and Effect Grid for 30-minute TV Anthology Episode: *La Couchette (Inside No. 9, 2015, BBC TV)*

30-Minute TV Anthology – La Couchette (Inside No. 9, 2015, BBC TV)

Content:	What Happens . . .	Effect:	How We the Reader / Audience Feel . . .
PLOT:	Getting to sleep on a sleeper train travelling through France	TONE:	Our world, but with heightened, surreal moments
THEME:	'Hell Is Other People'	POINT OF VIEW:	The couchette's
SETTING:	Shared couchette	STYLISTIC DEVICES:	Single camera, ellipsis, reveals
CHARACTER (EXTERNAL):	Middle class, professional, independent, travellers	CHARACTER (INTERNAL):	Frustrated, harassed, selfish, venal, vulgar, human

Blood Oath

In reality, content and effect lie at the heart of any film or TV project we may embark on from the very beginning of its development. Their establishment in the script and its scenes is an ongoing part of the integral, evolving process of story development from first idea to the screen. Take my movie idea *Blood Oath* which took me to the Pilbara. In May 2004, I was working with Arista and Film Victoria in Australia on a feature film development programme involving teams of Australian and New Zealand filmmakers. In the coach on the way down from the venue where the weeklong residential workshop had been held, I sat next to a New Zealand screenwriter:

```
INT. COACH, VICTORIA, AUSTRALIA — DAY

Scenery flashes by.

SIMON (40s) is sitting next to NICK (30s). They chat amiably.

                         NICK
               Enjoy the workshop?

                         SIMON
               Very much. You?

                         NICK
               Yeah. We all did.
Pause.

                         NICK (CON'T)
               So what you doing next?

                         SIMON
               When we get to Melbourne, I'm flying
               to Perth. I'm hiring a car at the
               airport then driving north to meet up
               with my brother Matt and his family.
               They're in the middle of a two-year
               trip round Australia so we've arranged
               to meet at a remote campsite. In two
               days' time. Should be fun!

Simon smiles at Nick.

Nick is staring at him — a mix of disbelief and concern.

                         SIMON
               What?

                         NICK
               What if they're not there when you
               get there?

Silence...
```

The prospect of driving 500 kilometres in a low-budget Hyundai Getz rental car to a remote campsite in the middle of nowhere to meet my brother and his family on an agreed day only for them not to be there had genuinely never occurred to me. But this premise – 'What if you agree to meet your brother and his family at a campsite on a given day and they're not there' – was the catalyst for the idea that became *Blood Oath* and a movie script that would take me to Cannes, California, Perth, and the Pilbara.

The seeds of many of the key aspects of its content and effect are evident even in the earliest iteration of the idea, long before it became a script and scenes:

TABLE 7.6 Content and Effect Grid for *Blood Oath, 2004 Film Idea*

Blood Oath (initial idea, 2004)

Content:	*What Happens . . .*	*Effect:*	*How We the Reader / Audience Feel . . .*
PLOT:	What if a man arranges to meet his brother and family at a remote campsite in the Australian outback and when he arrives, they're not there?	**TONE:**	Our world initially, then increasingly remote and unsettling
THEME:	Family, ghosts, fathers and sons, resilience, sins of the past	**POINT OF VIEW:**	Generally Martin's (the main character)
SETTING:	Western Australia, remote campsite, surrounding outback	**STYLISTIC DEVICES:**	Mystery, suspense, shock moments, unease
CHARACTER (EXTERNAL):	Urban, businessman, loner, fish-out-of-water, innocent	**CHARACTER (INTERNAL):**	Determined, desperate, resilient, has a big secret

Some interesting similarities and differences can be identified when we look at the opening scenes in different drafts of the script and then compare how the content and effect of the story developed over time:

BLOOD OATH (1st draft, 2007)

EXT. OUTBACK, WESTERN AUSTRALIA — DAY

The sun bakes the red earth as far as the eye can see.

This is a big place — big, empty, endless.

EXT. ROCKY OUTCROP, OUTBACK — DAY

Coarse vegetation sprouts in the middle of nowhere.

ANGLE ON:

Something crawling through the undergrowth. A bird? A large lizard? An animal of some kind?

It is a MAN: 30s, white, wearing only baggy undies and caked in red dust. Flies kiss his cracked lips. He flicks an "Aussie Wave" at them, mumbles, crawls on.

We can't make out what he's saying at first. Breathless, laboured, he's telling himself a story:

> MAN
> Teacher's talking... To a class
> of five-year-olds. About
> Easter... Eggs, bunny, chicks.

Still crawling...

> MAN (CONT'D)
> Tells 'em about Jesus... Good
> Friday... The Crucifixion...

Scraping himself along in the heat...

> MAN (CONT'D)
> How Jesus's body is taken down
> from the cross. Put in the Tomb.
> A great, big stone is rolled
> across the entrance. Kids
> listen... Eyes wide, mouths open.

WHEEZING now...

> MAN (CONT'D)
> Teacher tells them about the
> Resurrection... Mary and the
> disciples go to the Tomb on
> Sunday... Find the Tomb open...
> The stone rolled back.

Grits his teeth, forces himself on...

                    MAN (CONT'D)
         Inside, sitting up alive, is the
         man himself. Jesus.

His BREATHING is getting more and more laboured...

                    MAN (CONT'D)
         The kids gasp! Teacher smiles.
         Smug. Addresses 'em in his best
         teacher's voice:
            (Mimics Teacher)
         "Now, class. What do you think
         Our Lord's first words to his
         friends were?"

Fresh blood streaks his sides...

                    MAN (CONT'D)
         Silence. They're all thinking.
         The teacher basks in the moment.

Stops crawling, turns onto his back. His stomach is red
raw.

                    MAN (CONT'D)
         A hand goes up at the back of the
         class — Susie's hand. He beams
         indulgently at the little girl.
            (Mimics again)
         "Yes, Susie?"

The Man mimics Susie, throwing his arms out: a magician.

                    MAN (CONT'D)
         "Ta — da!"

The Man shields his eyes from the burning sun — then
LAUGHS.

                    MAN (CONT'D)
         Ta — bloody — da...

The laughter turns into a RATTLE, and overwhelms him...

                                DISSOLVE TO:

INT. MODERN OFFICE, SYDNEY — NIGHT

The same man — MARTIN APPLEBY — addressing a bunch of
OFFICE WORKERS. Urbane, dressed in a smart suit, in
charge, he's a million miles away from the first scene.

                    MARTIN
          So have a bit of patience while
          these changes are implemented.

Cynical young FACES eye one another: they know corporate-speak
when they hear it.

                    MARTIN (CONT'D)
          Yeah, I know. You've heard it
          all before. New bosses always
          say it's going to be different...

TABLE 7.7 Content and Effect Grid for *Blood Oath, 2007 Script*

Blood Oath scenes 1–3 (2007 draft)

Content:	*What Happens . . .*	*Effect:*	*How We the Reader / Audience Feel . . .*
PLOT:	A man in his underpants crawls through the harsh red outback; the same man in a city office	**TONE:**	Ironic, heightened then a more recognisable version of our world
THEME:	Resurrection, resilience, being an outsider, arriving	**POINT OF VIEW:**	Generally follows Martin (main character) and his POV
SETTING:	Western Australian outback, modern Sydney office	**STYLISTIC DEVICES:**	Harsh red landscape, mystery, glass city, heightened, contrasts
CHARACTER (EXTERNAL):	Fish-out-of-water, ironic, desperate, businessman, new	**CHARACTER (INTERNAL):**	Loner, *in extremis*, resilient, urbane, new leader

BLOOD OATH (producer's locked-off pre-production draft, 2009)

                                        FADE IN:

EXT. BUSH — NIGHT

A GIANT FULL MOON

Illuminates the white "ghost gums" — eerie.

FOUR FIGURES emerge below through the bush — a man and woman (late 20s) — BREATHING HEAVILY — both carrying a young child which clings to them, owl-eyed.

The Figures stop, their faces indistinct in the light. Their fear is palpable as they gaze behind them.

> WOMAN
> (hopeful)
> We've lost them.

The man adjusts the heavy backpack slung over his shoulder — peers into the dark — half-smiles, relieved.

> MAN
> Yes... I think so.

At that moment two lights can be seen, pursuing them —

CAR HEADLIGHTS? TORCHES? SOMETHING ELSE?

> WOMAN
> Oh, God...

The child in her arms starts crying. The man puts his finger to its lips, gentle — SHUSHES it.

> MAN
> We have to be brave. All of us.

The little boy nods.

> WOMAN (O.S.)
> Look.

The lights are brighter — closer now. The woman stares at the man — terrified.

> WOMAN (CONT'D)
> Don't let them get us. You promised.

> MAN
> (avoiding her eye)
> Come on. The car's this way...

He plunges into the bush. The woman follows...

FADE TO BLACK.

MAIN TITLES — "BLOOD OATH"

EXT. SYDNEY HARBOUR, AUSTRALIA — DAY

The setting sun casts soft light on one of the world's
great views — Sydney Harbour, Bridge and Opera House.

INT. SKYSCRAPER, SYDNEY HARBOUR — DAY

A bunch of YOUNG OFFICE WORKERS stand in a boardroom
overlooking the view, listening to STEVE RENWICK, (40,
large, sweating, trendy suit).

                  STEVE RENWICK
        So, all in all he's done a pretty
        good job while he's been here...

Steve indicates the good-looking, well-dressed,
charismatic Englishman (30) next to him.

MARTIN SHARMAN

                  HECKLER
        Yeah, for a "Pom".

LAUGHTER round the room. The Heckler (SHANE) feigns a posh
voice — taking the piss.

                  HECKLER (CONT'D)
        From the "Old Country"...

                  STEVE RENWICK
        Thanks for that, Shane, mate.

                  HECKLER
        No worries, Stevo.

He grins at his MATE — smug. Martin gazes at Shane.

```
                    STEVE RENWICK
          So, ladies and gents, let's hear
          it for Martin Sharman.

Steve leads the APPLAUSE — gestures to Martin to speak.

                    MARTIN
          Thanks, Steve...

He eyes the young faces — stems the APPLAUSE — modest.

                MARTIN (CONT'D)
          I've had a great time here. Short,
          but sweet. I reckon we've achieved
          a heck of a lot in three months.

Nods around the room... Martin indicates Steve.

                MARTIN (CONT'D)
          And I'm handing over to a good guy.

                    HECKLER
          Right — 'coz he ain't a "Pom"!

MORE LAUGHTER. Martin — good-natured — smiles too.
```

TABLE 7.8 Content and Effect Grid for *Blood Oath, 2009 Script*

Blood Oath scenes 1–3 (2009 draft)

Content:	*What Happens . . .*	*Effect:*	*How We the Reader / Audience Feel . . .*
PLOT:	A family fleeing from unknown pursuers in the outback at night	**TONE:**	Ghostly, threatening, remote, recognisable, urban
THEME:	Fear, keeping promises, resilience, job done, leaving	**POINT OF VIEW:**	Close-up, omniscient, Martin's (main character)
SETTING:	Western Australian outback, modern Sydney office	**STYLISTIC DEVICES:**	Full moon, mystery, thriller, chase, urban, modern, contrasts
CHARACTER (EXTERNAL):	In danger, scared, desperate, businessman, successful	**CHARACTER (INTERNAL):**	*In extremis*, resilient, linked, urbane, confident, charismatic

According to my notebook at the time,[3] this is how I viewed the content and effect of Blood Oath in terms of the potential genres as I was working on the 2009 draft:

TABLE 7.9 Content and Effect Grid for *Blood Oath Genres, 2009 Script*

Blood Oath (2009)			
Content:	*What Happens . . .*	*Effect:*	*How We the Reader / Audience Feel . . .*
PLOT:	Thriller / supernatural	**TONE:**	Thriller / horror / supernatural
THEME:	Family drama / coming of age	**POINT OF VIEW:**	Thriller / horror
SETTING:	Horror	**STYLISTIC DEVICES:**	Thriller / Horror
CHARACTER (EXTERNAL):	Thriller / detective	**CHARACTER (INTERNAL):**	Family drama / coming of age

There are evidently a lot of genres at work here, with potentially mixed success. But one aspect of this grid is worth bearing in mind when it comes to the development of the content and effect of your own script and its scenes. The genres identified in the "Theme" section – family drama / coming of age – are the same as those in the "Character (Internal)" section. Often, the thematic question of what your story is really about is reflected by and plays out in your main character's internal emotional Need.

Content – *What Happens*

The plot has evolved in development from the surreal one suggested in the original opening to the more genre-based thriller / horror one of the 2009 version, planting elements of the ghost story that's to come. Both opening scenes incorporate the 'mystery for the viewer' hierarchy of knowledge to draw the reader into the story and characters and involve them in the story world, such as "Who is this man in his undies and why is he crawling through the outback?" and "Who is this family, why are they on the run, and who (or what) is after them?"

The themes in both versions have similarities – resilience – but the themes are clearer and more fully developed in the 2009 version, as one might

3 Darwin, Northern Territory, Australia, 5 April 2009.

expect given that the project had been optioned and was in active industrial development for some time.
- **The settings** are the same – initially versions of the remote Western Australia outback, then the more familiar urban modernity of Sydney. The
opening scene in the 2009 version was also influenced by my recce in the
Pilbara in 2008, with its highlighting of the full moon and ghost gums
(gum trees).
- **The characters' external (Want) characteristics** are more heightened in the
first draft: the man in the outback is presented as a 'fish out of water',
juxtaposing his situation with his comic monologue. There are also differences in the businessman character between the two versions. In the first
version, the party celebrates his new arrival in post; in the later version,
the party is to celebrate the end of his time in post.

Effect – *How We the Reader / Audience Feel*

- **The tone** of the two versions has key differences, reflecting the change in the
story and characters from version to version in development. The first
draft is heightened and ironic, whereas the later preproduction draft is
more visceral and threatening, indicative of the genre. Both versions relocate to the more familiar and recognisable urban world of the city to further the set-up of the story and its main character.
- **The point of view** from draft to draft generally favours the character we will
come to know in both as Martin. However, in the first draft, the POV feels
more subjective and closer to Martin; in the later version, it is, initially at
least, more omniscient and objective, not least because Martin isn't in the
opening scene.
- **The stylistic devices** in both versions reflect the different story types and
genres at work. The 2007 draft highlights the harsh red landscape, the
incongruity of the man crawling through it in his underpants;[4] the 2009
draft features the thriller / horror conventions of a chase at night under a
full moon.
- **The characters' internal (Need)** qualities in these opening scenes have some
similarities – characters in extremis, urbane, leaders – but also differences.
In the 2007 version, Martin is the new as yet unknown boss, the bringer
of change; in the 2009 version, he is at the end of his term of office, so

---

4 Revisiting this character and his situation, it is worth noting that the 2007 scene predates the
pilot episode of *Breaking Bad* (2008), which opens with another character (Walter White) in
a desert in his underpants.

known and familiar to his team, with workplace banter to match. He has evidently already brought change.

These features and more besides combine in every scene of your film and TV script to establish and create the tone, genre, and atmosphere of the world of your story.

The World of the Story

The opening title of my lecture on the world of the story is: "The story world – Where your characters <u>live</u>". From the very beginning of our work on their stories, I encourage my students and writers to view the universe their characters are going to inhabit as an active, involving, consistent one that envelops and surrounds them and affects / is affected by everything they do rather than as an imposed, formulaic, distant one. We want our characters' lives to play out scene by scene within an immersive, pervasive, ever-present story world rather than in front of the backdrop of a story world as if this world was scenery painted on a stage flat behind them.

Our story world is a subjective and particular milieu that is unique to each film or TV show we create and write, and we have to establish the specific rules of this world for the reader early on in a script and then make sure we stick to them. The nature of the story and its world in the scenes of our script reflect the essence of some of the reasons why we tell stories in the first place:

- to make sense of the world around us
- to make sense of the past
- to make sense of the present
- to make sense of the future
- to prepare us for the journey ahead – the journey that starts now and is always into the unknown
- to make sense of ourselves

The nature of the story and its world in the scenes of our script also reflects our innate desire to try and understand the meaning of things:

- to explain the world to ourselves – local stories
- to explain our world to other people – universal stories
- to engage, entertain, warn, amuse, remind
- to show us how to grow up
- to show us there is a better way
- because we have to tell stories – to keep the demons at bay
- because we alone of all species can

Here is a list of some of my favourite film and TV shows. It is not exhaustive; new films and TV shows arrive on the list, others leave it. It ebbs and flows depending on my mood and the stage of my life, but it is indicative:

Little Miss Sunshine (2006)	*E.T.* (1982)
Muriel's Wedding (1994)	*Sideways* (2004)
The Office (2001–3, UK)	*Unforgotten* (2015)
The Seven Samurai (1954)	*Some Like It Hot* (1959)
Withnail and I (1987)	*Toy Story* (1995)
Modern Family (2009–20)	*Breaking Bad* (2008–13)
Ozark (2017–22)	*The Killing* (2007–12)
Fleabag (2016–19)	*Schitt's Creek* (2015–20)
Edge of Darkness (1985)	*Erin Brokovich* (2000)
The Lives of Others (2006)	*Blade Runner* (1982)
The Walking Dead (2010–22)	*Dad's Army* (1968–77)
Gladiator (2000)	*The Sacrifice* (1986)
Call My Agent (2015–20)	*Lupin* (2021-)
The Others (2001)	*Klute* (1971)
Juno (2007)	*Fargo* (2014-)
Jaws (1975)	*Singin' In The Rain* (1952)

Can you see any links or connections between this selection of my favourite films and TV shows in terms of a) the character types and b) their story worlds? These denote the themes I often respond to and the effect they have on me – and they can be found in my own work.

Character Types

It is, I'm sure, no surprise to you by now that many of the films and shows I respond to involve families of sorts – actual blood-related families or ensembles of characters that serve to act as families. These 'families' are usually dysfunctional in some way, and the characters within them are under some kind of pressure – either collectively or individually.

I am also drawn to stories that are about unknown people who are not famous but are thrust into the spotlight for some reason, often as a result of meeting or coming into contact with a more famous – or infamous – character. This is the case with my own script *Boney and Betsy* (1997) in which a 12-year-old unknown and ignored British girl on St. Helena becomes the interlocutor for Napoleon Bonaparte, the most feared man alive.

I respond to stories that are about characters who are forced to act, quick-witted, resourceful, dogged, and resilient – and who are comic in some way. I am also interested in character types who are flawed but ultimately moral.

None of this is revolutionary or earth-shattering. It's not meant to be. But it does give me a framework and a guide in terms of the thematic approach I take in my own screenwriting and scene-writing, and the effect that I want the characters and content of my scripts and their scenes to have on a reader or audience.

Story Worlds

By the same token, I am drawn to certain types of story worlds in the stories I watch and the stories I choose to write. Given the character types I've just described, it is no surprise that these story worlds are often domestic and familiar to us, housing as they do some kind of 'family'. They are usually located in our world – or a version of our world – and they tend to be realistic and tonally consistent.

That doesn't mean I only respond to the same tone, but once the tone of a story is established, I generally like it to be consistent and coherent throughout. As I say to my students, they can write a two-hander between two people set in the room we're in and I won't believe the characters and situation if the tone is off or uncertain; on the other hand, I can read a scene about someone who stands up in the middle of class, suddenly sprouts wings, and flies out the window and believe the possibility of this if it's set up properly and its tone is credible and plausible. As always, it depends on its execution.

So I will buy into a story world if it evidently knows what it is on the page. I respond to contemporary story worlds, period ones, heightened ones, and futuristic ones, and I've written scripts about characters located in story worlds such as these. For me, the overriding principle is that whatever the characters, plot, and situation, the world of the story must be recognisable in some way and serve the characters.

On that basis, what are your favourite film and TV shows, and what links the character types and story worlds in these? In what ways are these reflected, explored, exposed in your own scripts and scenes? How do their features combine to establish the genre, tone, and atmosphere of the chosen world of your story scene by scene?

Applying the Story World to Your Scenes

As you are developing and writing your script and its scenes, keep asking yourself the following questions scene by scene:

- Does the story world reflect your character?
- Does the story world enhance your character?
- Does the story world challenge your character?

- Does your character inhabit the story world?
- Does your character belong in the story world?
- Does your character change the story world?

There is also an overriding question for each of these: how does the world of your story do this?

When I assess a script in an industrial or educational capacity, the 'World of the Story' is usually a key criterion in that assessment. Effective scripts should provide the following:

1. The creation of a coherent story world, with consistent genre[5] and tone.
2. The presentation of this world in a way that sets out with clarity the rules of engagement for both the characters within the script and the creative practitioners who might produce the work.
3. A command of the functions and dynamics of image and sound required in presenting involving and engaging screen drama on every page.

In mediocre scripts, one or more of these key features is lacking or underdeveloped in a fundamental way.

In effective scripts, regardless of their length, intended mode of production, or type – feature, short, TV drama, sit-com, soap – these features are evident in every scene. They matter because, in due course, they are going to help establish the *mise-en-scène* of your work when it is brought to the screen.

Mise-en-Scène

The term *mise-en-scène*[6] is commonly used to refer to how a scene comes together and tells its story within the context of the visual style of the overall screen story. It influences – and is also influenced by – the tone, genre, and atmosphere of the images (and associated sounds) that have been chosen to be shared with us. It has come to mean everything that we see within the frame of the film or TV show we are watching, a prevailing concept for film and TV academics and auteurs.

In reality, the *mise-en-scène* that is produced on the screen is ultimately established and provided by – inspired by – the screenwriter and what they originally put down on the page. The content in a scene, the effect of that

---

5 The increasing intersection of genre means that few contemporary films or TV drama are limited to a single genre. Mixing the conventions and tropes of different genres can also lead to tonal innovation. Key to this is the relationship between the main genre, which generally defines the story world, and the other genre(s).

6 Derived from French and meaning 'to put into the scene', *mise-en-scène* has been used since the early 19th century to discuss visual style on stage and also, a century later, in film.

content, and the story world these invoke all combine to establish the initial parameters for the *mise-en-scène*.

In the same way that a musical score by a composer motivates and inspires creative collaborators, such as a conductor and musicians, to bring the notes on its pages to life, so a script and its scenes should motivate and inspire its director, crew, and cast.

Core constituents that are integral to every scene we write provide fundamental elements that are interpreted and organised by the director to be filmed. These will be visible on screen, portrayed in due course by the actors, lighting, sets, costumes, make-up, and other features of the image that exist independently of the camera and the processes of filming and editing.[7]

If the *mise-en-scène* in a produced screenwork reflects the style or 'voice' of a particular director – such as a Wes Anderson film or a Jane Campion TV drama – then the first assembly scene by scene in a script of all the elements that will contribute to its *mise-en-scène* reflects the 'voice' or style of its writer.

Get the content, its effect, and the intended story world right scene by scene, and the chances are a writer will begin to locate and project their 'voice'.

Conclusion

Our characters live in the world of our story. They create this story world through their actions, behaviours, conflicts, and decisions in every scene. Likewise, the story world also creates character.

In *Jaws* (1975),[8] widely acknowledged to be the first 'blockbuster' movie, Sheriff Martin Brody, newly arrived on Amity Island from the city, is afraid of water (his 'shadow'). Once it becomes clear that his family is threatened by the shark that's started killing holidaymakers, Brody is forced out onto the water to face his nemesis. At the climax of the film, he dangles just above the seemingly limitless ocean from the mast of the sinking *Orca* in order to kill the monster and free himself and his loved ones. He releases his shadow and, in doing so, resolves his Need. At the end of the film, he and Hooper paddle back towards Amity Island clinging to wreckage surrounded by water.

Character and story world, content and effect, intersect and intertwine in every single scene in the movie to create difficulty for Brody, represented by:

- his new job on Amity Island
- his wife Ellen

---

7 *Film art: an introduction*, David Bordwell and Kristin Thompson (originally published 1979).
8 Novel by Peter Benchley published in 1974. Film released 1975, dir. Steven Spielberg.

- his sons Michael and Sean
- Mayor Vaughn and the town council
- the mother of the boy that's taken by the shark
- the water
- the shark
- Brody himself – his 'shadow' (fear of water)

TABLE 7.10 Content and Effect Grid for *Jaws*, 1975

JAWS (1975)

Content:	What Happens . . .	Effect:	How We the Reader / Audience Feel . . .
PLOT:	A shark terrorises an island community and its new cop	TONE:	Our world, recognisable, unease, dread, fear, terror
THEME:	The family, fish-out-of-water, greed, overcoming the monster	POINT OF VIEW:	Subjective, Brody's, omniscient, also the shark's POV
SETTING:	Amity Island and the surrounding water	STYLISTIC DEVICES:	Unseen monster, shock moments, superhuman, horror feeling states, final battle
CHARACTER (EXTERNAL):	Cop, custodian, family man, city guy, fish-out-of-water	CHARACTER (INTERNAL):	Conflicted, compromised, needs to do the right thing, his nemesis

When our characters and their story world are seamlessly interlinked and interwoven in this way scene by scene, as they are in *Jaws*, this, in turn, creates engagement and emotion in our readers.

Postscript: Marysville, Victoria

The Arista / Film Vic script development workshop I referred to earlier in this chapter took place in a small country town called Marysville, 100 kilometres north of Melbourne, Australia. In May 2004, we took over the local hotel for a week and worked on film projects with talented Australian and New Zealand writers, producers, and directors. We went for silent walks through the local bush. We had script meetings in the local coffee shop. We always looked forward to our workshops there.

On 7 February 2009, the whole town was devastated in the Black Monday Murrindindi Mill bushfire. It is reckoned that 45 people died in Marysville

IMAGE 7.5 Entrance to the Marysville Hotel, March 2009 ©Simon van der Borgh

IMAGE 7.6 Indoor swimming pool, Marysville Hotel, March 2009 ©Simon van der Borgh

and its surrounds. All but 14 buildings were destroyed. Six weeks after this terrible event, I was asked by a friend who lived nearby to go up there with her. She needed to show someone who knew the place what had happened to her community and talk about it.

I always imagined that I would return there one day to take part in another workshop at the hotel. I never dreamt it would be to pay my respects to the place and the people who died there so tragically that day.

Style – Scene-Writing Exercise

"Content and Effect" Scene Exercises

As we've discussed in this chapter, the notion of 'content' and 'effect' provides us with a handy way of summarising key elements of our story and its specific chosen world to the reader in the style and approach that we want.

TABLE 7.11 Content and Effect Grid for Scene-writing Exercise

Content:	*What Happens . . .*	*Effect:*	*How We the Reader / Audience Feel . . .*
PLOT:	*Can be told in a sentence or less . . .*	TONE:	*How the writer wants the reader to interpret their attitude to the story*
THEME:	*The implicit recurring idea conveyed scene by scene*	POINT OF VIEW:	*The viewpoint chosen by the writer for the story*
SETTING:	*Where the story / scene happens*	STYLISTIC DEVICES:	*The narrative elements and techniques the writer uses to reveal the story*
CHARACTER (EXTERNAL):	*Can equate to the character's external physical Want (i.e., their goals, objectives)*	CHARACTER (INTERNAL):	*Can equate to the internal emotional Need (i.e., their desire, shadow, flaw, wound)*

Step 1 – *Choose an idea or any type of script you may be working on and create a "Content and Effect" grid for it.*

Step 2 – *Use the grid you've created in Step 1 to identify the genre / genres at work in this script or idea. As you work on this, ask yourself:*

- Is the genre clear in each category?
- Do you have a main genre for each category?
- Do you have more than one genre? What genres?
- Which categories have the same genre?
- How many categories are labelled "drama"? What do you mean by "drama" in terms of the intended world of your story?
- What happens to the overall idea and its story world if you change the approach or genre in a category – for example, 'tone' changes from black comedy to horror, or 'point of view' changes from 'subjective' or 'close-up' to 'omniscient'?

Step 3 – *Now use the grid for a scene you've written for this idea. This can be a scene in an existing script – or better still, a new scene you've written inspired by your progress through the earlier chapters in this book! Ask yourself:*

- Do the short descriptions in your scene grid reflect the short descriptions in your idea / script grid?
- Do the scene genres in the categories reflect the overall genre(s) of the story and world that you're envisaging?

8

THEME

What's Your Scene _Really_ About?

Introduction

As I began to work more and more as a screenwriting teacher and script developer, this took me to many different locations and involved collaborating with a variety of people on their stories. I was privileged to work with new, emerging, and experienced storytellers – writers, directors, producers, actors, students, teachers, programme organisers – from northwest England to the Northern Territory in Australia.

As a commissioned and produced feature film writer, I was familiar with the core components of a screenplay and its scenes. But working with other writers and filmmakers, helping them find the best way to identify these core components in their ideas and projects and apply them, whatever their level of knowledge and experience, inevitably clarified my approach to my own writing and my own teaching.

So far, we've focused on analysing the elements that are integral to pretty much every scene we may work on or write – character, action, dialogue, setting, formatting – and discussed each of these in their own chapters. We've concentrated on the fundamentals of a scene that help establish its context and content, such as:

- where we are
- when we are
- what we are looking at
- who we are looking at
- what we are seeing
- what we are hearing

DOI: 10.4324/9781003293927-9

However, these are not standalone elements. Improving our knowledge and mastery of them will almost certainly improve our scene-writing. But this is not the end product or the final destination *per se* of this approach to scene-writing.

Core elements like action and dialogue do not exist in isolation, no matter how well-written they may be. Indeed, sometimes well-written action and dialogue are seductive and can initially mask significant issues within the scene. To be effective, they need to be applied so that they are integrated and layered in every scene, coming together to create a unified story world for the plot and for the characters in that plot.

Many helpful questions can be asked throughout the scene-writing process to help us analyse and improve the scenes we may be writing or working on. But time and again, wherever and whoever I am teaching or working with, we return to two questions, above all:

1. What's your scene about?
2. What's your scene _really_ about?

In this chapter, we're going to look at what a scene may really be about and how we can identify this and hard-wire it into our scenes to improve the dramatic and emotional impact our scene-writing can make in order to heighten the overall effect of our film and TV writing as a whole.

What Are Our Characters and Scenes Really Saying?

When I enrolled at the Maurits Binger Film Institute (MBFI) in Amsterdam in September 1996, I was the only British filmmaker selected for its inaugural 5-month development programme. Surrounded by younger, sharper European filmmakers with their smart clothes and their even smarter contemporary film ideas, I felt like a 'fish out of water' with my English period film idea *Boney and Betsy,* inspired by Napoleon Bonaparte's final exile after the Battle of Waterloo in 1815 to the island of St. Helena and the unlikely friendship he struck up there with Betsy Balcombe, a 12-year-old English girl whose father was working on the island.

During the programme, we were visited by several notable filmmakers. One of these was Hungarian director István Szabó. His movie *Mephisto* (1981), a re-imagining of the Faust story set in 1930s Nazi Germany and starring Klaus Maria Brandauer, won the Academy Award for the *Best Foreign Language Film* in 1982. Brimming with themes and subtext, it had a big effect on me and, at the time, was one of my favourite films. So I was looking forward to meeting one of my heroes.

As one might expect, István was charisma personified. We all gathered to meet him and discuss our projects with him and hear what he had to say.

Picture the scene back in early 1997 . . .

IMAGE 8.1   First script development cohort at the MBFI, Amsterdam, 1996. The author is sitting on the right in the front row.

```
INT. LARGE MEETING ROOM, MBFI, AMSTERDAM — DAY

THIRTY STUDENTS around a large table. SIMON (35) is also there.

SITTING IN THE MIDDLE — ISTVAN SZABO (58)

                    ISTVAN SZABO
              Thank you all for letting me read
              your ideas.

Istvan smiles. The Students smile back.

                    ISTVAN SZABO (CONT'D)
              They are all terrible.
                    (with emphasis)
              Ter-ri-ble.

The Students stop smiling.

                    ISTVAN SZABO (CONT'D)
              Except for one.

The Students eye one another: whose idea is the "one"?

Simon closes his eyes. It won't be his...
```

```
                    ISTVAN SZABO (CONT'D)
          The one about the little English girl
          and Napoleon. On the island together.
          Now, my friends, this is a movie!

Simon opens his eyes. Disbelief.

                    ISTVAN SZABO (CONT'D)
          Whose story is this?

Every other student is staring at Simon. Also in disbelief.

                    SIMON
          Um, it's, er, mine.

                    ISTVAN SZABO
          Well done. You have found a great idea.

Istvan smiles at Simon. Simon smiles back. Huge relief.
```

Now I could – should, perhaps – stop the scene of this anecdote here.
At Simon's moment of triumph. His moment of validation and recognition. Maybe even his moment of change and transformation. Except that this wasn't how the conversation ended. It wasn't the end of the scene, merely its midpoint. So we must carry on, into its second half, and then on into its third and final part, its 'consequences' part. The scene must carry on, to clarify its context, subtext, themes – and for us to understand what it's _really_ about:

```
Istvan gazes at Simon.

                    ISTVAN SZABO
          Where did you find it?

                    SIMON
          From my father. He told me about it.
          He's always been a big fan of Boney.

Istvan nods at this. Warm.

                    ISTVAN SZABO
          Just one thing...

                    SIMON
          Of course.
```

                        ISTVAN SZABO
            To improve your story...

                        SIMON
            Thank you...

                        ISTVAN SZABO
            All the way through the film, they should
            be building a wooden gibbet on the cliff.

Simon, taken aback: has he heard him right?

                        SIMON
            A... gibbet?

                        ISTVAN SZABO
            A gibbet. A great big wooden gibbet.
                (into his stride)
            Then, after she has betrayed the British,
            The little girl should be taken by them and hung
            from this gibbet. Until she is dead.
                (warming to his theme...)
            At the end of the film, we see the crows pecking
            out her eyes.

ON SIMON

Stunned. Shocked. Appalled.

                        SIMON
            But... But it's a family film.

                        ISTVAN SZABO
            Indeed so.

Istvan turns away. Addresses the group.

                        ISTVAN SZABO (CONT'D)
            Now, time for coffee.

My all too brief moment of triumph (such as it was) was snatched away –
'auteured' in front of my very eyes by the epitome of an auteur director. But
at least it gained me the sympathy – respect, even – of my fellow participants.[1]

---

1 My cohort at the Binger generously recognised the journey I and my project made on the programme at our final dinner when they gave me an award titled: 'Person Most Likely to Succeed'.

They began to realise that there was more to my project and me than it had initially seemed. There was more to the subtext (a 30-something director trying to change direction, become a writer, taking some big decisions to try and do this) than was evident from its context (a typical English period film set, as so often, in the age of the British Empire).

Suffice to say, none of the many drafts of *Boney and Betsy* that I have written since this encounter for the numerous producers that have optioned the project over the years in the UK, US, and Australia have ever ended with a scene of Betsy being hung by the British as a traitor. But thinking about it now, given that the film remains as yet unproduced, perhaps they should have . . .

What Is Your Scene *Really* About?

One of the ways to help us work out what our scene is really about is to identify and clarify the core dramatic elements and ideas that are at work within a scene:

- subtext
- theme
- tone
- emotion
- tension
- rhythm
- need
- love
- anagnorisis

Please don't be put off or feel intimidated by this long, academic-sounding list! As we'll see, many of these elements are interconnected and related. They are inherent in the scenes we write every day, and you'll very likely be installing them in your work already. So view the following as a kind of checklist.

Subtext

The word 'subtext' often confuses writers when it is referred to by people discussing their script, for example, "some of the scenes lack subtext". Used as a shorthand for something else – your scene isn't working, your script isn't working, you the writer aren't working – 'subtext' is easy to say but much harder to identify and fix. When asked what they mean by this or how they suggest the writer might add some subtext, the silence in the room can be deafening. The inference being it is the writer's job to fix it and others will know when it is fixed.

So let's try and take some of the mystique out of this. In a scene, there are three types of subtexts that may be in play for us to consider using:

1. The subtext created by the ongoing 'dialogue' that takes place between a character and the reader (audience) in which the reader is encouraged through the scene-writing to infer or fill in the gap between a character's words and their actions (i.e., a character says one thing but then does another) – we tell the reader one thing, but we show the reader another in the scene.

    In my 'István Szabó at the Binger' scene, the description and reaction of Simon through the scene – a) on his own / 'fish out of water', b) fearing the worst, c) disbelief at having his idea praised, d) shock at István's suggestions – creates a subtextual 'dialogue' between the Simon character and the reader.

2. The subtext that exists between characters in the scene (i.e., the buried meaning of what two or more characters are actually saying – implying – to each other).

    In the 'István Szabó at the Binger' scene, there is potentially plenty of subtext and buried meaning between the characters in it, between a) Simon and his fellow Students, b) the Students and István, and c) Simon and István. The subtext between Simon and István Szabó evolves from a) Simon's excitement at meeting his hero, b) Simon's fears about what his hero thinks about his idea, c) Simon's hopes when his hero praises his idea, to d) Simon's shock at his hero's suggestions. As we see in this scene, subtext is also established, reinforced, changed by the evolving status between the characters in it, and, in particular, the status[2] of Simon, which moves from low status to high status then back to low status again.

3. The subtext that exists between the writer of the scene and the reader where the writer is communicating a meaning and exploring a theme to the reader through the characters and their actions. The audience may then infer a meaning from the consequences of these actions, a meaning that is not necessarily shared by the characters in the story.

    This is harder to establish in a one-off scene like my 'István Szabó at the Binger' scene, but hopefully, the reader gets a sense that there is a lot at stake for the Simon character in this scene. As I revisit this anecdote for

2 See Chapter 2 on 'Character' for more information about status.

this book, a theme that is evident to me now is the notion and meaning of 'Sacrifice':

1. The sacrifices my family made so I could be at the Binger and write my script.
2. The sacrifice I was prepared / not prepared to make about my characters and my idea in the light of an Oscar-winning director's feedback.
3. The sacrifice Boney had to make in my story to save Betsy at the end.

I'm not suggesting that much, if any, of this information is in the scene as written and presented to you here. But it was – it is – in my mind as its writer, which is a starting point for a conversation. Because subtext arises in a script via the ongoing conversation that is taking place between the writer and reader throughout the scenes of that script and the way that these are then interpreted and understood. The screenwriter places clues in the scenes within the story, and the reader is able to deduce their meaning and fill in the gaps of their own accord.

Theme

In screenwriting, theme generally refers to the broader unifying subject of a story or the meaning of the experience that we have just read or watched. Not to be confused with a 'thesis' or 'proof' about an idea, the theme indicates a value or concept which surrounds, permeates, and unifies the events and actions within a particular story.

Ideally, it can be expressed in one word distilled into the simplest possible statement to indicate what the story is really about, for example: trust, greed, power, evil, responsibility, self-acceptance, family, or, indeed, sacrifice, as I suggested about my 'István Szabó at the Binger' anecdote.

Over the years, I've become less adamant that the theme has to be summed up in a single word. But no matter how convoluted and sophisticated the story, there should be one central element, a focal point around which all the machinations of the story and plot revolve.[3] This thematic element should be present throughout the main character's story, its subplots, and its scenes. Reflecting the theme, in some way, scene by scene adds resonance to the simplest of stories and unity to the most complex.

---

3 In early screenwriting manuals, a strong 'theme' was given central importance. In most of the great silent films, such as *Sunrise* (F.W. Murnau, 1927) and *City Lights* (Charlie Chaplin, 1931), the theme was paramount.

This is particularly true in multi-character, multi-plotline, long-running TV series in which the breadth, scale, and ambition of even the most convoluted narratives can be unified and enhanced by thematic consistency and cohesion from scene to scene.

A common theme in returnable drama is the 'family'. Series like *Succession* (2018–23), *Modern Family* (2009–20), *Breaking Bad* (2008–13), *Ozark* (2017–22), *The Office* (UK, 2001–03), *Game of Thrones* (2011–2019), *Schitt's Creek* (2015–20), *The Sopranos* (1999–2007) and *E.R.* (1994–2009), to name just a few[4] revolve around the lives of a version of a dysfunctional 'family', a group of people tied together in some way in the home, castle, workplace, fantasy world, school, hospital, motel, remote town, spaceship, their assorted lives linked by time, place, and situation if not by blood. Some aspect of 'family'– happy, unhappy, envious, loving, destructive, united, rivalrous, binding, etc. – should be present thematically in some way in every scene in shows like these alongside an additional thematic element that is particular to that series – greed, revenge, crime, resurrection, love, and so on.

The theme is generally the central idea – the big idea – which inspires and then powers a film or TV story. It may be an underlying statement or assumption about an aspect of life. It may be the moral, philosophical, political, or spiritual idea that is propelling the writer to write in the first place. It can be expressed in the form of a universal truth, for example, united we stand; love conquers all; who dares, wins; all for one and one for all; every woman for herself; we are only as strong as our weakest part.

The mistake we can make as writers is to think that we have to know what the theme of our script is from the get-go. Sometimes, it is not until I've written the first draft and read through its scenes and discussed it with other people that I am able to realise what the theme actually is. It suddenly occurs to me that although I'd thought my new idea was about a forgotten composer, or a wannabe cowboy, or a famous painter on the run, it turns out that it's really about fathers and sons or parents and children – imaginative storytelling is anchored to lived experience. Yet again. When I've identified the theme, I start going through the script scene by scene to see if it is present in each scene in some way. Because the art of writing is . . . rewriting.

One way of finding or identifying the theme of your story is to ask yourself:

- What makes you angry?
- What do you feel passionate about?

---

4 I mention these shows in particular only because they have been much referenced by my students in class over the years around the world.

- What do you feel guilty about?
- What do you want to say to an audience about the 'human condition'?
- How are you using your story, your protagonist, your antagonist, to exemplify all these feelings?
- In what way are any of these ideas present and active in your script's scenes?

The theme(s) in your script may be evolving, evasive, and mercurial as the scenes unfold because the characters in those scenes and their story arcs are evolving, evasive, and mercurial. But, just as you will reach some sort of conclusion about your characters and their arcs by the end of your story, you will reach a conclusion about your theme(s), too – and so will your reader. Ultimately, your theme is the truth about the world contained in your story and conveyed by your story, scene by scene.

Tone

Tone is another key element in scenes that often gets confused and confusing. Writers regularly refer to the tone of their work as if it were its genre(s) and *vice versa*. I've found that the simplest, easiest, and most memorable way to explain tone to my students and writers is via what's become known as the 'Simon van der Borgh Tone Chart'.

IMAGE 8.2   The 'Simon van der Borgh Tone Chart' being demonstrated to students in class, York, April 2024 ©Christopher Leaman

INT. LECTURE ROOM — DAY

STUDENTS in rows: staring at SIMON standing out front, facing them.

                SIMON
        The easiest way to explain tone
        to you is to use what I call the
        Simon van der Borgh tone chart.

He extends both his arms, stretching them out straight on
either side of his body.

A Student looks bemused.

             SIMON (CONT'D)
        Now, where my left hand is...
          (Wiggles his left hand)
        Imagine that's the most ultra-realistic,
        drama-doc style story there is. Truth,
        24 frames per second personified. A
        naturalistic version of our world. Maybe
        a crime story, social drama, an urban
        story. You know the sort of thing.

Students nod: they do know.

Simon now wiggles his right hand.

             SIMON(CONT'D)
        Now, where my right hand is at the
        other end of the chart, this is the
        most fantastic, heightened tone
        imaginable. The kind of tone where a
        bunch of Greek islanders can sashay
        down a hill in time singing an ABBA
        song, dance along a wooden dock
        together and then do a perfect
        choreographed dive into the sun-kissed
        blue Aegean Sea.[5]

Simon smiles. Wiggles both hands: his Tone Chart.

---

5 This is memorably and enjoyably done in the jukebox musical romantic comedy *Mamma Mia!* (2008).

<pre>
                    SIMON (CONT'D)
        What you have to do is decide where
        the tone of your story is. And then stick
        to it. Is it close to my left hand, i.e.
        favouring realism? Or is it close to my
        right hand, i.e. favouring the fantastic?
        Or is it somewhere in the middle, near my
        heart, say? In which case, it may be a
        combination of the two, a kind of
        heightened realism or magical realism —
        our world, but with a twist.
</pre>

As one, the students leap to their feet and CHEER.

Simon acknowledges their applause by wiggling his fingers. He
bows. Modestly.

Okay, I admit it. I made the last two action lines up. They are my fantasy, my poetic reimagining.

The point is, the tone of a film or TV story can range from the fantastic (e.g., action-adventure, musical, fantasy) to the realistic (e.g., war, melodrama, social drama), from the ironic (e.g., screwball comedy, satire) to the totally involving (e.g., thriller, horror, detective). But, bear in mind, this kind of division is illustrative and not fixed. After all, horror stories can be fantastic, or ultra-realistic, or ironic, or involving, in their overall intended tone. Likewise thrillers, dramas, comedies, and so on.

At its most basic level, tone is often referred to as being either 'light' or 'dark'. István Szabó's suggestion that Betsy should be executed in the final scene of *Boney and Betsy* would certainly have darkened the tone of that script.

A hallmark of confident, assured, and engaging screenwriting is the ability to keep the desired tone consistent scene by scene throughout the particular story regardless of developments, changes, and complications in its plot, narrative, and genre.

Emotion

A core objective of identifying and projecting in our scenes what the story is really about is that when this is done effectively, it can create emotion in the reader.

I cannot overstate the importance of this. Industry readers of all types, roles, and levels in the film and TV industry read a lot of scripts. I once met an agent at William Morris in LA who read 30+ movie scripts every weekend. And that was in their time off. So a reader will forgive flaws in a script if it creates some kind of emotional response in them. We want our scenes to provoke a conscious mental reaction such as anger or fear or hope in the reader because this may encourage them to cross over from being objective, analytical, or sceptical about our work to being subjective, engaged, and curious about it.

As they say in Hollywood: "There are 100 reasons to say 'no' to a script and only ever one reason to say 'yes' to it: because you love it". The effective use and creation of some kind of intended emotional response in a script, scene by scene, increases our chances of a reader feeling that 'love' and engaging with our work. It may provide the starting point of a conversation and a relationship that could lead to who knows where.

Tension

We discussed in an earlier chapter that one of the ways of creating emotion in the reader and eliciting some kind of visceral response in them to what they are reading is through the creation of tension. We also discussed how the three hierarchies of knowledge and what the audience (A) knows in a scene in relation to what the characters (C) know can create layers of tension.

Tension is a mental, emotional strain for the reader or viewer, a pleasurable anxiety or apprehension resulting from watching an uncertain, undecided, or mysterious situation. It consists of hope for a desired outcome and, simultaneously, fear that the opposite will happen. As we have seen in this book, it is usually identified or implied by a scene-specific "Will . . .?" question in each scene, such as, "Will Simon be able to explain his definition of tone to his students?"

When I'm discussing the subject of tension and its release with writers and students, I propose that the dynamic movement of the spectator's engagement operates on three levels:

- cognitive
- emotional
- physiological

Cognitively, the reader's or viewer's mind is engaged in scenes by questions about what is happening or what will happen in them, and this tension is resolved when those questions are answered. A new tension is created when a new question is posed in a new scene.

Emotionally, readers and audiences experience tension and release when anxieties about what they hope and what they fear for the characters and stories they are watching are created, provoked, and calmed.

Physiologically, the movement between the turbulence and instability created by action and sound and a return to stability creates the experience of
tension and release at a kinesthetic[6] or physiological level.

Rhythm

Editors define rhythm on-screen as time, movement, and energy or emphasis
shaped by timing, pacing, and the phrasing of dynamics to create cycles of
tension and release.[7]

Given that the editor is often referred to as the second writer of a film or
TV show, it stands to reason that it is helpful to a script and its prospects if
the first writer – its screenwriter – is also aware of the importance of rhythm
in the scenes we're writing.

The interpretation and understanding of a scene and what it may really be
about can inevitably be affected by the timing, pacing, and phrasing of the
words on each page.

Once again, the art of writing is . . . rewriting.

Need

We've talked about character Need – the subconscious, emotional, internal
desire within the main character (and within other characters in the story
depending on the format and type) – throughout this book because its concepts and effects are influential in so many core aspects of scene-writing.

A character's Need is different from their Want (external physical goal).
Indeed, it is usually opposed to this, thereby creating tension and conflict,
comedy, and tragedy. It is often at the centre of what the story and its scenes
are _really_ about, not least because this Need reflects, explores, creates its
theme and subtext. Within a character before the screen story starts, it's what
they come to learn during that story as a consequence of the events in the plot
and what they have to recognise, respond to, and resolve in the final act. Ideally, it is present in some way in every scene, subconsciously or consciously.
Our characters ignore their Need at their peril.

Need Equals Love?

Working in development on a variety of projects, productions, stories, and
story types, I began to realise that a common thread ran through all of them

---

6 Kinesthetic: learning and experiencing through feeling or doing; it is particularly associated
   with this when that feeling or doing is sensory and involves movement.
7 _Cutting rhythms: Intuitive film editing_ by Karen Pearlman, Focal Press/Routledge, 2009.

regardless of budget, plot, genre, or tone. In all these stories, character Need could be equated in some way to a version or aspect of 'Love'.

At the beginning of their particular screen story, the protagonist and other key characters very often lacked love in some way – love of another, love of self, love of life, and so on – and their emotional arc through the story, scene by scene, culminated in them having to address or resolve this lack in some way. Or else.

So Need could be equated to Love as a general concept: internal, emotional, desired, life-affirming – but also repetitive. Because one 4-letter word is as meaningful or meaningless as the writer chooses to interpret it. If love represents the theme of our story and its scenes, then what kind of love, specifically?

As is often the case, I discovered that help – and revelation and instruction – lay in the writings and ideas of the Ancient Greeks. If a Need does equate to Love, then the more specific Greek words for love and their differing notions and concepts might offer us more helpful and distinctive terms to use when it comes to defining the specific Need, flaw, or lack within a character and add layers and meaning to these.

In *The Four Loves*,[8] writer, philosopher, and theologian C.S. Lewis considers four different types of love from his Christian viewpoint:

- affection or *storge* in Greek
- friendship or *philia*
- erotic love or *eros*
- charity or *agape*

Using these as a starting point to consider how different versions of love might equate to character Need, I identified at least ten words in Greek that equate to the English word 'love'. Each one potentially offers a distinctive way of defining and interpreting character Need. And each of them provides another potential layer for us to draw on as we work on what our script and our scenes are really about.

1. Storge

In the Greek-English lexicon,[9] *storge* equates to affection – the love of a parent to a child and of a child to its parents. It indicates unconditional love, an acceptance of things, and putting up with them. Another meaning is 'loving

---

8 *The four loves* by C.S. Lewis (published by Geoffrey Bles, 1960).
9 *Greek-English lexicon*, H. G. Liddell and R. Scott, Oxford University Press, 1843.

the tyrant', a definition a parent who has spent time with a small child can relate to. *Storge* can be humble, modest, no airs, homely, unconditional. The poet Ovid[10] offers illumination: "If you would be loved, be loveable." C.S. Lewis warns that if we try to live by affection alone, affection can "go bad on us".

In *As Good As It Gets* (1997), misanthropic writer Melvin is unable to display or accept affection from others. Carol, the kindly waitress who serves him every day, represents a threat to his *status quo*. As he becomes more engaged with her and her sick son, he needs to be able to display *storge* and acquire empathy if he is going to be able to move to *eros* and attain a deeper, more equal, erotic love with Carol.

2. Eros

Eros is the Greek expression of love with which we may be most familiar because of its association through the ages with intimate, erotic, passionate, physical love. *Eros* can signify sexual passion and desire or suggest an appreciation of beauty within a person. A much-explored Need of characters in romances, rom-coms, and beyond, *eros* is the most mortal of loves and, consequently, the most fickle. As a Need, *eros* offers a warning about dangerous love, the perils of uncontrollable, fiery, mad love. Erotic love can be a force for good – a life-maker – or a force for bad – a life-breaker. Because *eros* exists in characters that want not another character *per se* but <u>one particular character</u>. Therein lies its allure, its magic, and its danger.

In *Anna Karenina* (2012), Anna is married to the well-regarded but cold Karenin, just about existing in *storge* until she falls for the dashing and dangerous Count Vronksy. *Eros* consumes Anna with consequences for her, her status in patriarchal 19th-century Russian society, and her sense of self – her *philautia* (see #5). Anna breaks the rules but her suppression of *eros* and return to *storge* (her *status quo*) is more than she can bear, resulting in her tragic outcome.

3. Philia

Philia equates to friendship: dispassionate, non-erotic love, love among equals. Exalted through human history, *philia* was independent – defiant – of nature, raising us to the level of gods and angels. In some cultures, *philia* retains a mythic quality. In Australia, it corresponds to 'mateship', originally

---

10 *Ars Amatoria* 7 (The Art of Love, written in 2 CE by Roman poet Ovid (43 BCE -17/18 CE).

a male-centric philosophy forged through new world hardship then enshrined in the national psyche because of the Gallipoli campaign[11] in World War I.

In *Muriel's Wedding* (1994), the accepted male-centric notion of 'mateship' is subverted in Muriel, who receives scant affection or *storge* at home from her domineering father or her bewildered mother and also experiences little success or satisfaction in her pursuit of *eros*. But she does come to understand the importance of *philia* and puts this into action, liberating her best mate, the wheelchair-bound Rhonda, from the living death that is Porpoise Spit and taking her with her to Sydney.

Classified by Aristotle[12] as a virtue, *philia* suggests a deep friendship – loyalty to friends, family, and community. A key element of *philia* is equality, unlike *storge,* which often highlights an inherent differing status in its participants. C.S. Lewis contends that *philia* is the least natural of loves – the least instinctive, organic, biological, gregarious, the least necessary. But *philia* is a mark of civilisation, enabling communities not just to live but to live well.

4. Agape

Agape denotes decency and common sense, goodness. C.S. Lewis equates it to God's love and Christian love, reflected by the New Testament notion of 'Charity'[13] – selfless love for others, brotherly love, selflessness, or universal loving-kindness in Buddhism. Having *agape* also indicates an empathy for others. Often described as Christian love or God's love,[14] *agape* is the fundament of Christianity in the New Testament, for example, reflected in the philosophical idea of 'loving thy neighbour'. In film and TV stories, *agape* often features in the journey of the misanthrope to be able to love others and to exhibit brotherly love.

In *The Lives of Others* (2006), highly skilled East German Stasi agent Gerd Wiesler is ordered to spy on Georg Dreyman, bugging his flat and listening in on Dreyman's life in pursuit of evidence against the playwright. But even Wiesler is not immune to the power of love, both *eros* and *agape*, ultimately sacrificing his own career to protect Dreyman and his lover and allow him to publish the truth about the doomed communist regime. Wiesler's *agape* may

---

11 On 25 April 1915, 16,000 Australian and New Zealand (ANZAC) troops landed as part of an Allied campaign to capture the Gallipoli Peninsula. More than 2,000 were wounded or killed on the first day. The Gallipoli campaign was a military failure, but the characteristics that the ANZACs displayed throughout – bravery, ingenuity, endurance, and mateship – have come to be celebrated as defining characteristics of the Australian personality. https://www.nma.gov.au/defining-moments/resources/gallipoli-landing.

12 *Nicomachean Ethics* by Aristotle, circa 340 BCE.

13 See 1 Corinthians 13: 1–13.

14 *The Sermon on the Mount,* Gospel of St. Matthew, 6: 5–7.

result in his disgrace, but that is a price worth paying for doing the right thing and showing humanity brotherly love.

As well as C.S. Lewis's four loves, there are other distinctive types of love that Lewis didn't address in his text that are commonly found in film and TV stories:

5. Philautia

Translated as 'love of self' or 'love of the self', *philautia* can reflect the bad and the good in a character. On one hand, *philautia* equals narcissism. But *philautia* also means being able to love and appreciate other people because you love yourself in the right measure. This so-called 'self-compassion' widens the ability to love others. According to Aristotle: "All friendly feelings of others are expressions of a man's feelings for himself".[15] By the same token, unfriendly feelings about others are also expressions of a character's feelings for herself or himself.

Philautia also reflects the one hidden character question in development that potentially lies behind every story: "How does your character feel about herself or himself?" And how will they mend the wound / flaw / fear that lies beneath this feeling? In drama, as in real life, people can love themselves too much or too little, and there are consequences for both.

In *Silver Linings Playbook* (2012), bipolar sufferer Pat is released into the care of his father and wants to reconcile with his ex-wife Nikki, who has a restraining order on him. He begins a relationship with depressed widow Tiffany that develops as they share a passion for dance. *Eros* and *storge* are at play throughout the film, but it is *philautia* that represents the Need of both Pat and Tiffany and that they individually have to face up to and resolve to have a future together.

6. Ludus

Ludus is playful love, young love, for example, the love between children. It can take the form of flirtation between young lovers or involve drinking, banter, dancing, going out. Playing games, engaging in casual conversation, or gossiping with friends are all forms of *ludus*. Many film characters have to engage with *ludus* and rediscover their need for play and flirtation before they are able to move to the deeper more needful loves signified by *eros* and *philautia*. *Ludus* is a transformative love that the protagonist often needs

---

15 Chapter 4, Book IX, *Aristotle's Nicomachean Ethics*.

to rediscover or go through on their journey to reach something deeper and more meaningful.

In *The Full Monty* (1997), *ludus* emerges when Gaz and five other unemployed steel workers are driven by circumstances to form a male striptease act. *Ludus* is the unifying Need as each of the characters discovers or rediscovers their own individual Need, be it *eros* (Lomper, with Guy), *storge* (Gerald), or *philautia*, which Gaz needs to restore within himself before he can do 'the full Monty' in front of everyone who knows him.

The hard-wiring of *ludus* into stories like this may help to explain their 'feel-good' factor – and their consequent connection with audiences of all ages and nationalities and their phenomenal box office and critical success.

7. Pragma

Pragma means longstanding love, the notion of 'standing' in love as opposed to 'falling' in love. Mature and established, *pragma* represents the *status quo* for older characters in seemingly stable, happy relationships. They have their love and their deeper Need tested in some way before re-emerging with the *pragma* that exists between them restored, reinforced, renewed, or changed forever. *Pragma* stories are often circular in nature, with characters emerging wiser and more alive as a result of the journey. Inevitably, *eros* is the enemy of *pragma*.

In *45 Years* (2015), Kate and Geoff exist in *pragma* as they plan a party to celebrate their 45th wedding anniversary. However, one week before the celebration, a letter arrives for Geoff. The body of his first love has been discovered, frozen in a glacier in the Swiss Alps. Long-buried *eros* and its secrets intrude suddenly to threaten their *pragma* and everything Kate has invested in and believed about her marriage.

So far, the loves discussed have been generally positive. But Love has its flipside.

8. Mania

Mania equates to obsessive love and is dependent, highly emotional, dangerous, and destructive. Mania is a warning for us all. It is what can exist when other Loves and Needs such as *eros, philia, philautia,* and *storge* are ignored or unresolved and go wrong.

In *Being John Malkovich* (1999), married puppeteer Craig uses a portal into the head of the eponymous character to pursue his desire for coworker Maxine, losing perspective and reason along the way. *Eros* and *philautia* are casualties as Craig increasingly ignores his Need and descends into *mania* and self-loathing, trapped as he is forever in the head of Maxine's and his wife Lotte's love child Emily.

9. *Epithumia*

Epithumia equates to strong desire or lust and is a more extreme and overtly dangerous version of *eros*. *Epithumia* can draw characters draw together and pull them apart with destructive effects on them and others around them. Like *mania*, *epithumia* offers a warning of what can happen to us if we fail to recognise or respond to purer loves – that is, to our Need.

Jagged Edge (1985), *Fatal Attraction* (1987), and *War of the Roses* (1989) portray characters whose *epithumia* goes wrong with dangerous and devastating effects. Given the dates of these films, *epithumia* may be more active at certain times in our history than others, such as the 'Greed is Good'[16] 1980s.

10. *Eunoia*

Eunoia equates to kindness, thinking well of others, altruism. Characters with *eunoia* have benevolent feelings of goodwill from one to another, verging on the saintly. For that reason, they tend not to be dramatically very interesting in and of themselves. For quizzers,[17] the most interesting thing about *eunoia* is that it is the shortest word in English with all five vowels in it. But this is unfair. *Eunoia* offers opportunities for creating comedy when it is centred around some kind of comic discrepancy at play in the story and scenes, causing characters and their functioning Loves and Needs to become increasingly dysfunctional.

In *Blackadder's Christmas Carol* (1988), kindly Ebenezer Blackadder initially brims with *storge* but ultimately decides <u>not</u> to save the Scratchit family in Dickensian London after he is turned into a cruel miser having seen visions of his needy ancestors and descendants at Christmases past, present, and future, a comic reversal of the traditional Scrooge journey from bad to good.

Bringing Different Types of 'Loves' Together

In *The Shining* (1980), Jack Torrance loses sight of *agape* for his wife and son as he is consumed by his increasingly distorted *philautia* born out of his frustrations as a writer, his secrets, and his sins of the past. However, Wendy is strengthened by her own *storge* for her son Danny, and this compels her – enables her – to defeat the 'monster' that her husband has become.

In *Withnail And I* (1987), Withnail revels in his *philautia*. The existing *philia* between him and Marwood keeps them together albeit in a dysfunctional, co-dependent, and potentially destructive relationship. But, as the story develops, the evident *ludus* between the two unemployed actors cannot

---

16 Catchphrase based on movie character Gordon Gekko's line, "Greed, for lack of a better word, is good" from *Wall Street* (1987).
17 People who take part in pub quizzes, etc.

sustain and gives way to different versions of *philautia*, represented positively in Marwood's case – he auditions successfully for a play, is cast as the lead, gets his hair cut, leaves forever – and negatively in Withnail's case: he ends the film performing Hamlet in the rain to the wolves of Regents Park Zoo, doomed never to move on.

The notion that love can be misguided and go wrong is a powerful one when creating appropriate and forceful antagonists for our main characters, too. Colonel Nathan R. Jessup in *A Few Good Men* (1992) has a misguided dangerous *philia* and *philautia* – his love of country and of self – that inspires *storge* in his soldiers to deadly effect. Jessup's perverted 'love' endangers the very values he has spent his life protecting.

Anagnorisis

Originally identified by Aristotle in the *Poetics*, anagnorisis refers to the unexpected, surprising, life-changing discovery that a character makes about themselves, resulting in a transformation in them from ignorance to knowledge in the final part of their story.

For the screenwriter, this kind of insightful recognition by their characters can be gold dust for their script – and for their career. It is that moment in a key scene in the final act of a film or TV drama when a character has made a critical discovery about themselves (usually to do with their Need or flaw), has a sudden awareness of the real situation, and acts on this. It often gives them new insight into a relationship with their main antagonist and into themselves.

The Anagnoretic Moment

A major turning-point and a key scene in the story, the anagnoretic moment is when the main character, storyteller, and audience come together and experience a shared feeling of identification and emotion.

We will all have our favourite anagnoretic moments, that moment in that scene in a film or TV drama when the plot, action and dialogue align to create anagnorisis and we feel the strongest level of emotion. These are some of my favourite examples.

Toy Story (1995)[18]

In the final sequence of scenes in *Toy Story* (1995), toy cowboy Woody and toy space ranger Buzz are trying to catch up with the removal truck and

---

18 *Toy Story* script (draft: "File copy – RED"). Original story by John Lasseter, Pete Docter, Andrew Stanton, Joe Raft, Screenplay by Joss Whedon, Andrew Stanton, Joel Cohen and

Andy's car. Stuck together, desperate, in danger of both being left behind forever, they light a rocket with Sid's match and shoot up into the air. Woody is fearful – until Buzz uses his wings to just about keep them airborne.

>   WOODY
>   Hey, Buzz!! You're flying!!
>
>   BUZZ
>   This isn't flying. This is falling
>   — with style!
>
>   WOODY
>   Ha ha!! To Infinity and Beyond!!

By acknowledging that Buzz is actually flying – a constant source of conflict between the two through the story – Woody finally recognises his Need to be generous and show the qualities, the virtues (as Aristotle might say), of a true leader.

The genius of the scene is that Buzz has his own Need, too – he needs to realise he is really just a plastic toy like everyone else. He recognises this when he tells Woody that it isn't flying, it's falling with style. In this moment of anagnorisis for both characters, we share their connection, emotion, friendship – their *philia*. It is a triumph of screenwriting.

Little Miss Sunshine *(2006)*[19]

Richard has managed to get Olive and the rest of his family to the 'Little Miss Sunshine' pageant. As he sits in the audience, the music plays: "hard driving and nasty. It is completely different to the other pageant music we've heard so far." Olive starts her routine up on the stage and Richard begins to realise the nature of the dance her grandfather (his late father who Olive reveals innocently to the MC is "in the trunk of our car") has been teaching her in private.

As Olive begins to do pelvic thrusts to the music, the MC and others try to get her off the stage, forcing Richard to take action. He invades the stage and protects his daughter, dancing alongside her and enabling her to kick ass as chaos reigns around them. He finally displays true *storge* towards his daughter, which, in turn, enables him to recognise his own *philautia* and love

---

Alec Sokolow. 1996 Academy Award Nominee, **Best Writing, Screenplay Written Directly for the Screen.**

19 *Little Miss Sunshine* (draft dated 10 September 2003) by Michael Arndt, 1996 Academy Award Winner, **Best Writing, Original Screenplay**

himself in the right measure. The other family members join them on stage, united as Richard recognises and responds to his need to understand that it is okay to be a 'loser' (his deepest fear). As the subtext of the film suggests, most of us are, in one way or another.

Blackadder Goes Forth (1989)[20]

The fourth and final series of this iconic BBC TV sit-com is set in the trenches in World War I. In the final episode, Blackadder, Baldrick, George, and Darling are preparing to go 'over the top' and engage the enemy, heading into German gunfire and certain death. They all display gallows humour about the inevitably of their situation and that they are scared to die. The ensemble takes their leave of one another and of us. There can be no more cunning plans from Baldrick or clever wheezes from Blackadder. It truly is the end – of them, the episode, the series, and the characters.

Even in their final moments, the characters continue to display *ludus* and *philia*, confirming their 'mateship'. Anagnorisis is accentuated as they charge forward into the fog of No Man's Land. The action in the scene switches to slow motion, and the much-loved characters fade out forever. Like the World War I soldiers they represent, from Ypres to Gallipoli, they are gone but not forgotten. It is the epitome of the definition of comedy: "Comedy = Tragedy + Time".

Creating Anagnorisis and Anagnoretic Moments in Our Own Scenes

These examples of anagnorisis create a high bar for us, and this can make our own efforts to try and create anagnorisis in our own work feel daunting. So how can we try and bring it all together in practice to ensure that our reader or audience understands what our work is really about?

In reality, anagnorisis is created through a fusion of character, action, dialogue, and story world. It isn't magic and it doesn't exist in isolation. The development of nuanced truthful credible characters, undertaking clear logical actions, supported by well-written revealing dialogue, located in an appropriate, believable, engaging story world, scene by scene, are all integral to the establishment of anagnorisis. Identifying the character's

---

20 *Blackadder Goes Forth* (1989, BBC TV). Written by Richard Curtis and Ben Elton. 1990 Winner BAFTA TV Award, **Best Comedy Series**, John Lloyd, Richard Boden, Ben Elton, Richard Curtis.

Need – and the specific nature of their unresolved Love – can help in this, too.

I will explain how I have tried to approach this over the years using a sequence of scenes. To do this, let us return to the Binger in Amsterdam.

Bringing It All Together

During my time at the MBFI, I focused on developing and writing the first draft of *Boney and Betsy*, my story about the unlikely friendship between a 12-year-old English girl (Betsy) and the most notorious man alive (Napoleon Bonaparte/Boney) on St. Helena in the South Atlantic, the most remote island on the planet.

Central to the plot is Boney's desire to try and escape from the island and Betsy's increasing involvement in this as his interlocutor (she's the only person on the island who can speak French), putting herself and her family in increasing danger.

The plot reaches its climax in the final part of the script when Napoleon manages to get on board a rowing boat taking him out to a waiting American ship and Betsy, her father William Balcombe, and her older sister Jane are captured by the British on the beach having helped Boney to escape:

EXT. MARTIN'S BOAT, WATER - NIGHT

Standing under the dancing tricolour, Napoleon watches events on the beach, his face pensive. Bertrand eyes him. (NB. *French dialogue indicated by italics*)

                    BERTRAND
          Your duty is to return to France. Your
          people need you. History needs you!

Napoleon continues to stare back to the shore.

EXT. WATER'S EDGE - NIGHT

Betsy is wriggling as Farnell tries to hold her still.

                    BETSY
          Let me go.

                    FARNELL
          Keep still, damn you!

William confronts Sir Henry Lyle.

> WILLIAM
> I shall complain about this to the
> proper authority.

> LYLE
> I am the proper authority.
>   (circling the prisoners)
> Back in England you'll be executed.
> The journey back, the long trial, seem
> such a waste of time and money.

Lyle stops behind Betsy, leans down, and whispers.

> LYLE (CONT'D)
> Why don't we save the Crown a
> fortune and kill you all now?

Jane GASPS. Betsy stands dead still. William is outraged.

> WILLIAM
> You wouldn't dare.

Lyle grabs William by the hair and pushes him down onto his
knees. Farnell does the same to Jane and Betsy.

> WILLIAM (CONT'D)
> You're both mad.

All three are kneeling. Lyle glances at Farnell.

> LYLE
> Order the men to reload.

EXT. MARTIN'S BOAT - NIGHT

Napoleon gazes at the figure of Betsy as she kneels on the
beach. She is getting smaller and smaller. Behind the Bal-
combes, Farnell forms the soldiers into a firing squad.

Martin is staring back too. Napoleon gestures to him to turn
the boat round. An oar cuts into the water.

> BERTRAND
>   *No!*

Bertrand seizes the oar from Martin. The boat rocks.

                    BERTRAND (CONT'D)
        I have a wife and children too.
        I have a family...

Napoleon grabs him, holds him tight, whispers to him gently.

                    NAPOLEON
        It's over, my dear General. All over.
        It's time for me to do the right thing.

Bertrand releases the oar slowly and starts to weep. Napoleon
eyes Martin.

                    NAPOLEON (CONT'D)
        Come on, man! Row faster...

The boat veers sharply and turns back to shore.

Boney has his anagnorisis, his moment of insightful recognition, when he's
on the rowing boat and it looks like he's escaped. Yet, despite the entreaties
of his companion Bertrand, who followed him into exile, he decides to turn
back to try and save Betsy. Reputedly responsible for 2,000,000 deaths in
Europe, Napoleon is a complex, ruthless, driven character who is ultimately
out for himself for much of the script. Driven by his *philia* (his love of country), his *philautia* (love of self) and *agape* (love of others) are non-existent
when he arrives on the island, defeated, exiled from his homeland, forcibly
removed from his family. Meeting Betsy and encountering her innocence, her
goodness, and her family begins the process of repair to these and helps him
recognise and resolve his internal emotional Need.

   However, this is not the end of the story. To resolve the drama. Betsy, too,
must have her anagnorisis, her moment of insightful recognition.

EXT. WATER'S EDGE - NIGHT

Embers glow. A Soldier dumps on more wood and it crackles into
life. Soldiers march Bertrand, Les Cases, Monterry and Martin
across the beach past Anne and Alexander who are untying William and Jane.

Betsy, rubbing her wrists, is interpreting for Lyle.

                    BETSY
        He's furious about the way we've been
        treated. He's going to write to King
        George and complain about you both.
            (a beat)
        And he'll tell him about Albert too.

Betsy eyes Farnell, who looks away. Lyle sneers.

>   LYLE
> His letter can travel on the same ship
> as you.
>   (explaining to Betsy)
> You can't stay here. I'm banishing you from
> the island. And your family.

Betsy, shocked, indicates Napoleon.

>   BETSY
> But who'll do the talking for Boney?
> He'll never speak to you.

>   LYLE
> I shall enjoy the silence.
>   (to Farnell)
> Prepare to escort General Bonaparte to
> Longwood House. I shall meet you there.

Lyle walks off. Farnell goes to gather his men.

Betsy, left alone with Napoleon, looks at him.

>   BETSY
> It's all over.

>   NAPOLEON
> I prefer to think that things are
> just beginning for us both.

>   BETSY
> What will you do here?

>   NAPOLEON
> I will think of something. Dictate my
> memoirs to Bertrand. Read books. Talk
> to the flowers in my garden.

>   BETSY
> That's what people do when they get old
> and retire.

Boney smiles at her and touches her cheek softly.

>   NAPOLEON
> Exactly.

Tears well up in Betsy's eye. Boney puts his hand gently on her shoulder.

> NAPOLEON
>
> It has been an honour to know you.

Betsy tries to wipe her eyes, but the tears are flowing too fast. Napoleon pulls a hankie from his pocket. He checks that no-one is watching them. Farnell is too busy berating his troops. Napoleon slips something off his finger, wraps it in the hankie and passes it to Betsy.

> BETSY
>
> Thanks.

She opens the hankie. Lying there, shining, is the GOLD SIGNET RING. She looks at him questioningly.

> NAPOLEON
>
> The time has come for my son to have the
> Bonaparte ring. As I will not be able to
> give it to him myself, I want the bravest
> person I know to do it for me.

Betsy looks at the ring. Farnell and his troops are marching across the sand towards them. She closes the hankie and tucks it up her sleeve. She embraces Napoleon.

> BETSY
>
> He'll get it, I promise.

> NAPOLEON
>
> I know he will.

Farnell and his men stop nearby.

> BETSY
>
> I'll never forget you.

> NAPOLEON
>
> And I won't forget you, Betsy Balcombe.
> In the dark nights, when the ghosts of
> the dead howl around me, I will think
> of you.
> (a beat)
> You have given me courage to face the
> darkest night of all when it comes, as
> it surely will.

```
Napoleon and Betsy gaze at one another for the last time. He
salutes her crisply. She salutes him back. Then he takes his
place in Farnell's armed escort.

                         FARNELL
               Squad! Quick march.

The men start marching and Napoleon is taken away.

Tears fall down Betsy's cheeks. As she watches Napoleon disap-
pear from her life forever, a hand gently touches her shoul-
der. She turns and sees Jane, who is crying too. Betsy and her
sister hug.

The two girls are joined by William, Anne and Alexander. The
Balcombe family stands united together on the beach, staring
at Napoleon Bonaparte until he is swallowed up by the darkness.

                                         FADE TO BLACK
```

Conclusion

For Betsy, her friendship with Boney is life-changing. She has suddenly found herself at the centre of the world, playing her part in history. However, meeting someone like Napoleon and being his friend is not without consequences. Innocent people, such as Boney's chef Albert, die because of people like Bonaparte. Betsy comes to realise this – her insightful recognition, her moment of anagnorisis.

Betsy's story is really an exploration of the end of childhood, of childish games, of innocence. Her *ludus* with Boney is over and is giving way to something else. She is also being exiled – off the island, away from her new friend and her home, back to England. She may never feel *philia* (love of country) – indeed the Balcombe family were unable to settle in England and emigrated to Australia – but her *storge* (affection) is restored, reuniting her with her family and, in particular, with her sister Jane.

But Betsy has achieved more besides. Her friendship with Napoleon, her brief moment in the spotlight, and the consequences of this mean that her *philautia* – her love of self – is now in the right measure, enabling her, like Boney, to be able to face whatever may be to come.

Theme – Scene-Writing Exercise

"Theme" Exercise

The notion of theme can be elusive and complicated. Imposing a theme on work too early can be counterproductive, fixing that work too early or taking it in an unintended or unwanted direction. On the other hand, ignoring the theme altogether can mean the actions and dialogue of characters from scene to scene seem random and disconnected.

Step 1 – *Take a character and scene you're working on, or one you may have written for an earlier chapter. Think about who they are, where they are, what they are, when they are, how they are.*

Step 2 – *Imagine this character back in their past, in a situation or scene that predates any of the story and script you are writing about and that they are in.*

Step 3 – *Write a short scene that reveals the greatest moment for that character in their life – their happiest moment so far.*

Step 4 – *Now write a short scene that reveals the worst moment for that character in their life – their unhappiest moment so far.*

Step 5 – *Read these two scenes and compare them. Your protagonist in them may be markedly different in age, location, circumstance, situation. But what links them? What word links them and unifies their story and their world?*

Ask yourself:

- *Does this word represent the theme of their story – of your story?*
- *To what degree is this word or theme present in the key scenes in your script, the story about this character?*
- *How does it reflect the internal emotional Need of the character?*
- *Which of the Greek 'loves' (reflecting a character's Need) are in your scenes? If they're not, can you add one or more in some way?*

9

THE SEQUENCE

How Do We Join It All Together?

Introduction

In previous chapters, we looked at the scene and how it exists and functions as an individual unit of action. We focused on the key elements that are integral to and active in every film and TV scene we are likely to write regardless of the length of the script or its form. We also looked at different types of scenes and what their use can offer the screenwriter, such as the 'seduction' scene, the 'introduction of the main character' scene, and the different sorts of dialogue scenes that are available to us.

However, it is also important for us to remember that individual scenes rarely stand alone. A scene is almost always part of a larger sequence of scenes, interconnected units in sequences of dramatic action that interlink to advance the characters, story, and plot in some way. If most stories start with a character with some kind of problem, then the same is true at the start of the scenes in that story. Characters enter the scene with a problem that they carry – often reluctantly – from one scene to another.

The specific functions of a sequence of scenes at different points in the script contribute to the dynamic of the particular story, regardless of the length of that script or the screen it may one day appear on. As we have discussed, the script plays a vital part in the realisation of that story. The nature of film and TV production means that scenes are often filmed out of sequence. Economies of scale imposed by time and money hard-wire a need for efficiency on the shooting schedule. This means that all the scenes in that particular location, or involving that particular actor, or that particular piece of equipment, have to be shot on the same day or days regardless of where those scenes may actually come in the script. The script, with its sequential

DOI: 10.4324/9781003293927-10

telling of the story from first to last scene, is the one document throughout the development, pre-production, production, and post-production process that tells the whole story, in the correct order, for everyone involved, whatever their role or level of involvement.

When I was in St. Petersburg in 2005 writing the production and shooting drafts for *In Tranzit*, it was announced that we had secured John Malkovich to play the role of Pavlov. The excitement this generated was tempered by the fact that he was only available for three specific weeks during the shoot. This meant that all his scenes, involving different locations and seasons of the year, had to be shot in a single block, and so out of order as far as the narrative of the movie's story was concerned. Some of this was easy to navigate. Some of it was harder: scenes involving Malkovich in the final sequences of the script that were set in the spring and reflected an actual and metaphorical thawing in the lives of the Soviet women running the transit camp and their male German prisoners had to be shot in February in the middle of the Russian winter. The importance of the screenplay in showing and telling the story scene by scene in sequence for everyone involved came into sharp focus.

The Sequence

The existence of the sequence in screen stories, its specific functions in that story depending on where it is located, and the core elements it involves are important parts of the screenwriter's toolkit. I was first introduced to the concept of the 8-sequence approach providing a feature film story with its core structure at the MBFI in 1996 by David Howard,[1] and I continue to use this approach today in my teaching and my own screenwriting to help me plot and structure my film and TV scripts. Over the years, I have modified this approach in my own teaching so it can be incorporated into writing TV dramas and sit-coms, and even short films.[2]

Much of the early work on identifying the importance of sequences in screen storytelling and establishing a dramatic theory to explain this was done by screenwriting teacher Frank Daniel,[3] whom David Howard studied with. Another Frank Daniel student, Paul Gulino, has written a book titled *Screenwriting: The Sequence Approach* that is worth checking out for more on this. There are also more and more websites online that address sequences and the sequence approach. Some of these are more helpful – and accurate – than others.

---

1 Professor David Howard, USC, *Tools of Screenwriting*, Souvenir Press Ltd; Main edition (29 September 2011).
2 See B, C, D in *The Sequence* Appendix for teaching material about film and TV sequences.
3 Frank Daniel (1926–96), Czech-American screenwriter and teacher.

For the purposes of this book and its specific focus on scene-writing, I am going to share with you my version of the sequence approach. I acknowledge with gratitude the teaching and instruction I've received about this in the past from Howard, other screenwriting teachers that I've studied with and worked with, and, of course, Frank Daniel himself, a man I never met but, given the role he has played in my life as a screenwriter and teacher, would very much have liked to.

The Sequence Approach

As you read this section, remember that, like you, I am a storyteller. I have shared this approach many times since 1996 with screenwriters, filmmakers, and students around the world, from Liverpool to Lithuania and Alice Springs to York. Inevitably, there is some poetic licence in it, a little bit of myth, even. But there is also a great deal of truth. The point of admitting this to you is not to undermine what I'm saying or challenge you to work out what may be fact and what may be fiction. Rather, it is to encourage you to embrace the essence of the story. The sequence approach has served me very well over the years as a writer, teacher, script consultant, audience member, and consumer of screen stories, and I hope it does the same for you.

Historically, movies were shown in reels. I just about can remember the changeover of these during the projection of movies in my local picture house in the 1970s. In the early years of cinema, the first films were 'one-reelers' – so-called because one reel of film was the physical limit that the earliest technology of an edited film and its projection method could sustain. The 'one-reeler' had a maximum running time of 11–12 minutes[4] and consisted of a single 'reel' – or sequence – of dramatic action. In many ways, it was the precursor of the short film today: what goes around comes around.

Screen storytelling has always depended on and been driven forward by technology. Whatever stage of technology we are in when you read this – digital production, virtual production, augmented reality (AR), virtual reality (VR), artificial intelligence (AI), or the as-yet-un-invented production methods and realities still to come – the existence and use of technology has defined the length, type, and nature of the screen stories we've been able to tell. Technology has always driven the medium, including screenwriting, rather than the other way around. If there weren't the means to make and screen films and TV stories, screenwriters wouldn't need to exist. We'd all be playwrights, epic poets, or singers of ballads and tellers of sagas instead.

---

4 1000 ft of 35-mm film spliced together ran for around 11 minutes, a duration that became associated with the length of film sequences in longer-form moving pictures.

And ultimately, what drives the technology and, therefore, all of us is the audience.

Early filmmakers soon discovered that audiences liked – loved – watching flickering moving images projected in front of them in the dark. They cherished being transported out of their daily lives. And they soon wanted to watch films that told stories that lasted longer than 'one-reelers'. They <u>demanded</u> this. And if the history of the world has taught us anything, it is that where there's demand, there is opportunity and money to be made by other people. So 'one-reelers' became 'two-reelers', became 'four-reelers', became 'eight-reelers', as the available technology continued to develop, allowing for the making and the projection of longer and longer films and for the telling of longer and longer screen stories.

During the Silent Era,[5] the 'eight-reeler' – eight reels of dramatic action linked by fade-ins and fade-outs for each reel – became the template for long-form moving pictures. Each reel – often a mini movie in its own right – represented a particular sequence of action within the longer film it was situated. As well as an overall structure for the whole film, there was an inherent structure for each sequence. Like screen stories as a whole and the scenes within them, their sequences have beginnings, middles, and ends and involve set ups, goals, tensions, dramatic questions, complications, conflicts, midpoints, reversals, culminations, resolutions, and twists into the next part of the story – the next sequence.

Although movies no longer have fade-outs between the reels, it is useful for us to be able to understand the existence of and the notion of sequences. Dividing a 90–120-page screenplay into a series of sequences or chapters enables us to navigate our way through the script by working on it in smaller sections, typically 10–20 minutes long, each with

- its own sequence-specific dramatic question, (i.e., "Will . . . ?")
- Six sequence-specific dramatic beats / plot events to support this tension
- its own heading or arena for the action and where it takes place, such as "The Wedding", "The Funeral", "The Road Trip", "The Chase", or "The Love Sequence".[6]

Similar sequential structural elements also exist in TV dramas. The template for TV drama was initially provided by the theatre, reflecting the 'live' performative nature of the early TV drama outputs. But as film and its more

---

5 The Silent Era relates to the era of cinema before the invention and use of synchronised sound, in particular, dialogue. The increasing use of dialogue in movies following *The Jazz Singer* (1927) resulted in a requirement for this dialogue to be written – leading, in turn, to the invention and use of the screenwriter!

6 Historically, the fifth reel or sequence featured the main love story of the film, which was often the main subplot in a traditional Hollywood genre movie.

portable technology began to influence the ambition and execution of TV dramas such as police procedurals, the sequence approach became embedded in its writing and structure. Its presence can be located and identified throughout TV drama worldwide today. A 1-hour TV drama episode, running 44 to 56 minutes, contains 4 sequences of 10–15 minutes each, with 1 sequence in Act 1, 2 sequences in Act 2, and 1 sequence in Act 3.

This is all very well, I can hear you say. Enough of the history lesson. How does it work in practice?

A Sequence of Scenes

To illustrate this for us, I have created a sequence of scenes with a beginning, a middle, and an end. It could be a sequence in a film or TV drama. Or it could be the single sequence of a short film, reminiscent of the 'one-reeler', where the structure and form of moving pictures all started. Its purpose is to show the scene-by-scene approach a) to the writing and development of a typical sequence and b) to each of the scenes in that sequence and to share with you the ideas, intentions, comments, and questions I ask myself – and any other writer – when working on this integral, often hidden, dramatic element.

I am also focusing on process here and analysing the scenes as I would for any script and its writer. During this process, I realised that some of the scenes would be improved by a rewrite or a revision. Rather than do this prior to my analysis, I have left them as is so that you can see this process of analysis in action.

If you'd like to read the unannotated sequence before my scene-by-scene analysis of it and make your own mind up about it and its scenes, you'll find it in the Appendix[7] at the end of this chapter. I've tried to incorporate many of the scene-writing ideas and principles we've discussed in this book in these scenes, so why not have a go at analysing them before you read my take on this?

Scene Analysis Questions

As you read, keep asking yourself the key dramatic scene-related questions that I am always thinking about and asking myself or my students and writers:

1. Whose scene is it?
2. What is their specific external physical goal or objective (want) in it?
3. What is the specific question of the scene?
4. What are the 6 beats in the scene?
5. How do these beats give the scene its 3-part structure: a) set up; b) conflict; c) consequences?
6. Which of the three hierarchies of knowledge are at play in the scene?

---

7 Appendix A, *Magic Hour by Simon van der Borgh*; 12-page sequence/short film script.

7. Where does the scene take place?
8. What event or new piece of information spins us into the next scene?

Sequence Analysis Questions

Similar questions are also in play when considering the sequence as a whole:

1. Whose sequence is it?
2. What is their specific external physical goal or objective (want) in it?
3. What is the overall dramatic question linking the action in the sequence?
4. What are the 6 beats in the sequence?
5. How do these beats give the sequence its 3-part structure: a) set up; b) conflict; c) consequences?
6. Which of the three hierarchies of knowledge are at play in the sequence?
7. What event or new piece of information spins us into the next sequence?
8. What is the overall heading or arena that unites the sequence?

Case Study: "Magic Hour"

Please note I have followed industry practice and not used scene numbers in this sequence for what I am still regarding as work in progress, or work still in development.

MAGIC HOUR
by
Simon van der Borgh

FADE IN:

EXT. LANDSCAPE - DAY

Winter light.

Then

A SOUND: an ALARM

Scene 1 – "In the Beginning" – Introduction to Story World

I am trying to create the sense of the curtain parting to reveal the world of the story within to the audience and draw them into this world. Given the characters and story to come, I want to introduce the notion of light, imagery, the cinematic, photography, and winter. There is no dramatic question for this scene. Establishing tone and atmosphere are more important at this stage, and I am deliberately vague about what we might actually be looking at in the scene, beyond "Landscape" and "Winter light". I want to give the director and the DoP reading the script encouragement – poetic licence – to interpret this in their own way and make the scenes their own – to begin to invest in my characters, story, and world. The ALARM sound is intended to intrude (and drag us into the next scene).

```
INT. BEDROOM - DAY

The same ALARM.

In the gloom: GRAHAM (50-something, large, seen better
days) lies in bed. Wide awake. Staring up at the ceiling.
On the bedside table, the ALARM continues to ring...
```

Scene 2: "Meeting Graham" – Introduction to Main Character

The diegetic sound of the alarm links the scenes, taking us into a bedroom and introducing a man (GRAHAM) to us in his routine/ordinary world. We can't be sure if he is going to be the main character of this sequence yet. But there is a dramatic question of sorts for him in the scene: Will the man turn off the alarm? He doesn't. At this stage, I am primarily thinking about this scene in terms of how it introduces the character of Graham the first time we see him in the story. What do we learn about him? What ten adjectives can be used to describe him (reinforcing the ones in the descriptor in brackets)? Middle-aged, preoccupied, reluctant to get up, catatonic, frozen . . .

Note that I give minimal description about the room itself beyond the fact that it's day outside, gloomy inside, there's a bed, ceiling, and something with an alarm on the bedside table (I am planting the bedside table and drawing attention to it for an upcoming scene). Unless there is a specific item or prop in the room that is relevant to the story and plot, the look and feel of the room is up to the director, art director, production designer, DoP, etc. – it is someone else's creative or technical decision.

```
INT. BATHROOM - DAY

Graham, eyeing himself in the mirror. Feels his stubble.

                                                   CUT TO:

Graham, wet-shaving.
```

Scene 3: "Close Shave" – Preparation for a Meeting

The shaving scene is intended to suggest that Graham is getting ready to go out. He's preparing for a meeting of some sort and whoever he's meeting won't like the stubble on his face. This is a nod to my own personal experience.

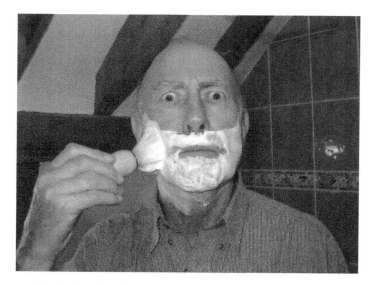

IMAGE 9.1 My father Jonathan van der Borgh: "Shave every morning before breakfast!" circa 2005.

My father, a disciplined and habitual wet-shaver, encouraged with varying degrees of success his five sons[8] to be the same, to the point where it became a family joke. As we say in screenwriting: write about what you know.

```
INT. BEDROOM - DAY

Graham irons a shirt.

Ties a tie.

Puts on a jacket.
```

Scene 4: "Dressing Up" – Masquerade

The sense that Graham is preparing for some kind of key meeting is reinforced in this scene. He is getting dressed in clothes that are traditionally seen as formal – shirt and tie, jacket – suggesting that he is going out to meet a particular someone or do a particular something.

When I met costume designer Ruth Myers[9] in Los Angeles with Peter Medak and we interviewed her for the feature-doc *The Ghost of Peter Sellers*,

---

8 Me, Peter, James, Adam, and Matthew.
9 Interview with Ruth Myers, 5 March 2016, Los Angeles. Oscar-nominated for *The Addams Family* (1992) and *Emma* (1997), Myers was the costume designer on Medak's ill-fated *Ghost in the Noonday Sun* (1974).

she told me: "The function of costumes is to aid the story. They're a key part of the storytelling" – great advice that I took forward into my screenwriting and scene-writing teaching.

I am implying that Graham is masquerading as someone he's not. As a result, there is status at work. Such is the nature of the meeting and / or the person he is going to meet that Graham feels obliged to take action and dress up for it and pretend to be a version of himself that the person he is due to meet expects him to be. This suggests low status in terms of how Graham may be perceived – or, more accurately, how he perceives himself. We can also add more words to describe how he is being introduced to us: formal, old-fashioned, buttoned-up, precise, practical, can iron a shirt.

```
INT. HALLWAY - DAY
```

```
Graham walks towards the front door. Sees himself in the
mirror. In his Sunday Best. A dog's dinner...
```

```
He pulls off the tie. And the jacket. Angry. Stares into
the mirror. Breathing heavily. Heads back upstairs.
```

Scene 5: "A Dog's Dinner" – Inner Conflict

This short mini-sequence of introductory scenes (1–5) is linked by a dramatic question running through them: "Will Graham get up and get himself ready to go out?" It's not the most dynamic of dramatic questions, but it does reflect a domestic activity that most of us can relate to. Having set it up and drawn the reader into familiar territory, I then want to reverse this in this scene by having Graham react badly to seeing himself in the mirror. This is a personal moment that no one else would normally witness: the camera allows us to be voyeurs observing it. The scene reveals a sense of self-loathing and anger in Graham about getting dressed up in his Sunday Best for a meeting he is not looking forward to. It's also meant to make us wonder why he has responded like this. What or who off-screen has the power, the influence to make him react like this?

```
INT. BEDROOM - DAY
```

```
Graham is sitting on the bed. Staring at the bedside table.
```

```
He slides open the drawer. Gazes at something inside:
```

```
A SMALL HANDGUN
```

```
He reaches in. Picks it up. Puts it into his pocket. [Sequence
Beat #1]
```

Scene 6: "The Gun" – Pivotal Moment / Twist / Advertising

As we see in this scene (the final scene of this mini-sequence), Graham's reaction to seeing himself in the mirror has an even darker effect than just taking off his tie. It makes him change his plan – or get his plan back on track, maybe – forcing him to go upstairs again and get the gun in the (planted) bedside table.

When I initially wrote this sequence as a short film, there wasn't a gun in it at all. But as I began to consider it for inclusion here to illustrate a sequence of scenes, I wanted to increase the stakes and the dramatic tension of the overall piece. Adding a gun seemed like a good way to do this visually and quickly. My writing students often include guns in their scenes when I set them writing tasks, so I decided to replicate their decision-making. To paraphrase the great Russian playwright Anton Chekhov,[10] if you plant a gun in the first act, you must use it in the final act.

This is effectively the end of the first mini sequence of scenes in "Magic Hour" as a whole. In terms of the 6 dramatic beats in the sequence, Graham taking the gun and putting it in his pocket [#1] is (for me) Sequence Beat #1 of 6, the 'Inciting Incident' of the sequence. It changes Graham's *status quo* in this sequence. The gun introduces the notion of external conflict. In the first five scenes, the dominant hierarchy of knowledge for the reader is 'mystery for the viewer': we the audience (A) <u>know less than (<)</u> what the character (C) knows. Initially, from what we are watching, we only really know that the man is reluctantly shaving and getting dressed up to go out. Once the gun is revealed and he takes the gun and puts it in his pocket, 'mystery for the viewer' is joined by another hierarchy of knowledge – 'mystery' or dramatic tension. Because we the audience (A) <u>know what (=)</u> Graham (C) knows: He has put – hidden? – a gun in his pocket. This raises the stakes, increasing the potential for conflict and creating tension.

```
I/E. CAR - DAY

MUSIC PLAYS. Graham drives along. He is dressed once more in
the tie and jacket. Resigned to the day ahead.
```

Scene 7: "Driving to the Meeting" – Transition Scene

We locate Graham in his car, driving somewhere (we don't know where yet). However, we suspect the gun is in his pocket (we haven't seen him remove it from there), so the third hierarchy of knowledge is underway here, too.

---

10 Anton Chekhov (1860–1904). Plays include *The Seagull*, *Uncle Vanya*, and *Three Sisters*. Chekhov wrote in several letters to aspiring writers that if you say in the first chapter that there is a rifle hanging on the wall, in the second or third chapter it absolutely must go off. If it's not going to be fired, it shouldn't be hanging there.

Because now that Graham is out in public, we the audience (A) <u>know more than (>)</u> the people (C) that the character may encounter know – which creates 'suspense' or dramatic irony.[11]

In the action description, it says: MUSIC PLAYS. Note that I don't specify the song playing, if indeed it is a song. Unless a particular piece of music has a specific and integral dramatic function in the story and the plot, then it is not the screenwriter's job to specify what is playing on the radio in this scene beyond the fact that it is 'music'. So I avoid specifying songs and pieces of music from the get-go. If I wanted to suggest the mood, I might put CLASSICAL MUSIC PLAYS or COUNTRY MUSIC PLAYS.

```
I/E. CAR - DAY

Graham pulls up in a tree-lined suburban street. Large houses.
Nice area. Well-to-do.

He looks out through the windscreen:

A LARGE RESIDENTIAL HOME

He stares at it.

He opens the glove compartment. Takes the handgun from his
pocket, places it inside the recess. Closes it again.

Checks his watch. Then gets out of the car. Slowly.
```

Scene 8: "Arriving at His Destination" – New Location / New Situation

We establish Graham arriving outside a large residential home. The purpose of this scene is to encourage the reader or audience to ask questions about this new location / situation for Graham: Where are we? What is this home? Who lives there? Who has Graham come to meet? Why does he leave the gun in the car?

While re-reading this scene and analysing it, I see that there isn't much of a dramatic question in it. In a rewrite, I might fix this by showing him taking the gun out of his pocket earlier, before he looks out of the window, introducing the gun as the conflict that creates the tension of the scene – "Will Graham . . . or won't he?" – for example:

---

11 NB. 'Suspense' can also create comic irony: we see someone eating a banana and throwing the skin on the ground. We know it's on the ground. Someone else walking along doesn't know. We watch them approach the banana skin. They skid on it. Some of us laugh.

Revised scene 8:

```
I/E. CAR - DAY


Graham pulls up in a tree-lined suburban street. Large houses.
Nice area. Well-to-do.

He takes the handgun out of his pocket.

He looks out through the windscreen:

A LARGE RESIDENTIAL HOME

He stares at it. Then at the gun.

He opens the glove compartment. Places the handgun inside the
recess. Closes it again.

Checks his watch. Then gets out of the car. Slowly.
```

This creates a more specific question of the scene: "Will Graham take the gun with him?" He doesn't – posing another question: Why doesn't he take it?

```
EXT. AVENUE - DAY

Graham turns into the driveway towards the large dwelling.
Past a sign:

"THE CEDARS — A CARE HOME of QUALITY"
```

Scene 9: "The Cedars" – Exposition

We are shown a key element of exposition about the nature of the "large residential home". Exposition is the information the reader / audience needs to know to understand the story. It's a care home. What's the nature of the care it provides? Who lives there? What's their connection with Graham? Why take a gun to go visit them?

```
EXT. FRONT DOOR, "THE CEDARS" CARE HOME - DAY

Graham stops by the door. RINGS the buzzer. Waits.

THROUGH THE LARGE BAY WINDOW

He becomes aware of someone staring through the glass. At him.
But not seeing him.
```

This is PHILIP (late 70s, dapper, a ladies' man, well-groomed).

Graham half waves at him. No response from Philip.

Graham presses the BUZZER again. The front door opens, revealing NURSE SHARP (30s, takes no prisoners).

                    NURSE SHARP
          I'm coming...

She realises who it is.

                    NURSE SHARP (CONT'D)
          Oh. Graham.

                    GRAHAM
          Hello, Nurse Sharp.

She stands there. An immovable object.

                    GRAHAM (CONT'D)
          Can we talk?

She stares at him. Allows him to cross the threshold.

Scene 10: "An Unexpected Visitor" – Introduction of New Characters

This is the first time we see PHILIP, the character who will be the main antagonist for Graham in this sequence (though we don't know that or his relationship to Graham yet). The fact that Graham half-waves at Philip suggests they may know one another. Philip's total lack of response is also indicative.

Again, the dramatic question for the scene is not as clear or active as it could / should be. In my mind, it centres around Graham getting into the home – "Will Graham be able to enter the home?" NURSE SHARP is the external conflict to this – the gatekeeper – and her reaction to seeing Graham on the doorstep suggests that she is not expecting him. She is not as warm or welcoming as we might expect her to be to a visitor of one of her residents – begging the question "Why?" Note that Nurse Sharp is not going to be Graham's main antagonist in this sequence. Her function is to be the force of antagonism for Graham here, in these scenes at this particular point of the story, an obstacle that creates difficulty for Graham that he has to overcome.

This is the beginning of Graham crossing the threshold, leaving his ordinary, routine world and entering the extraordinary, specific world of the sequence and, potentially, the script and story as a whole. Nurse Sharp is a gatekeeper in more ways than one.

```
INT. NURSES' STATION - DAY

At the sink a young NURSE (20) scrubs a used commode. One of
many piled up...

Nurse Sharp enters, followed by Graham.

                    NURSE SHARP
          All the rooms are busy. So we'll have to
          chat in here.

Graham nods. She eyes him. Pointed.

                    NURSE SHARP (CONT'D)
          Long time, no see. [a]

                    GRAHAM
          I've been busy. Away. Working.

                    NURSE SHARP
          We like to have notice. About visits.

                    GRAHAM
          Of course. How is he?

                    NURSE SHARP
          Philip's had a happy week.

                    GRAHAM
          Great. Can I see him? Philip? [b]

                    NURSE SHARP
          Apart from Thursday.

                    GRAHAM
          Oh.

He knows what that means.

                    NURSE SHARP
          One of his films was on the telly. It
          confused him. Upset him. That's the
          trouble with Aphasia. He can't express
          himself. Even if he knew what he wanted
          to express.
```

                        GRAHAM
          I know the feeling.

Dark humour. She ignores this.

                      NURSE SHARP
          Why are you really here, Graham? **[c]**

                        GRAHAM
          It was his birthday.

                      NURSE SHARP
          We know. We had a cake. Yesterday.

                        GRAHAM
          I've booked a table. For lunch.

At the sink, the young Nurse scrubs another commode...

                      NURSE SHARP
          He doesn't eat much lunch.

                        GRAHAM
          At his favourite place. We used to go
          every Sunday. In the good old days.

She is still unconvinced. He gazes at her.

                    GRAHAM (CONT'D)
          His doctor said it might do him good
          to visit some familiar places.

She is listening...

                    GRAHAM (CONT'D)
          Please, Jenny. **[d]**

Behind them, the commode cleaning continues. Noisy.

                    GRAHAM (CONT'D)
          He's my dad. I miss him. **[e]**

                      NURSE SHARP
          What time would you get him back?

Graham smiles. **[f]**

Scene 11: "Seducing Nurse Sharp" – Seduction Scene

This is one of the key scenes in the sequence. After all, if Graham doesn't get Nurse Sharp to let him take his father out, then the rest of the action in the scenes and sequence can't happen. The story stops. I've set the scene in a location that is not conducive to 'seduction' – the place where nurses rinse out and wash up patients' commodes (bedpans); this happens throughout the scene, providing opportunities for the intrusion of images and sound into the 'seduction'.

Scene questions:

1. Whose scene is it?

   Graham's. He has the biggest objective – winning over Nurse Sharp.

2. What is his specific external physical goal or objective (want) in it?

   Graham wants Nurse Sharp to agree to let him see his father.

3. What is the specific question of the scene?

   Will Graham get Nurse Sharp to agree to let him see his father?

4. What are the six beats in the scene?

   a. *"Long time, no see" Introduction of conflict / inciting incident*
   b. *"Can I see him?" Want / main objective*
   c. *"Why are you really here?" Midpoint / furthest from main objective*

   This results in a reversal / change of strategy: "I've booked a table. For lunch."

   d. *"Please, Jenny" Culmination*
   e. *"He's my dad. I miss him." Twist*
   f. *She tacitly agrees. Graham smiles. Resolution*

5. How do these beats give the scene its 3-part structure:

   a. *Set up: Nurse Sharp and the location are cold, unfriendly.*
   b. *Conflict: Winning Nurse Sharp over.*
   c. *Consequences: Graham not only gets permission to see his father but also to take him out for lunch.*

6. Which of the three hierarchies of knowledge are at play in the scene?

   a. *A<C: we know less than Nurse Sharp about Philip and how he is*
   b. *A=C: we know the same as Graham – we know about the gun*
   c. *A>C: we know more than Nurse Sharp – we know about the gun*

7. Where does the scene take place?

   In the busy nurses' area where they wash out used patient commodes

8. What event or new piece of information spins us into the next scene?

   Not only is Graham allowed to see his father but he's allowed to take him out of the care home for lunch.

Exposition:

We learn some important exposition via the 'seduction':

- Graham hasn't visited his father Philip for some time.
- Graham isn't getting the red-carpet treatment from Nurse Sharp.
- Caring for elderly residents (even illustrious ones) is not glamorous.
- Philip used to work in the film industry.
- Philip has aphasia (a brain disorder that affects communication).
- Nurse Sharp is suspicious of Graham and his motives.
- Philip has just had a birthday.
- Graham wants to take his father out to lunch at his favourite place.
- Philip's doctor said an outing like this might be good for him.

Seduction strategies:

What strategies does Graham use to 'seduce' Nurse Sharp into letting him see his father?

- He's been busy, away, working (this doesn't work).
- He is sympathetic – he understands his father's condition (this doesn't work).
- It was his father's birthday (this doesn't work).
- He's booked a table for lunch (this doesn't work).
- He invokes the good old days, the past (this doesn't work).
- The doctor said visiting familiar places might do some good (this begins to work).
- He appeals to her on a personal level – as "Jenny" (this works some more).
- He appeals to her empathy – he misses his father (this seals the deal).
- He succeeds in the seduction – and wins the scene.

As this list indicates, a seduction is progressive. It usually starts external and impersonal and becomes more internal, more personal in order to win over the scene's antagonist.

Status:

In the scene, Nurse Sharp is high status – she rules the care home and is the gatekeeper to its residents. Graham is low status – reinforced by the location he is taken into, a place where commodes are being cleaned of urine and excrement. This means Graham has to work even harder to 'seduce' Nurse Sharp. Although we don't see him in the scene, Philip has a status, too – higher than Graham's, lower than Nurse Sharp's.

In a scene like this, one character often moves in a straight line, the other character in a wavy line.[12] Nurse Sharp is the straight-line character – clinical, indomitable, reliable, truthful, professional, consistent, resistant, protective. Graham is the wavy-line character – mercurial, unreliable, inconsistent, lying, deceitful, manipulative, unprofessional. The wavy-line character has to work hard to seduce the straight-line character. The effective use of his wavy-line characteristics ultimately enables Graham to achieve his goal, overcome straight-line Nurse Sharp, get her agreement that not only can he see his father but he can also take him out for lunch, and win the scene.

```
EXT. FRONT DOOR, RESIDENTIAL HOME - DAY

Graham waits.

Nurse Sharp appears with Philip.

                    NURSE SHARP
              Here he is...

She hands Philip over to Graham. She eyes the two well-dressed
stiff-upper-lip men.

                    NURSE SHARP (CONT'D)
              Don't get up to any mischief, you two!
              See you at five. Have fun!

The front door closes. [Sequence Beat #2]

Graham eyes Philip.

He moves away from the door. Philip follows.
```

---

12 Steve Kaplan introduced me to the concept of straight-line and wavy-line characters in his comedy writing masterclass at the Australian Film Television and Radio School in 2012.

Scene 12: "Philip" – Main Antagonist / New Situation

This scene completes the set up of this sequence and establishes the dramatic tension of the sequence itself: "Will Graham have fun out at lunch with Philip?" (Sequence Beat #2 [#2]). Given what we know already – Philip's medical condition, Graham's long absence from visiting his father, Graham's own state of mind, and the fact that he's brought a gun – like Nurse Sharp – we may hope Graham will have 'fun', but we fear that he won't.

```
EXT. DRIVEWAY, THE CEDARS - DAY

Halfway down, Graham realises Philip isn't with him.

Philip is looking at the light. Deep. Watching it play on his
hand. Inspecting it. The colour temperature. Transfixed.

                    GRAHAM
             (curt)
        C'mon, dad. Or we'll miss the soup.

Graham takes his arm. Escorts him down the drive. Philip
acquiesces. Automatic. Locked in his own world.
```

Scene 13: "Get a Move On" – Planting / Element of the Future

This is an extension of Scene 12, showing us the two men suddenly together in the outside world and the challenge for Graham of communicating with Philip. We know that Philip worked in the film industry, and his evident fascination with light, colour, and colour temperature reminds us about this and reinforces it. These short scenes are linked by the dramatic question, "Will Graham get Philip to their lunch date in time for the soup?"

```
EXT. AVENUE - DAY

Graham unlocks the car. Opens the passenger door. Waits.

Philip approaches. Graham drums his fingers on the roof.
Philip gets in. Graham puts on Philip's seat-belt. Closes
the door.
```

Scene 14: 'Belt Up' – Main Character

This scene is a further extension of the new situation. We see that Philip exists in his own world. Graham has to wait for him and do a mundane task like putting on a safety belt for him. Getting to where they're going in time for the soup will be touch-and-go.

```
I/E. CAR - DAY

Driving. Silence. Graham eyes Philip. Philip is staring out
the window at the light, shadow, shapes. Entranced.

Graham puts on the radio. MUSIC plays. Focuses on the road.

Philip fiddles with parts of the dashboard. Pushes a button.
The glove compartment pops open.

INSIDE

The handgun. Philip reaches for it. Takes it. Eyes the light
catching the metal. Then points it at Graham.

Graham realises.

                        GRAHAM
            What the hell... Give me that.

He snatches the gun. Stuffs it in his pocket. SLAMS the
glove compartment shut. Philip is already staring back out the
window.
```

Scene 15: "Philip Finds the Gun" – Open Conflict

Initially, this feels like a transition scene – Graham driving Philip to their lunch date – but in reality, one wouldn't need a scene just to relocate them to the hotel. To save time, money, the cost of rigging up a car, shooting on the road, etc., we could use an ellipsis here and cut straight to the hotel. So this scene only works, is only fundamental to the characters, action, and story, if it shows and tells us something new.

Given that we know that there is a gun in the glove compartment – we've seen Graham put it there – I want to explore the idea: What if Philip found this gun? The open conflict the gun causes – confirmed by Graham's reaction – serves several dramatic purposes:

- It reminds us about the gun.
- It shows us Philip's reaction to the gun: he initially studies it like it's a film prop.
- Philip suddenly pointing the gun at Graham is an unexpected twist.
- Graham's reaction reinforces the fact that the gun is a dangerous weapon.
- Graham puts the gun in his pocket. And we know it's there.
- The event increases our fears about this outing.

```
EXT. HOTEL - DAY
```

```
The car pulls up outside the hotel. The sort that does a tra-
ditional Sunday lunch.
```

Scene 16: "Arriving for Lunch" – Establishing Main Location

This scene confirms that Graham has got them to the lunch venue (and the key location in Act 2), resolving the dramatic question running through this mini-sequence of scenes. But are they in time for soup?

```
INT. DINING ROOM, HOTEL - DAY
```

```
Graham and Philip enter the sparsely filled room. THE MANAGER
(60s) greets them. Warm.
```

```
                    MANAGER
          Hello, Philip. It's been ages.
               (to Graham)
          Usual table?
```

```
Graham nods. She shows them to the table by the window.
```

```
Graham and Philip sit. The Manager pushes in Philip's seat.
Unfurls a napkin for him. She doesn't hand them menus.
```

```
                    MANAGER
          Soup, followed by the roast beef?
```

```
                    GRAHAM
          Thank you. [Sequence Beat #3]
```

```
She leaves. Philip is staring across the room. Watching the
dust dancing in its light...
```

Scene 17: "The Usual Table" – Exposition

The Manager greets Philip by name but not Graham, reinforcing the low status of Graham compared to his father, who was – is – someone notable. We learn

- Philip is familiar to and known to the Manager by his name.
- He hasn't been there for a long time.
- He has a "usual table" by the window.
- Graham follows his father. In his shadow: their *status quo*.

- The Manager is used to being attentive to Philip.
- She remembers what he (*ergo* they) always orders.

Arriving at their usual table is the Midpoint (Sequence Beat #3 [#3]) of the sequence – the closest that Graham gets to his external physical Want / goal in the sequence: taking his father out for lunch. This leads us into the Midpoint Reversal:

                                                          LATER

Philip eats some bread. Slowly.

Graham is aware of A COUPLE (70s) hovering by the table.

Fans. The Woman smiles at him. And especially Philip.

                          WOMAN
                We loved all his movies.

                          HUSBAND
                All of them.

                          GRAHAM
                Thank you...

                          WOMAN
                Even the depressing ones.

                          HUSBAND
                Especially the depressing ones!

Silence. Hoping they will move on. But they still hover.

                          WOMAN
                Does he talk much about the old days?

                          GRAHAM
                He can't talk.

                          WOMAN
                Oh.

                          GRAHAM
                He hasn't said a word for five years.

Silence. They stare at Philip. Locked in.

                        HUSBAND
         He did his talking through the camera.

Graham eyes the Man. About to say something. Checks himself.

                        GRAHAM
         Our soup'll be here soon.

The Woman nods.

                        HUSBAND
         Can we have an autograph?

                        GRAHAM
         That's not possible.

                        WOMAN
         A photo, then.

She hands Graham her mobile phone. She and her husband go round
and stand either side of Philip. Like he's a trophy. They both
smile. Graham takes the photo.

Philip is oblivious.

                    WOMAN (CONT'D)
             (retrieving her phone)
         Does he see Sir Richard much?

A beat.

                        GRAHAM
         He hasn't seen him for six years.

                        WOMAN
          I guess he lives a long way away.

                        GRAHAM
         He lives two blocks from Philip's home.
         Philip's <u>care</u> home. He's never been to
         visit him once - the man whose pictures
         won him all his Oscars.

A long silence.

Philip chews his bread. Puts a chunk in his jacket pocket.

Scene 18: "Fandom" – Exposition and Revelation

Another key scene, which I load with exposition, meaning, and subtext in the dialogue with the two elderly movie fans, serves to remind, reinforce, and provoke Graham's long-standing feelings about the past, setting up and inciting what is to come in future scenes. I intentionally make the fans intrusive; I've observed this many times in the past when I've been out with well-known actors, directors, and musicians, who are often viewed as public property even when they're being private. The two fans are evidently unaware of Philip's condition, and they also fail to pick up on the increasing tension in Graham. Their focus is on Philip; Graham is secondary, his interlocutor.

We learn:

- Philip worked in the movies for a long time.
- He made films people remember and loved – even the depressing ones.
- Philip can't talk; he hasn't spoken for 5 years.
- He can't sign an autograph – so Graham has to take a photo of them with Philip.
- The Oscar-winning director that Philip worked with has never been to visit him.
- Philip was responsible for the pictures – a Director of Photography.
- Philip is oblivious to all this. He puts some bread in his pocket (planting for later).

There is intended to be a sense of escalation in the dialogue as this information comes out, reflecting the increase in Graham's anger, frustration, animus. This is not the first time their lives have been invaded and he's been second-fiddle to his father.

In a rewrite, I might make the photograph a 'selfie', increasing the sense of invasion and intrusion by the fans into their privacy.

```
                                                    LATER

Still waiting for their soup. Graham is having a drink. It's
loosening his tongue. He scowls at Philip.

                          GRAHAM
                It's your fault, of course.

A sip...

                          GRAHAM (CONT'D)
            The great photographer! If only they knew...
```

Another sip...

                    GRAHAM (CONT'D)
          The terrible father. Holding me back.
          Ruining my life.

He hisses at Philip.

                    GRAHAM (CONT'D)
          It was only ever about you. And your
          so-called art...

Sound of CHINA. A Soup Tureen is placed on the table. Ladle.
Bowls. The Waitress beams at them.

                    WAITRESS
          Tomato.

                    GRAHAM
          His favourite.

The Waitress ladles soup into a bowl.

Scene 19: "Father / Son" – Hidden Conflict

Note that I do not use slug lines / scene headings for these scenes in the script itself. Being a first draft, I use LATER as a shorthand to move the story and plot along at this stage, to increase the sense of ellipsis as they eat lunch in the same location and Graham gets more and more frustrated and angry about "the great photographer" versus "the terrible father".

However, once the sequence / script is locked off and moves from development into pre-production, I then add a scene heading / slug line to every scene and also a scene number to ensure that each scene is specified, recognised by production software, and in the schedule, system, etc.

                                    LATER

Philip is eating his soup, SLURPING it.

This irritates Graham.

                    GRAHAM
          Do you have to make such a racket?

Philip carries on eating and SLURPING. Like a machine.

> GRAHAM (CONT'D)
> Was it all worth it? The missed birthdays
> and wedding anniversaries? All those
> little affairs on set? D.C.O.L. Doesn't
> Count On Location. Except that it did.
> Every time. You were the one who drove her
> to drink, not us.

Another SLURP.

> GRAHAM (CONT'D)
> Even when Mike took his own life, you
> didn't come home. Couldn't leave the
> shoot, you told her. Not even for your own
> son's funeral. Too many people depending
> on you. They needed the great photographer.
>> (raised voice)
> Well, so did we!

ACROSS THE ROOM

DINERS are looking at Graham.

The Manager clocks him. Begins to come over...

> GRAHAM (CONT'D)
> They say the booze killed her. But we know
> the truth, you and I, don't we. She died
> of a broken heart. And you broke it.

Philip. Silent. Impassive.

The Manager reaches the table. She assesses Graham.

> MANAGER
> Everything alright?

> GRAHAM
> Fine.
>> (beat)
> Lovely soup. **[Sequence Beat #4]**

SLURP.

Scene 20: "The Great Photographer" – Open Conflict

I start the scene with the running 'gag' of the soup, using this to push time
forward, link the story world and also reveal character, highlighting Philip's

lack of awareness and Graham's mounting anger as the past returns to the present. I tell my students that every character has a secret hidden away somewhere. Graham has a big one: he has a gun literally hidden in his pocket. As these scenes reveal, Philip has some big secrets, too, even if he is no longer aware of them. His illustrious career was evidently destructive for his family and catastrophic for his other son Mike and his wife, Mike and Graham's mother. Graham is still haunted, still damaged by this, and holds his father responsible for their tragedies. This reinforces Graham's wound and his resulting internal emotional Need – the need to forgive (if not to forget), come to terms with the past and move on, love himself in the right measure – which lies at the heart of everything in this sequence. Although Graham tries to keep a lid on his emotions, his feelings escalate into open conflict towards the silent Philip, only increasing his anger and drawing the attention of the other diners and the Manager to his heated words. The sense of frustration and hopelessness is reinforced by the scene ending back where it started: with the soup. (Sequence Beat #4 [#4])

LATER

The Waitress is clearing the table.

Philip is staring out through the large window.

The light outside has changed again.

Graham sips coffee. Feels his pocket. Where the gun is.

Scene 21: "A World Apart" – Aftermath / Decision

The aftermath of the lunch. Philip is preoccupied by the ever-changing light outside; Graham is preoccupied by the hidden gun. The audience should be thinking: What next? Is Graham going to use the gun? If so – When? Where? How?

EXT. PARK – DAY

Magic Hour. Graham and Philip walk round the park.

Graham is steering his father away from other people.

Scene 22: "In the Park" – New Location / Establishing

This scene used to have one line in it, establishing the new "park" location. I added the second action line after I introduced the handgun into the sequence, to maintain the tension and the feeling in us that there is still the possibility of harm coming to Philip.

```
EXT. POND, PARK - DAY

They sit on a bench on the far side of the large duckpond.
Graham looks around: no-one else is about.

THEY ARE ALONE

He takes the handgun out of his pocket. Weighs it in his hand.
Considers it. The sunlight catches it. Glinting.

                    GRAHAM (CONT'D)
            Magic hour... [Sequence Beat #5]

Philip nudges him. He hands Graham the chunk of bread he took
earlier. Graham rests the gun on his lap. Tears off a piece,
gives it to Philip. Philip throws it for the ducks.

                    GRAHAM (CONT'D)
            Light like this won you your Oscar.

Ducks QUACK and FIGHT for the bread.

                    GRAHAM (CONT'D)
            I hope it was all worth it.

Graham hands Philip more bread. Philip throws it, silent.

Graham stands. Eyes the gun. Hurls it out into the middle of
the pond. It hits the water. Sinks...
```

Scene 23: "Magic Hour" – Climax / Recognition

Following on from the previous scene, I also 'punched up' the first action lines in this scene, to sustain the tension and our fears for Philip and Graham. The question of the scene is: "Will Graham use the gun?" But at the moment when he reveals the gun, he is caught up by the same thing that preoccupies his father – light, reflection, colour temperature, "Magic Hour".[13] (Sequence Beat #5 [#5]). For a brief moment, the two men are linked.

---

13 "Magic Hour" refers to the period of the day before sunset and after sunrise when the sun is lower than 45 degrees in the sky and the light creates cooler tones. At "Golden Hour", the light is warmer: red, orange.

Philip remains oblivious to any threat. He reveals the bread he took earlier during lunch, paying this off. He asks (wordlessly) Graham to tear some off, which Graham does. As he watches Philip feed it to the ducks, Graham realises the futility of his plan (if indeed the gun ever was really a plan). He doesn't use the gun. Instead, he comes to a decision (remember, decisions reveal character). He throws it away, into the middle of the pond.

EXT. "THE CEDARS" CARE HOME — NIGHT

Graham escorts Philip up to the front door. Rings it.

They wait for Nurse Sharp. Graham stares at his father.

The door opens. Nurse Sharp smiles at them.

> NURSE SHARP
> Five o'clock on the dot. Had fun?

Graham evades her eye. She turns.

> NURSE SHARP (CONT'D)
> Same time next Sunday...

She goes back inside. Expecting Philip to follow her.

But he doesn't. He stares at Graham.

Graham looks at his father.

Philip is staring at him. Really staring at him. Looking at him. Into his eyes. His soul.

Graham stares back.

Out of nowhere:

> PHILIP
> I love you.

ON GRAHAM. Stunned.

Philip, locked in again.

He disappears inside the Care Home after Nurse Sharp.

```
The door closes. Leaving Graham alone in the dark.
```

```
Graham stares at the wooden door where Philip stood. He gently
touches it. [Sequence Beat #6]
```

Scene 24: "I. Love. You." – Anagnorisis / Resolution

Ultimately the whole sequence (or short film) comes down to this scene and its moment of anagnorisis or insightful recognition for the main character. What I like about it is that, like the anagnoretic moment in *Toy Story* that we discussed in an earlier chapter, there is a double anagnorisis. Graham's anagnorisis is set up by the moment of insightful recognition that Philip displays, when, suddenly, briefly, the curtain of aphasia lifts. Despite his condition, despite Graham's frustrations through the day, despite the gun, he tells his son that he loves him. And as quickly as the curtain lifted, it closes again. The effect on Graham is profound (Sequence Beat #6 [#6]).

I was told this story many years ago by a man to whom some of these events happened. His locked-in father who hadn't spoken a single word to anyone, including him, for five years suddenly turned to him, after a difficult day out together full of one-way recrimination, frustration, and anger, stared at him, into his soul, and told him that he loved him. It was the last thing he ever heard his father say.

Write about what you know. And if you don't know, write about what someone else knows.

```
EXT. CAR — NIGHT
```

```
Graham walks to the car. Unlocks it. Gets in.
```

Scene 25: "Back to the Car" – Aftermath

Graham returns to the car. We are wondering what the effect of the previous scene and his father's unexpected three words to him might be . . .

```
INT. CAR — NIGHT
```

```
Graham stares through the windscreen at the care home.
```

```
He starts to weep.
```

```
The radio PLAYS
```

FADE TO BLACK.

THE END

Scene 26: "Catharsis" – New Situation

This effect is revealed to us in the final scene. Graham starts to weep. Letting out the past. Beginning to come to terms with it. Taking the first tentative step to resolve his need, move on, heal himself, I like to think. I like to hope.

Sequence Questions

Let's revisit the sequence questions:

1. Whose sequence is it?
   Graham's
2. What is his specific external physical goal or objective (want) in it?
   Graham wants to take his father out of the care home for lunch (so that he can have it out with him once and for all – at gunpoint if need be).
3. What is the overall dramatic question linking the action in the sequence?
   Will Graham have fun out at lunch with Philip? (This is a loaded question. "Fun" is how the Nurse expresses her hopes for the outing. We already know Graham views it differently – so much so he's brought a gun.)
4. What are the Six Sequence Beats in the sequence?

   a. Putting the gun in his pocket.
   b. Getting Philip out of the home.
   c. The usual table at the hotel.
   Midpoint Reversal: the fans reminding Graham about the past
   d. You broke her heart (killed her) / "Lovely soup".
   e. Magic Hour.
   f. "I love you". Graham weeps.

5. How do these beats give the sequence its 3-part structure?

   a. Set up: going to the care home and getting Philip out.
   b. Conflict: lunch at the usual table.
   c. Consequences: Magic Hour.

6. Which of the three 'hierarchies of knowledge' are at play in the sequence?
   A<C: we know <u>less than</u> Graham because he knows all about his family's past
   A=C: we know <u>the same as</u> Graham because we know he has a gun
   A<C: we know <u>less than</u> Nurse Sharp about Philip's life now, in the home
   A>C: we know <u>more than</u> Nurse Sharp because we know Graham has a gun
   A<C: we know <u>less than</u> the hotel manager, who was there in the old days
   A<C: we know <u>less than</u> the elderly fans because they know Philip's movies
   A>C: we know <u>more than</u> the fans etc because we know Graham has a gun
   A>C: we know <u>more than</u> Philip about everything – or do we?

7. What event or new piece of information spins us into the next sequence?
   Despite – perhaps, because of – the tension, anger, past enveloping their lunch, Philip has a moment of insight when he tells Graham he loves him – releasing Graham and allowing him to begin to come to terms with the past and let out his emotion – allowing him to love himself in the right measure.
8. What is the overall heading or arena that unites the sequence?
   "Magic Hour"? "Sunday Lunch"?

Conclusion

A Sequence = Dramatic Action in 16 Questions

In practical terms, a movie script is really a series of consecutive interconnected dramatic questions scene by scene. The 16 questions for the "Magic Hour" sequence reveal this and the movement and flow of the drama:

- Will Graham turn off the alarm? YES
- Will Graham get up and get ready to go out? YES
- Will Graham take the gun with him? YES/NO
- Will Graham get Nurse Sharp to let him into the care home? YES
- Will Graham get Nurse Sharp to agree to him seeing his father? YES
- Will Graham (and Philip) have fun? NO (the sequence question)
- Will Graham get Philip there (to the hotel) in time for the soup? YES
- Will Philip pull the trigger? NO
- Will the Manager give them Philip's usual table? YES
- Will the Woman fan (ansd her husband) get to talk to their hero? NO
- Will Graham provoke Philip into a response? NO
- Will Graham get Philip to say if it was all worth it? NO
- Will Graham get Philip to a quiet place in the park? YES
- Will Graham use the gun? NO
- Will Graham get Philip back into the care home without issue? YES/NO
- Will Graham let Philip's words to him sink in? YES

As this book suggests, our work on scenes, sequences, and scripts is never really completed. Working on this sequence for it and reviewing it to ascertain the questions, I made myself the following notes as we went along about things that will need addressing in the next draft.

- Continue to research aphasia.
- Revisit all the scene-specific dramatic questions and make sure they are as clear, active, accurate as they should be.
- Does the dramatic question reflect whose scene it actually is?

- How many scenes is Graham having to react in – (i.e., it's another character's scene)? We often learn more about a character from how they react to something.
- Where necessary, either revise the question to better reflect the action intended in the scene or rewrite the scene to better reflect the desired question.
- Check each scene and its specific function as a scene – expositional, open conflict, hidden conflict, seduction, pivotal, etc.– in its own right and as part of the sequence.

The art of writing is, as ever . . . rewriting.

Sequence of Scenes – Scene-Writing Exercise

"Sequence" Exercise

As we have discussed in this chapter, a sequence provides us with the means of revealing the story to the reader scene by scene.

Choose a sequence or a short film you are working on. Go through it scene by scene and analyse it using the same questions I asked myself about the scenes in "Magic Hour". Can you answer these questions? If not, think about why not.

1. *Whose sequence is it?*
2. *What is their specific external physical goal or objective (Want) in it?*
3. *What is the overall dramatic question linking the action in the sequence?*
4. *What are the six sequence-specific beats in the sequence?*
5. *How do these beats give the sequence its 3-part structure: a) set up, b) conflict, c) consequences?*
6. *Which of the three hierarchies of knowledge are at play in the sequence?*
7. *What event or new piece of information spins us into the next sequence?*
8. *What is the overall heading or arena that unites the sequence?*

Think about:

- the overall heading or arena that links the scenes in this sequence
- the shape, pattern, type or 'genre' of it
- the specific question for each scene or 'mini-sequence' of scenes in your sequence
- how these questions reflect the story and its action, movement, flow, drama, that you intend to reveal to us

10

RECAP AND CONCLUSION

Why Isn't This Scene Working? How Can I Make It Work Better?

Introduction

Writing the first draft of a film or TV script of any length requires commitment. Whether you're writing a short film script as part of your course or to make over a weekend with your friends, whether you're working on the pilot episode of your new TV drama or sit-com idea, or you're writing a new 'spec' movie screenplay that could be the one, it takes time. A day, days, weeks, months, years even.

A couple of my 'spec' film scripts took me more than ten years to write from initial idea to first draft script. Not because I'm a particularly slow writer. I write fast when I know what my story is about and what I'm doing. The trouble is, it can take years to know what my story is about. Coming up with an idea is one thing. Believing in it enough to dedicate the hundreds of hours required to turn it into a viable TV script or feature film screenplay is quite another.

When you meet people outside the film and TV industry and they find out you're a screenwriter, the first thing they always ask is: "What have you written?" Once that is out of the way, they ask: "Where do your ideas come from?" I also have an answer for that. Often, they will then say that they've always wanted to write a script . . . if they had the time. They've got a great idea. Would I like to write it for them? For free. They'll even share the credit. When I politely decline, they move away to talk about cars or pensions to someone more interesting. Like a dentist. Or a management consultant.

Nothing beats the thrill of typing "The End" on a new first draft. Finishing a new script of any length is always an achievement. As I read through its scenes, the sense of accomplishment and excitement is unrivalled in my

DOI: 10.4324/9781003293927-11

experience – a brief period of joy and hope. One of my screenwriting teachers used to say that the first draft of anything we ever write is always our favourite because we can imagine it in our heads as the best version of our original idea.

What a shame for us, then, that writing for the screen is a collaborative process! Its success or failure as an enterprise ultimately depends on the involvement, to varying degrees, of dozens – hundreds – thousands in the case of a $100M+ special effects–driven franchise film or long-running TV series – of other people to transport our original idea from script to screen.

Once other people read your script, give you feedback on it, or become professionally involved, then the process of sharing your idea begins. To paraphrase Ernest Hemingway,[1] as I remind my students in pretty much every class or session we undertake together: "The art of writing is . . . rewriting."

So how do we approach that rewriting when it comes to our script and its scenes?

The Art of Writing Is . . . Rewriting

You've written the first draft, and now someone is telling you to start rewriting it: "The script is good, but . . .", "It might make more sense if . . .", "What if she did this . . . ?", "I don't understand why this happens . . .", "Your script would be much better if . . ."

Over the years, I've heard comments like these and many more besides. No matter how experienced or inexperienced a writer you are, they can feel like a hammer blow. Especially when they are delivered tactlessly or don't make sense. It's as if the commentator hasn't actually read the script (sometimes, they haven't!). A development exec I once met took great delight boasting about the 3-hour script sessions he used to do with screenwriters without having actually read their scripts.

Of course, it also depends who the reader is. If it's your partner, your mother, or your best friend, that's one thing. If it's your teacher or the other students working on your short film with you, that's another thing. If it's your agent, an actor, or the producer who is interested in optioning your script by paying you money to own the project for a defined period of time to try and get it made, that's another thing again.

Navigating your way through all this is tricky.

Rewriting someone else's project is just as complicated and difficult as rewriting your own. Some years ago, I was brought on board a movie to do a new draft of the script. The producers and director had read *Boney and Betsy* and

---

1 "The only kind of writing is rewriting." *A Moveable Feast* by Ernest Hemingway (1899–1961). Published posthumously in 1964.

liked my work. They thought I'd be the ideal writer for their period film which was stuck in development. I was commissioned to do a new draft and spent several enjoyable weeks immersing myself in the project. Based on a true story, I read a biography about the subject, met his elderly sister, pored over his letters and diaries. I spent productive days in London with the director, over from LA, working on our ideas for the new version. I then wrote the new draft, typed "The End", and sent it off, full of joy and hope. I got an overwhelmingly positive response from the producers and director to it. It was a breakthrough draft, the project had taken a big step forward, we were going out to cast with it . . . A week later, my agent got a one-line fax from LA telling me I'd been fired.

Julian Fellowes' advice to me that you're only really a screenwriter once you've been fired by Hollywood didn't cheer me up much.

Questions to Answer

Certain questions get asked regularly in development meetings and writing classes when we are discussing script drafts of any type of length.

The very day I wrote this section, I did a class with some of my undergraduate filmmaking students at York talking through their 5-minute films scene by scene and the following questions kept coming up:

- Where is this scene specifically located?
- What's the slug line?
- Who is in the scene?
- Whose scene is it?
- What is the specific dramatic question of the scene?
- What is the character trying to do (want/goal) in the scene?
- How do we know . . . what the character is thinking, feeling, imagining, etc.?
- Would this scene work better as two shorter scenes, with a different dramatic question for each scene?
- How are you using ellipsis to shorten scenes and push the plot forward?
- Does your idea feature the most important five minutes in the life of your character? If not, why not?

Recurring questions like these are commonplace in scene and script development. Likewise, issues. As I was planning this book, I began to make a note of the most common writing and rewriting issues that kept coming up when I was reading, analysing, marking, or advising on feature film screenplays, TV drama scripts, sit-com pilots, 30-minute scripts for assessment, and short films for production. We have considered many of these in earlier chapters, but I include them here by way of a recap and checklist for when you're writing your own scenes or working with a writer or a student on theirs.

Writing and Rewriting Checklists

1. **Layout, formatting, and presentation of the scene and script**

   a. You only get one chance to make a first impression with your script and its scenes.

   b. Avoid presentation errors such as typos, spelling mistakes, omitted words, incorrect grammar, poor syntax, etc.

   c. Avoid apostrophe misuse, (e.g., their / there / they're; you're / your; its / it's; lets / let's)

   d. Don't just rely on your spell-checker. Proofread your scenes. If you have issues in this area, please ask someone to help you do it.

   e. Use CAPITALS for the character's name (or job/function if there is no name) when we meet them in the action line in a scene for the first time in the script.

   f. Provide that new character's age and a brief 3–4 word unique, memorable, eye-catching descriptor of them in brackets, to locate new characters in the mind of the reader, for example, SIMON (60s, seen better days).

   g. Don't use CAPITALS in dialogue for emphasis (e.g., if someone is shouting) or when mentioning a character by name for the first time.

   h. Avoid one scene running into another scene – for example, a change in location, time, action – without a scene heading / slug line to signify this change.

   i. Avoid imposing scene numbers too early during development. Give yourself and your draft script the flexibility to be able to respond to feedback, ideas, notes – to be open to cutting scenes and adding scenes as may be required in the new draft to improve it.

   j. Use CAPITALS for key sounds and sound effects in the scene.

   k. Don't use parentheses in dialogue to replace an action line. Write action in an action line.

   l. Don't use parentheses to tell us the feeling state of the character speaking. The action and dialogue should reveal this to us.

   m. Don't use parentheses to tell us how the dialogue should be delivered or interpreted. We should be able to understand this from the character's actions and what they are saying. (Also, this kind of imposed direction irritates actors).

   n. <u>Avoid parentheses whenever possible!</u>

2. **Style in every scene**

   a. How many different images do you see in your head when you write or read an action line or paragraph?

b. What are the 'Subject' – 'Verb' – 'Object' in these action lines?

- Subject = who or what are we looking at?
- Verb = how does who/what we are looking at develop? static, moving, etc.?
- Object = how are we looking at it? what is the context / frame in which we're looking at it: close, wide, from above, below, etc.?

c. Scene-writing avoids 'narrative' storytelling, or writing that

- is like a novel or a short story – passive, past tense, internal, descriptive
- contains information we don't see or hear on screen
- makes us ask "How do we know?" – what the character is thinking, feeling, remembering?
- infers the interior hidden world or psyche of the character
- is over-described, with adjectives, adverbs, repetitions
- tells us the story

d. Scene-writing is all about 'dramatic' storytelling, or writing that

- is like a movie, TV drama, or short – active, present tense, external, concise
- contains information we see or hear on screen
- ensures we know because we see or hear what the character is doing, saying
- reveals the exterior active world or psyche of the character
- focuses on what we're looking at – Subject, Verb, Object
- shows us the story

e. Avoid overlong action lines and over-described details in those lines.

f. Avoid so-called 'laundry lists' in action lines describing details in the scene that are generally irrelevant to the characters, story, plot, and action.

g. Action paragraphs in scripts should be 1–5 lines MAX. I prefer 1–3 lines MAX. More space on the page makes scenes and scripts easier and faster to read for everyone on set.

h. Focus the reader's attention on a key moment, element, character, prop, or revelation to us in the action in the scene. Privilege that key information in CAPITALS with its own line of action, for example:

```
THROUGH THE WINDOW

OUTSIDE

INSIDE THE CAR

THE GUN

A RATTLESNAKE
```

    i. Words like 'slightly', 'a bit', 'quite', 'a little', 'rather', 'somewhat', etc. weaken your writing and qualify its potential impact.

    j. An action or activity like "She boils a kettle" is described in just four words but actually takes a minute or two in real time to happen. Use ellipsis to shorten actions and activities like these.

    k. Avoid repeating words from the slug line – for example, the location (INT. APARTMENT – DAY) – in the first line of action: Kobe enters the apartment.

3. Meeting your characters

    a. What do we learn about your main character in the opening scenes?

    b. What do we find out about their world, their situation, their *status quo*, their big problem? How do we find this out?

    c. Why does their story start today, with this scene?

- Who do we meet?
- Where do we meet them?
- When do we meet them?
- How do we meet them?
- Why do we meet them?
- What is their big problem?
- What is their big secret?
- When is their story going to start?
- How is it going to start?

    d. What ten words can we identify in the early scenes to describe the main character?

    e. What is their 'most' – the thing they are the 'most' in their world? In this book, we've met Ellie (the most determined to do her dive in her world), Graham (the most determined to have it out with his father Philip once and for all in his world), and Diana (the most cannibalistic in her world).

    f. What words describe the other characters? Do they have a 'most'?

    g. What is the status of each character in the scene?

    h. What is the specific function of each character in it?

    i. Is there a seduction going on in the scene? What is the seduction? Who is doing the seducing?

    j. Is a character taking action that is relevant to the plot or engaged in an activity (e.g., doing a crossword) that may be characterful but is additional to the plot? How long does this activity take in real time? How long does it take in film time?

4. The character's 'Want' – the context of the scene

Keep asking yourself (or your writers) 'Want' questions about each scene:

    a. What's the scene about?

    b. What is the specific dramatic action of this scene?

   c. What happens in it?

   d. What's the scene's context: who, what, where, when, why, and how?

   e. What's the primary purpose of the scene: the one thing it has to achieve for you, your character(s), the story, and the script?

   f. Whose scene is it?

   g. What is that character's external physical Want or goal in the scene?

   h. What strategies is your character using to get what they want?

   i. What is the specific dramatic question of the scene: "Will . . . ?"

   j. Who or what is the antagonist in the scene?

   k. What's the conflict? Stakes? Jeopardy? Danger? Problem?

   l. In what way is the action in the scene 'life and death' for the character(s) even in a domestic comedy? If it's not, why not?

   m. Are Aristotle's Three Unities – Time, Place, Action – evident in some way? If not, why not?

   n. What are the key parts of the scene: 1) set up? 2) conflict? 3) consequences / resolution? Not all scenes have a resolution. For example, in a series of chase or escape scenes, there may be a twist into the next scene instead.

   o. What are the six beats in the scene?

5. The character's 'Need' – the subtext of the scene

Keep asking yourself (or your writers) 'Need' questions about each scene:

   a. What's the scene _really_ about?

   b. Is the internal emotional need of the protagonist of the scene present in some way?

   c. What is the protagonist of the scene doing?

   d. What is the protagonist of the scene _really_ doing? Or avoiding doing?

   e. What is the protagonist of the scene saying?

   f. What is the protagonist of the scene _really_ saying? Or avoiding saying?

   g. How is the theme of the story present in every scene in some way?

   h. How do the need, theme, action, dialogue combine or juxtapose with one another to create the subtext of the scene?

6. How do we know?

We can only know what we see or hear in the action or dialogue in the scene on screen in real time.

   a. How do we know . . . what a character wants in the scene?

   b. How do we know . . . what a character needs in the scene?

   c. How do we know . . . the age of the character?

   d. How do we know . . . what the character is thinking, thinking about, feeling, remembering, wondering, imagining, hoping for, fearing, and so on?

   e. How do we know . . . if a character is thinking back two years ago about their ex-lover, if they got up two hours earlier to prepare breakfast, if they are thinking about the meeting they will be having that afternoon, etc.?

    f. How do we know . . . the intended period, date, time, location, place, genre, story world, tone of the scenes?

    g. How do we know . . . where the action is?

    h. How do we know . . . when the action is?

    i. How do we know . . . it's 1990? 1996? 1890? 1490? 2590?

    j. How do we know . . . why it is set then? Why does it <u>have to be</u> set then?

    k. How do we know . . . what are we looking at on the screen when there are pages of dialogue?

7. Show vs tell: Action vs dialogue in the scene

    a. Don't show us what you are also telling us.

    b. Don't tell us what you are also showing us.

    c. Don't tell us in the dialogue what we should be seeing in the action.

    d. Don't tell us in the action what we should be hearing in the dialogue.

    e. Don't show / tell us what you have already shown / told us!

    f. If the scene is all dialogue – what are we looking at during it?

    g. If the scene is all action – what are we listening to during it?

    h. Don't make your dialogue too 'on the nose' and obvious. Find the balance between making sure we know stuff (exposition, requisite information, context) versus the audience finding out stuff (mystery, revelation, subtext).

    i. Dialogue mentioned in the action should be written as dialogue. Don't just write, "Amina babbles on about her life and how she never had a job she liked until now" or "Mo sings a funny song that makes them all laugh".

    j. Great dialogue is character-driven, characterful, and reveals character.

    k. Beware the fear of being understood – don't be too elliptical, evasive, vague, clever, clever-clever.

    l. Avoid the "Emperor's New Clothes"[2] syndrome – your scene's not really about anything, it's a triumph of style over substance.

    m. Why do we care? Engage? Sympathise? Empathise? Root for the character(s)?

8. Swearing in scenes

    a. Use swearing and profane language in dialogue carefully. Where possible, if possible, avoid it.

    b. The use of a well-placed, well-directed swear word can focus attention, make a point, reveal character, shock or amuse the reader.

---

2 *The Emperor's New Clothes* (pub. 1837) by Hans Christian Andersen. Folktale about an emperor obsessed with lavish new clothes who is duped by two conmen into wearing a suit that is invisible to stupid people. Parading through the city, it takes a child to shout out what everyone else knows: that he is wearing nothing at all.

c. However, I recently read a script with 17 C-words and 175 variants of the F-word in it. This extreme usage didn't deepen or elevate the character (a criminal); in fact, it lessened his status and diminished him on the page and in his scenes.

d. Strong dangerous characters like Mr. Blonde (*Reservoir Dogs*, 1992) and Alice Morgan (*Luther*, 2010–19) don't need to swear all the time. Indeed, the quieter and more polite a dangerous character is, the greater the threat and menace they exude.

9. **Effective scenes . . .**

a. Are a fusion of action and dialogue to create well-drawn characters, plot, and story world.

b. Feature key moments in real time in the lives of your characters.

c. Start at the latest possible moment *in media res*.

d. End at the earliest possible moment.

e. Employ ellipsis to push forward characters, story, action, plot, drama.

f. Use industry-standard formatting, layout, and presentation for their specific type –feature film, TV drama, TV soap, sit-com, or short film. Research the correct presentation approach and use the correct script template for your intended type of script.

g. Observe and adhere to industrial screenwriting conventions throughout.

h. Reveal exposition through conflict, or comedy, or both.

i. Are the windows for us to look in on your story world and its characters.

j. Are integral to your world-building because they answer who, where, when, how, what, and why.

k. Use a variety of common types and patterns – 'seduction', 'open conflict', 'hidden conflict', 'introduction of main character', 'introduction of antagonist', 'pivotal moment', 'escape' and so on – to show and tell your story in the best way.

l. Can help you make a first impression that may just change your life.

10. **Your first draft scene by scene**

a. Some poetry is okay in a 'spec' script – up to a point.

b. One page of properly formatted and laid out script = One minute of screen time.

c. Be consistent in formatting, presentation, layout – use screenwriting software.

d. We only know what we can see or hear on the screen.

e. Understand the rules and the logic you're creating for your story world. Stick to these scene by scene.

f. Do the locations, set up, story world you are creating match your characters? Or are you using these to misdirect us for a reason?

g. What is the light source in the scene? How are we going to see the action? Where is the light in the scene coming from? During the day? At night? Inside a space with no windows? Outside? Outside, underwater? In space?

h. What is the sound source in the scene? Is it seen? Unseen? Within the location? Beyond the location?

i. How are props being used? Does their use develop or change in some way? For example, does a knife start out in a scene as a kitchen instrument used to peel and slice an orange and end it as a deadly weapon?

j. Dialogue: identify its context (what it's about) versus its subtext (what it's really about)

k. Who or what is the source of the conflict in the scene?

l. What strategies do your characters use to obtain their goals? Are these subtle, direct, indirect, obvious, clumsy, menacing, violent, seductive, etc.?

m. Think about the precise meaning of words, for example, 'cuffs'. Are these handcuffs? Or cuff links? Or blows to the head?

n. Make your script the best read you can. Readers will be more responsive if they enjoy reading your work.

Tricky Questions

It takes courage to reveal your writing – which may contain your innermost secrets and deepest fears or your greatest hopes and wildest dreams – to other people. Inevitably, this can make writers feel insecure and question their work.

- Why are my scenes so boring?
- How do I make a scene less boring?
- Why is my dialogue too 'on the nose'?
- Why do all my characters sound the same?
- How do I cut down the dialogue?
- How do I make dialogue funnier, sharper, more characterful?
- How can I show what my characters are thinking?
- What should there be more of in a scene: action or dialogue?

Like all writers, I've pondered these questions, too. And I know that for as long as I continue to write, they will never be far away. Because they reflect the eternal fear of all writers that our work might be viewed as repetitive, dull, flat, ordinary, obvious, undramatic, predictable, or boring.

Improving our scene-writing by being able to review and rewrite our scenes is one tangible and proactive way of reducing these fears. Fundamental to this is improving the function, motivation, action, behaviour, and essence of our characters.

My response to these questions is always the same. Keep working on your characters. Locate and situate these clarified, enhanced, improved characters in your story and script scene by scene. The chances are, the rest will be clarified, enhanced, and improved, too.

Great Screen Characters

Great screen characters have many key traits. They

- are well-developed well-drawn individuals . . .
- and / or believable, recognisable archetypes . . .
- with depth, motivations and psychological complexity . . .
- who are flawed and wounded in some way . . .
- have big problems . . .
- face life-and-death conflicts and have to make difficult decisions . . .
- thereby going on big journeys and story arcs . . .
- generating interest, empathy, and emotion in the audience . . .
- creating powerful, dramatic, memorable, and engaging stories.

Creating truthful, memorable, complex, credible screen characters takes time and work. It means digging into their past – and into their present – and into their future. We have to identify and understand, scene by scene, the good points and the bad points of each of them, their strengths and weaknesses. We need to understand what makes them unique. What makes them vulnerable, interesting, and real. What their Achilles heel is. What their big secret is.

All Characters Have Secrets

Think of the movies, TV shows, and short films you like and respond to. Most of the protagonists in them have secrets – big secrets that they don't want other people to know. The bigger the secret, the better.

Ask yourself: in your script and its scenes

- What is your main character's big secret?
- When does this secret come out? In which scene?
- How does it come out?
- Why does it come out?
- What happens when it comes out?
- What is the effect of this on this character, other characters, story, and plot?
- How does it change the story afterward?

Interview Your Characters

One way of building or developing a character is to interview them. Imagine they are sitting opposite you. Maybe you're in a café, on a bus, at home, in a bar, in a prison. After all, where you are may well influence how you go about the interview or the answers you get. Is it a snatched conversation, in a rush, somewhere public? Or a leisurely one over a drink or a coffee somewhere? Do you have to be furtive, quiet? Or can you be open, carefree?

Ask them lots of questions. Try and find out their specific emotional, mental, physical, and social traits:

- What events in the past (school, home, work) have shaped them into the person they are today?
- What successes, failures, highs, lows, triumphs, traumas have moulded them into that person?
- How do they see themselves today?
- How do they want to be seen by other people?
- How do they think they relate to other people?
- How do other people actually see them and relate to them? (You have to ask another character this question).
- What underlying reasons are motivating them to make critical, specific decisions or behave in the way they do?
- What is your character's specific a) age, b) appearance, c) attitude, d) conduct, e) life dream, f) hope, g) fear, h) ambition, i) secret, j) flaw.

Here's an example that I came up with on 'spec' for a character: a) 50s, b) lots of 'bling', c) confrontational, d) bull in a China shop, e) to discover the greatest kid footballer of all-time, f) hopes this player is out there somewhere, g) fears time is running out to find them, h) pay off all their debts, i) they no longer love football, j) they always run into trouble, not away from it.

Here are some more ways to get to know your characters better:

- Ask them to tell you what they'd do in a certain situation.
- Create a biography for them.
- Put yourself in their shoes.
- If they were a colour, what colour would they be? Red? Blue? Pink? Beige?
- If they were a musical instrument, what instrument would they be?
- Is this musical instrument reflected in the way they behave, act, speak?
- What 5–10 words describe them when we first see them?
- What 5–10 words describe them at the end of their journey?
- Which words have changed? Why have they changed? How? When?

How Does Their Dialogue Reflect and Reveal Their Character?

- Transactional? *(strategic, it moves the story and plot forwards)*
- Revealing *(about them or other characters)*
- Poetic? *(symbolic, figurative, rhythmic, aspirational)*
- Metaphoric? *(meaning something else altogether, allegorical, emblematic)*
- Contextual? *(what the scene is about, explicit, part of the mise-en-scène)*
- Subtextual? *(what the scene is really about, implicit)*
- Silent? *(we can understand what is being said from the action alone that we're watching, 'pars pro toto' = a part of something that can be taken for the whole)*
- Diversionary? *(we are being deliberately misdirected or drawn away from truth about something)*
- Camouflage? *(disguising or hiding something in amongst something else)*
- Verbal action? *(dialogue we can see)*

Conclusion

While I was thinking about this chapter and working out what to put in it and how to conclude it, I became increasingly aware of the ongoing debate in the film and TV industry and beyond about artificial intelligence (AI) and the effect this is going to have on screenwriting and the screenwriter. Doomsday scenarios suggest that in the near-future, AI is going to create everything, decide everything, write everything. Writers will become redundant. Everyone will become redundant.

So I decided to put this to the test. I signed up for ChatGPT and asked the AI to write a couple of scenes for us – the types of scenes we have been discussing in this book. Here is that conversation and the outputs from it:

"Please can you write me a seduction scene for a film"

Within seconds, the AI provided this:

INT. LUXURIOUS PENTHOUSE – NIGHT[3]
The room is bathed in the warm glow of candlelight. Soft music plays in the background, adding to the romantic ambiance. ALEX, a charming and confident individual, stands near the window, gazing out at the city skyline. Across the room, EMMA, equally alluring, leans against the grand piano, watching him with a playful smile.

---

3 ChatGPT 3.5. Available at: chat.openai.com (Accessed: 28 February 2024).

EMMA:
You know, Alex, I've always found the city lights mesmerizing at night.

Alex turns to face her, his eyes locking onto hers with intensity.

ALEX:
Not as mesmerizing as you.

Emma's smile widens, and she takes a step closer to him, closing the distance between them . . .

I then typed in another request: "write me an open conflict scene."

Again, within seconds, the AI provided this:

INT. ABANDONED WAREHOUSE – NIGHT
The warehouse is dimly lit, with shafts of moonlight piercing through the broken windows, casting eerie shadows across the dusty floor. JAMES, a man consumed by rage, stands alone in the center of the warehouse, surrounded by crates and debris. His eyes burn with intensity as he clutches a loaded pistol in his hand.

JAMES:
(voice filled with venom)
You thought you could destroy everything I cared about. But tonight, the tables have turned.

James steps forward, his footsteps echoing in the silence of the warehouse...

As you read these two scenes, hopefully the scene-writing knowledge, skills, and tools you've acquired from reading this book were kicking in, helping you to analyse the scenes provided.

For a start, there are significant formatting, layout, and style errors in every line of both. The scenes weren't even presented in Courier 12, the most basic of all the screenwriting and scene-writing fundamentals. They are many other core scene-writing issues, too. They both rely on 'narrative' storytelling: they are over-described and tell us things we aren't seeing or hearing on screen. For example, how do we know Alex is "a charming and confident individual", Emma is "equally alluring", and that James is "consumed by rage", what his age is, his "voice is filled with venom"?

There is also a lack of other scene-writing fundamentals such as effective contemporary nuanced characters, diversity, dialogue we can see, creativity, imagination, and 'voice' in either excerpt. The AI scenes are obvious, stereotypical, lacking depth and development, full of clichés. They tell us the action rather than show it to us. Bottom line – they are boring.

Undoubtedly, AI is going to play an increasingly influential part on every aspect of our lives moving forward, including screenwriting. As this book recognises, screenwriters and our craft came into being in the first place as a result of technological development. We are a product of this, we are used to it, we understand it and its possibilities, and we have always been able to accept it, work with it, and use it to our advantage to write powerful relevant screen stories set in real and imagined worlds.

The temptation for students in particular to use AI to help them come up with ideas, write outlines or treatments, and write scenes is understandable. So I encourage them to look at the process of writing in this way:

- In 20–30 minutes, using writing exercises like the ones in this book, they can write their own original scene.
- In 10–15 minutes in class, the student can read aloud that original scene, listen to how their teacher and other students interpret and understand it, answer questions about it, explain their intentions in the scene, and get feedback on it.
- A 10–15-minute rewrite afterwards and the scene is transformed, without any AI to be seen. Or, perhaps, more accurately, unseen.

For now, and for the foreseeable future, we are better advised to spend our time thinking up, writing, and rewriting our own original scenes than spend the same amount of time relying on someone – somebody – something – else to do this for us.

As Chinese philosopher Xun Kuang advised 2,300 years ago: *"Tell me, and I will forget. Teach me, and I might remember. Involve me, and I will understand."*[4]

Action, dialogue, formatting, style, setting, style, and theme are only activated, brought to life, and given relevance and meaning by the characters at the heart of these elements.

Without involving, active, engaging, lovable, terrifying, heroic, antiheroic, likable, unlikable, truthful, deceitful, witty, hard-boiled characters in our scenes, none of those other elements ultimately matter. Who cares about layout, or formatting, or style, or world-building, or genre and tone if we don't care about the characters within. So it seems appropriate to end it where we started. With character.

---

4 Wrongly attributed to Benjamin Franklin, this saying comes from *The Xunzi*, a collection of the works of Chinese Confucian philosopher Xun Kuang (312–230 BCE). It was first translated by H.H. Dubs in 1928, 138 years after Franklin died. https://www.goodreads.com/quotes/7565817-tell-me-and-i-forget-teach-me-and-i-may

Understand our characters better, develop better characters, unleash them and set them free in our stories and story worlds, and we will inevitably write better scenes and better scripts.

THE END

APPENDIX A

MAGIC HOUR

by

Simon van der Borgh

FADE IN:

EXT. LANDSCAPE - DAY

Winter light.

Then

A SOUND: an ALARM

INT. BEDROOM - DAY

The same ALARM.

In the gloom: GRAHAM (50-something, large, seen better days) lies in bed. Wide awake. Staring up at the ceiling. On the bedside table, the ALARM continues to ring...

INT. BATHROOM - DAY

Graham, eyeing himself in the mirror. Feels his stubble.

CUT TO:

Graham, wet-shaving.

INT. BEDROOM - DAY

Graham irons a shirt.

Ties a tie.

Puts on a jacket.

INT. HALLWAY - DAY

Graham walks towards the front door. Sees himself in the mirror. In his Sunday Best. A dog's dinner...

He pulls off the tie. And the jacket. Angry. Stares into the mirror. Breathing heavily. Heads back upstairs.

INT. BEDROOM - DAY

Graham is sitting on the bed. Staring at the bedside table.

He slides open the drawer. Gazes at something inside:

A SMALL HANDGUN

He reaches in. Picks it up. Puts it into his pocket.

I/E. CAR - DAY

MUSIC PLAYS. Graham drives along. He is dressed once more in the tie and jacket. Resigned to the day ahead.

I/E. CAR - DAY

Graham pulls up in a tree-lined suburban street. Large houses. Nice area. Well-to-do.

He looks out through the windscreen:

A LARGE RESIDENTIAL HOME

He stares at it.

He opens the glove compartment. Takes the handgun from his pocket, places it inside the recess. Closes it again.

Checks his watch. Then gets out of the car. Slowly.

EXT. AVENUE - DAY

Graham turns into the driveway towards the large dwelling.
Past a sign:

"THE CEDARS — A CARE HOME of QUALITY"

EXT. FRONT DOOR, "THE CEDARS" CARE HOME - DAY

Graham stops by the door. RINGS the buzzer. Waits.

THROUGH THE LARGE BAY WINDOW

He becomes aware of someone staring through the glass. At him.
But not seeing him.

This is PHILIP (late 70s, dapper, a ladies' man, well groomed).

Graham half waves at him. No response from Philip.

Graham presses the BUZZER again. The front door opens, revealing NURSE SHARP (30s, takes no prisoners).

> NURSE SHARP
> I'm coming...

She realises who it is.

> NURSE SHARP (CONT'D)
> Oh. Graham.

> GRAHAM
> Hello, Nurse Sharp.

She stands there. An immovable object.

> GRAHAM (CONT'D)
> Can we talk?

She stares at him. Allows him to cross the threshold.

INT. NURSES' STATION - DAY

At the sink a young NURSE (20) scrubs a used commode. One of
many piled up...

Nurse Sharp enters, followed by Graham.

> NURSE SHARP
> All the rooms are busy. So we'll have to chat in here.

Graham nods. She eyes him. Pointed.

> NURSE SHARP (CONT'D)
> Long time, no see.

> GRAHAM
> I've been busy. Away. Working.

> NURSE SHARP
> We like to have notice. About visits.

> GRAHAM
> Of course. How is he?

> NURSE SHARP
> Philip's had a happy week.

> GRAHAM
> Great. Can I see him? Philip.

> NURSE SHARP
> Apart from Thursday.

> GRAHAM
> Oh.

He knows what that means.

> NURSE SHARP
> One of his films was on the telly. It confused him. Upset him. That's the trouble with Aphasia. He can't express himself. Even if he knew what he wanted to express.

> GRAHAM
> I know the feeling.

Dark humour. She ignores this.

> NURSE SHARP
> Why are you really here, Graham?

                    GRAHAM
            It was his birthday.

                    NURSE SHARP
            We know. We had a cake. Yesterday.

                    GRAHAM
            I've booked a table. For lunch.

At the sink, the young Nurse scrubs another commode...

                    NURSE SHARP
            He doesn't eat much lunch.

                    GRAHAM
            At his favourite place. We used to go
            every Sunday. In the good old days.

She is still unconvinced. He gazes at her.

                    GRAHAM (CONT'D)
            His doctor said it might do him good
            to visit some familiar places.

She is listening...

                    GRAHAM (CONT'D
            Please, Jenny.

Behind them, the commode cleaning continues. Noisy.

                    GRAHAM (CONT'D)
            He's my dad. I miss him.

                    NURSE SHARP
            What time would you get him back?

Graham smiles.

EXT. FRONT DOOR, RESIDENTIAL HOME - DAY

Graham waits.

Nurse Sharp appears with Philip.

                    NURSE SHARP
            Here he is...

She hands Philip over to Graham. She eyes the two well-dressed stiff-upper-lip men.

> NURSE SHARP (CONT'D)
> Don't get up to any mischief, you two!
> See you at five. Have fun!

The front door closes.

Graham eyes Philip.He moves away from the door. Philip follows.

EXT. DRIVEWAY, THE CEDARS - DAY

Halfway down, Graham realises Philip isn't with him.

Philip is looking at the light. Deep. Watching it play on his hand. Inspecting it. The colour temperature. Transfixed.

> GRAHAM
> (curt)
> C'mon, dad. Or we'll miss the soup.

Graham takes his arm. Escorts him down the drive. Philip acquiesces. Automatic. Locked in his own world.

EXT. AVENUE - DAY

Graham unlocks the car. Opens the passenger door. Waits.

Philip approaches. Graham drums his fingers on the roof.

Philip gets in. Graham puts on Philip's seatbelt. Closes the door.

I/E. CAR - DAY

Driving. Silence. Graham eyes Philip. Philip is staring out the window at the light, shadow, shapes. Entranced.

Graham puts on the radio. MUSIC plays. Focuses on the road.

Philip fiddles with parts of the dashboard. Pushes a button. The glove compartment pops open.

INSIDE

The handgun. Philip reaches for it. Takes it. Eyes the light catching the metal. Then points it at Graham.

Graham realises.

                    GRAHAM
          What the hell... Give me that.

He snatches the gun. Stuffs it in his pocket. SLAMS the
glove compartment shut. Philip is already staring back out the
window.

EXT. HOTEL - DAY

The car pulls up outside the hotel. The sort that does a traditional Sunday lunch.

INT. DINING ROOM, HOTEL - DAY

Graham and Philip enter the sparsely filled room. THE MANAGER
(60s) greets them.

                    MANAGER
          Hello, Philip. It's been ages.
               (to Graham)
          Usual table?

Graham nods. She shows them to the table by the window.

Graham and Philip sit. The Manager pushes in Philip's seat.
Unfurls a napkin for him. She doesn't hand them menus.

                    MANAGER (CONT'D)
          Soup, followed by the roast beef?

                    GRAHAM
          Thank you.

She leaves. Philip is staring across the room. Watching the
dust dancing in its light...

                                             LATER

Philip eats some bread. Slowly.

Graham is aware of A COUPLE (70s) hovering by the table.

Fans. The Woman smiles at him. And especially Philip.

                    WOMAN
          We loved all his movies.

                         HUSBAND
          All of them.

                         GRAHAM
          Thank you...

                         WOMAN
          Even the depressing ones.

                         HUSBAND
          Especially the depressing ones!

Silence. Hoping they will move on. But they still hover.

                         WOMAN
          Does he talk much about the old days?

                         GRAHAM
          He can't talk.

                         WOMAN
          Oh.

                         GRAHAM
          He hasn't said a word for five years.

Silence. They stare at Philip. Locked in.

                         HUSBAND
          He did his talking through the camera.

Graham eyes the Man. About to say something. Checks himself.

                         GRAHAM
          Our soup'll be here soon.

The Woman nods.

                         HUSBAND
          Can we have an autograph?

                         GRAHAM
          That's not possible.

                         WOMAN
          A photo, then.

She hands Graham her mobile phone. She and her husband go round
and stand either side of Philip. Like he's a trophy. They both
smile. Graham takes the photo.

Philip is oblivious.

> WOMAN (CONT'D)
> (retrieving her phone)
> Does he see Sir Richard much?

A beat.

> GRAHAM
> He hasn't seen him for six years.

> WOMAN
> I guess he lives a long way away.

> GRAHAM
> He lives two blocks from Philip's home.
> Philip's <u>care</u> home. He's never been to
> visit him once - the man whose pictures
> won him all his Oscars.

A long silence.

Philip chews his bread. Puts a chunk in his jacket pocket.

> LATER

Still waiting for their soup. Graham is having a drink. It's
loosening his tongue. He scowls at Philip.

> GRAHAM
> It's your fault, of course.

A sip...

> GRAHAM (CONT'D)
> The great photographer! If only they knew...

Another sip...

> GRAHAM (CONT'D)
> The terrible father. Holding me back.
> Ruining my life.

He hisses at Philip.

> GRAHAM (CONT'D)
> It was only ever about you. And your
> so-called art...

Sound of CHINA. A Soup Tureen is placed on the table. Ladle.
Bowls. The Waitress beams at them.

> WAITRESS
> Tomato.

> GRAHAM
> His favourite.

The Waitress ladles soup into a bowl.

                                                    LATER

Philip is eating his soup, SLURPING it.

This irritates Graham.

> GRAHAM
> Do you have to make such a racket?

Philip carries on eating and SLURPING. Like a machine.

> GRAHAM (CONT'D)
> Was it all worth it? The missed birthdays
> and wedding anniversaries? All those
> little affairs on set? D.C.O.L. Doesn't
> Count On Location. Except that it did.
> Every time. You were the one who drove her
> to drink, not us.

Another SLURP.

> GRAHAM (CONT'D)
> Even when Mike took his own life, you
> didn't come home. Couldn't leave the
> shoot, you told her. Not even for your own
> son's funeral. Too many people depending
> on you. They needed the great photographer.
>   (raised voice)
> Well, so did we!

ACROSS THE ROOM

DINERS are looking at Graham.

The Manager clocks him. Begins to come over...

                    GRAHAM (CONT'D)
          They say the booze killed her. But we know
          the truth, you and I, don't we. She died
          of a broken heart. And you broke it.

Philip. Silent. Impassive.

The Manager reaches the table. She assesses Graham.

                    MANAGER
          Everything alright?

                    GRAHAM
          Fine.
               (beat)
          Lovely soup.

SLURP.

                                                  LATER

The Waitress is clearing the table.

Philip is staring out through the large window.

The light outside has changed again.

Graham sips coffee. Feels his pocket. Where the gun is.

EXT. PARK — DAY

Magic Hour. Graham and Philip walk round the park.Graham is
steering his father away from other people.

EXT. POND, PARK - DAY

They sit on a bench on the far side of the large duckpond.
Graham looks around: no-one else is about.THEY ARE ALONE

He takes the handgun out of his pocket. Weighs it in his hand.
Considers it. The sunlight catches it. Glinting.

GRAHAM

Magic hour...

Philip nudges him. He hands Graham the chunk of bread he took earlier. Graham rests the gun on his lap. Tears off a piece, gives it to Philip. Philip throws it for the ducks.

GRAHAM (CONT'D)

Light like this won you your Oscar.

Ducks QUACK and FIGHT for the bread.

GRAHAM (CONT'D)

I hope it was all worth it.

Graham hands Philip more bread. Philip throws it, silent.

Graham stands. Eyes the gun. Hurls it out into the middle of the pond. It hits the water. Sinks...

EXT. "THE CEDARS" CARE HOME — NIGHT

Graham escorts Philip up to the front door. Rings it.

They wait for Nurse Sharp. Graham stares at his father.

The door opens. Nurse Sharp smiles at them.

NURSE SHARP

Five o'clock on the dot. Had fun?

Graham evades her eye. She turns.

NURSE SHARP (CONT'D)

Same time next Sunday...

She goes back inside. Expecting Philip to follow her.

But he doesn't. He stares at Graham.

Graham looks at his father.

Philip is staring at him. Really staring at him. Looking at him. Into his eyes. His soul.

Graham stares back.

Out of nowhere:

                         PHILIP
              I love you.

ON GRAHAM. Stunned.

Philip, locked in again.

He disappears inside the Care Home after Nurse Sharp.

The door closes. Leaving Graham alone in the dark.

Graham stares at the wooden door where Philip stood. He gently
touches it.

EXT. CAR — NIGHT

Graham walks to the car. Unlocks it. Gets in.

INT. CAR — NIGHT

Graham stares through the windscreen at the care home.

He starts to weep.

The radio PLAYS

                                        FADE TO BLACK.

                        THE END

APPENDIX B

8-Sequence Feature Film Story Structure

- There are typically eight sequences in a feature film screenplay:

  two sequences in Act 1 (20–30%)
  four sequences in Act 2 (50–60%)
  two sequences in Act 3 (20–25%)

- A sequence usually runs for 10–20 minutes. Each sequence has its own beginning, middle, and end with five or six key beats / plot events.

ACT 1:

Sequence 1 – set up and introduction: undisturbed status quo of main character / protagonist
#1: INCITING INCIDENT
Sequence 2 – building the dilemma, the collision (with the antagonist)
#2: MAIN TENSION, the main dramatic question (the **Want** of the main character) for Act 2 is established and articulated to the audience.

ACT 2:

Sequence 3 – elaborating on future obstacles. Introduce new characters. Initiate the subplot(s).
Sequence 4 – first serious obstacle is faced and overcome.
#3: MIDPOINT, OR the FIRST CULMINATION

The main character is closest (or furthest away in a tragedy / out of balance story) to getting what they <u>want</u> in the whole movie.

The **MIDPOINT REVERSAL** can happen at this point, provoked by the protagonist's **Need** which is beginning to emerge / intrude in the story.

Sequence 5 – Main subplot kicks in, as a break from or contrast to the main plot. Traditionally, this is often the 'love' sequence.

Sequence 6 – back on the main Act 2 **Want** storyline, leading to:

#4: MAIN CULMINATION. The main character has gone as far as they can go in trying to get what they want, and **failed or succeeded. Their** Want is replaced by their Need creating **a new dramatic tension** in Act 3.

ACT 3:

Sequence 7 – What the main character has learnt in terms of their need. What's going to happen at the end? How will things turn out?

Elaborating on the new dilemma leading up to **#5: THE TWIST / FALSE RESOLUTION / SACRIFICE**. This looks like a solution, but it isn't.

Sequence 8 – What actually happens; outcome and **#6: RESOLUTION**.

APPENDIX C

The 8-Sequence Feature Film (90–120') Breakdown

- 1-page MAX per sequence (8 pages MAX in total)
- Written in Courier 12
- Single-spaced, 6–8 paragraphs per page.
- Think about whose sequence is it and structure the action of the sequence around the external goal / objective / desire of this character.
- What is the dramatic tension of the sequence? "Will Woody . . . (or won't he)?"
- Express / frame the overall action in the sequence as a heading
- At the start of each sequence, express the specific dramatic tension of the sequence as a question.

TOY STORY[1] (1995)

ACT 1 TENSION: *Will Woody keep his place as Andy's favourite toy?*

SEQUENCE 1: "ANDY'S PARTY" – *Undisturbed 'status quo' of main character.*
Seq. 1 Q: "Will Woody and the toys get through Andy's party?"

---

1 *Toy Story* (1995), Screenplay by Joss Whedon, Andrew Stanton, Joel Cohen, and Alec Sokolow, directed by John Lasseter.

SEQUENCE 2: "BUZZ" – *Building the dilemma, collision with the antagonist.*

Seq. 2 Q: "Will Woody regain his place of honour on Andy's bed?"

ACT 2 MAIN TENSION: *"Will Woody defeat Buzz and restore his status quo as Andy's favourite and the leader of Andy's toys?"* Woody's WANT.

SEQUENCE 3: "WOODY'S PLAN" – *Elaborating on future obstacles. Introduce new characters.*

Seq. 3 Q: "Will Woody get rid of Buzz?"

SEQUENCE 4: "PIZZA PLANET" – *First serious obstacle faced and overcome.*

Seq. 4 Q: "Will Woody find Buzz and bring him back home?"

SEQUENCE 5: "SID'S BEDROOM" – *Main subplot kicks in.*

Seq. 5 Q: "Will Woody and Buzz survive Sid together?"

SEQUENCE 6: "YOU'RE A TOY!" – *Back on the main storyline.*

Seq. 6 Q: "Will Woody revive Buzz so they can get home?"

ACT 3 TENSION: *"Will Woody (show true leadership and) get him and Buzz back to Andy in time (before Andy and the toys move)?"*

SEQUENCE 7: "THE GREAT ESCAPE" – *What the main character needs to learn.*

Seq. 7 Q: "Will Woody save Buzz from Sid?"

SEQUENCE 8: "THE CHASE!" – *What actually happens. Outcome and resolution.*

Seq. 8 Q: "Will Woody (and Buzz) catch up with Andy?"

APPENDIX D

The 4-Sequence Returnable TV Drama Episode (45–60') Breakdown

- 1-page MAX per sequence (4 pages MAX in total)
- Written in Courier 12
- Single-spaced, 6–8 paragraphs per page.
- Think about whose sequence is it and structure the action of the sequence around the external goal / objective / desire of this character.
- What is the dramatic tension of the sequence?
- Express / frame the overall action in the sequence as a heading
- At the start of each sequence, express the specific dramatic tension of the sequence as a question:

THE KILLING[1] (2007, #1.1 'DAY 1')

ACT 1

SEQUENCE 1: "FINAL DAY" – *Ongoing 'status quo' of 'A' Plot characters. New dilemma / problem / 'collision'. Story of the week.*
Seq. 1 Q: "Will Sara Lund get through her final day in Copenhagen unscathed?"

---

1 *Forbrydelsen* (2007). Season 1. 20 episodes x 55', DR TV-Drama, Danish Broadcasting Corp., Norsk Rikskringkasting (NRK), Sveriges Television (SVT) and Nordvision Fund (support). Denmark.

MAIN TENSION: *"Will police detective Sara Lund find the whereabouts of the owner of the blood-stained personal items before she emigrates to Sweden?"* Sara's WANT.

ACT 2 (A)

SEQUENCE 2: "THE FIRST CLUE" – *Elaborating on future obstacles. Introduce new characters. Activate B, C, and D Plots.*
Seq. 2 Q: "Will Sara identify the owner of the video rental card?"

ACT2 (B)

SEQUENCE 3: "NANNA IS MISSING" – *Story of the week to Act 2 culmination. Progression of other Plots.*
Seq. 3 Q: "Will Sara work out where Nanna is?

ACT 3

SEQUENCE 4: "FINDING NANNA" – *What actually happens. Resolution of story of the week. Main character continues to ignore need. Hook / Twist into next episode.*
Seq. 4 Q: "Will Sara get confirmation of the identity of the body in the submerged car?"

BIBLIOGRAPHY

Aeschylus (c472 BCE) *The Persians*. Translated by R. Potter. London: AJ Valpy (pub. 1833).

Argentini, P. (1998) *Elements of style for screenwriters*. Los Angeles, CA: Lone Eagle.

Aristotle (1996) *Poetics*. Translated by M. Heath. London: Penguin Books.

Aristotle (2012) *Aristotle's Nicomachean ethics*. Translated by R. C. Bartlett and S. D. Collins. Chicago, IL: University of Chicago Press.

Axelrod, M. (2014) *Constructing dialogue: screenwriting from* Citizen Kane *to* Midnight in Paris. New York; London: Bloomsbury Academic.

Baldick, C. (2015) *The Oxford dictionary of literary terms*. Oxford: Oxford University Press.

Beckett, S. (1983) *Worstward ho!* London: Calder.

Benedetti, J. (1998) *Stanislavski and the actor*. New York: Taylor & Francis Group.

Bettelheim, B. (1972) *The uses of enchantment: the meaning and importance of fairy tales*. Harmondsworth: Penguin Books.

Booker, C. (2004) *The seven basic plots: why we tell stories*. London: Continuum.

Bordwell, D. (2006) *The way Hollywood tells it: story and style in modern movies*. Berkeley: University of California Press.

Bordwell, D., Thompson, K. and Smith, J. (2016) *Film art: an introduction*. 11th edn. New York, NY: McGraw-Hill Education.

Caine, M. (1997) *Acting in film: an actor's take on movie making*. London: Applause Theatre Books.

Campbell, J. (2008) *The hero with a thousand faces*. Novato, CA: New World Library.

Cooper, P. and Dancyger, K. (2000) *Writing the short film*. Boston, MA and Oxford: Focal Press.

Crowe, C. (1999) *Conversations with Billy Wilder*. London: Faber.

Dancyger, K. (2001) *Global scriptwriting*. Boston: Focal Press.

Dancyger, K. and Rush, J. (2013) *Alternative scriptwriting: beyond the Hollywood formula*. 5th edn. Oxford: Focal.

Davis, R. (2016) *Writing dialogue for scripts*. 4th edn. London: Bloomsbury.

Douglas, P. (2011) *Writing the TV drama series: how to succeed as a professional writer in TV*. 3rd edn. S.l.: Michael Wiese Productions.

Edgar, D. (2009) *How plays work*. London: Nick Hern Books.

Ferguson, T. (2010) *The cheeky monkey: writing narrative comedy*. Richmond, SA: Hyde Park Press.

Field, S. (1994) *Four screenplays: studies in the American screenplay*. New York: Dell Pub.

Field, S. (2003) *The definitive guide to screenwriting*. London: Ebury.

Flinn, D. M. (1999) *How not to write a screenplay: 101 common mistakes most screenwriters make*. Los Angeles, CA: Lone Eagle Publishing.

Gulino, P. J. (2004) *Screenwriting: the sequence approach*. New York: Continuum.

Hauge, M. (2011) *Writing screenplays that sell*. London: Methuen Drama.

Hay, L. V. (2017) *Writing diverse characters for fiction, TV or film*. Harpenden, Herts: Kamera Books.

Hemingway, E. (1964) *A moveable feast*. London: Cape.

Howard, D. and Mabley, E. (2011) *The tools of screenwriting: a writer's guide to the craft and elements of a screenplay*. Introduction by F. Daniel. London: Souvenir Press.

Johnstone, K. (1981) *Impro: improvisation and the theatre*. New York: Routledge.

Johnstone, K. (1999) *Impro for storytellers*. London: Faber and Faber.

Jung, C. G. (1938) *Psychology and religion*. New Haven: Yale University Press, 1966.

Kaplan, S. (2013) *The hidden tools of comedy: the serious business of being funny*. *Studio* City, CA: Michael Wiese.

Kaplan, S. (2018) *The comic hero's journey: serious story structure for fabulously funny films*. Studio City, CA: Michael Wiese Productions.

Katz, S. D. (1991) *Film directing shot by shot: visualizing from concept to screen*. Studio City, CA: Michael Wiese Productions.

King, S. (2012) *On writing: a memoir of the craft*. New edn. London: Hodder.

Lewis, C. S. (1960/2016) *The four loves*. London: William Collins.

Liddell, H. G. and Scott, R. (1843/1996) *Compiled by a Greek-English lexicon*. Oxford: Clarendon Press.

Maras, S. (2009) *Screenwriting: history, theory and practice*. London: Wallflower.

McKee, R. (1999) *Story: substance, structure, style, and the principles of screenwriting*. London: Methuen.

McKee, R. (2007) *On dialogue: volume 1 – number 1*. Los Angeles: Writers' Quarterly.

Mercurio, J. (2019) *The craft of scene writing: beat by beat to a better script*. Midwest Book Review.

Mernit, B. (2001) *Writing the romantic comedy: from "cute meet" to "joyous defeat": how to write screenplays that sell*. New York: London Harper Perennial.

Moran, A. (2006) *Understanding the global TV format*. Bristol: Intellect Books.

Ovid (2CE) *Ars Amatoria 7*. Translated by R. Cormier as *Ovid's erotic poems: "Amores" and "Ars amatoria"*. Middletown: America Library Association.

Pearlman, K. (2016) *Cutting rhythms: intuitive film editing*. Burlington, MA: Focal Press.

Proferes, N. T. (2008) *Film directing fundamentals: see your film before shooting*. 3rd edn. Amsterdam; London: Focal Press.

Propp, V. (1968) *Morphology of the folktale*. Translated by L. Scott. Austin: University of Texas Press.

Propp, V. (2012) *The Russian folktale*. Translated by S. Forrester. Detroit: Wayne State University Press.

Reisz, K. and Millar, G. (1953/2010) *The technique of film editing*. 2nd edn. Burlington, MA: Focal Press.

Seger, L. (1990) *Creating unforgettable characters*. London: Henry Holt.

Seger, L. (1994) *Making a good script great*. London: Samuel French.

Snyder, B. (2005) *Save the cat! the last book on screenwriting you'll ever need*. Studio City, CA: Michael Wiese Productions.

Stanislavski, K. (1936) *An actor prepares*. Translated by E. R. Hapgood. London: Bles.

Stanislavski, K. (1948/2013) *Building a character.* London: Bloomsbury.

Stanislavski, K. (1957/2014) *Creating a role.* London: Bloomsbury.

Szabo, I. (1994) *Sources of inspiration lecture 4.* Amsterdam: Sources.

Thompson, K. (2003) *Storytelling in film and television.* Cambridge, MA: Harvard University Press.

Thornham, S. and Purvis, T. (2005) *Television drama: theories and identities.* Basingstoke: Palgrave Macmillan.

Tierno, M. (2002) *Aristotle's poetics for screenwriters: storytelling secrets from the greatest mind in Western civilization.* New York: Hyperion.

Vogler, C. (1998) *The writer's journey: mythic structure for writers.* 2nd edn. Studio City, CA: Michael Wiese Productions.

Welles, O. (1958) *A ribbon of dreams.* International Film Annual #2.

Weston, J. (1996) *Directing actors: creating memorable performances for film and television.* Studio City, CA: Michael Wiese Productions.

Other Sources

Arndt, M.; *Little Miss Sunshine* (draft dated 10 September 2003) by Michael Arndt.; https://www.dailyscript.com/scripts/LITTLE_MISS_SUNSHINE.pdf

ChatGPT 3.5. Available at: chat.openai.com (Accessed: 28 February 2024).

Cleary, S.; Stephen Cleary handouts as shared with participants on *Arista Genre* (London 2004), *Arista Development* (SvdB, Cyprus (2005) and *Dialogue* (Australia 2011) workshops.

Daniel, F.; Frank Daniel handouts as shared with participants on the MBFI (Amsterdam 1996) and North by Northwest (Denmark 1999, 2001) script development programmes.

DNA/Deoxyribonucleic acid (National Human Genome Research Institute website). https://www.genome.gov/genetics-glossary/Deoxyribonucleic-Acid#https://web.archive.org/web/20150807142608/http://www.pages.drexel.edu/~ina22/splaylib/Screenplay-Toy_Story.pdf

https://www.socreate.it/en/blogs/screenwriting/are-day-and-night-the-only-descriptions-you-can-use-in-a-slug-line.

https://www.storysense.com/format/headings.htm#

Lasseter, J.; *Toy Story* (draft: "File copy – RED"); Original story by John Lasseter, Pete Docter, Andrew Stanton, Joe Raft, Screenplay by Joss Whedon, Andrew Stanton, Joel Cohen, and Alec Sokolow. Available at: simplyscripts.com (Accessed: 16 March 2024).

https://web.archive.org/web/20150807142608/http://www.pages.drexel.edu/~ina22/splaylib/Screenplay-Toy_Story.pdf

Medak, P. and van der Borgh, S.; interview with Ruth Myers, 5 March 2016, Los Angeles for feature doc *The Ghost of Peter Sellers* (prod. Paul Iacovou, 2018).

Whitfield, N. (2012) 'Filmmaking is a death-defying act'; *Guide to Filmmaking, The Guardian*, 24 September 2010.

Wilson, J. (2022) Interview with Aaron Sorkin; *This Cultural Life*, BBC Radio 4, BBC Sounds. 2 April 2022.

Xun Kuang quote, *The Xunzi*, Chapter 11, Book 8, '*Ruxiao*'. Available at: https://www.goodreads.com/quotes/7565817-tell-me-and-i-forget-teach-me-and-i-may (Accessed: 17 March 2024).

Films

45 Years (Andrew Haigh, 2015).

A Few Good Men (Rob Reiner, 1992).

Amadeus (Milos Foreman, 1984).

Anna Karenina (Joe Wright, 2012).
As Good as it Gets (James L. Brooks, 1997).
Being John Malkovich (Spike Jonze, 1999).
City Lights (Charlie Chaplin, 1931).
Die Hard (John McTiernan, 1988).
Fatal Attraction (Adrian Lyne, 1987).
Gomorrah (Matteo Garrone, 2008).
Gosford Park (Robert Altman, 2001).
In Tranzit (Tom Roberts, 2008).
Jagged Edge (Richard Marquand, 1985).
Jaws (Steven Spielberg, 1975).
Jerry Maguire (Cameron Crowe, 1996).
Little Miss Sunshine (Jonathan Dayton and Valerie Faris, 2006).
Mama Mia (Phyllida Lloyd, 2008).
Mephisto (István Szabó, 1981).
Muriel's Wedding (P.J. Hogan, 1994).
Parasite (Boon Joon-ho, 2019).
Richard III (Richard Loncraine, 1995).
Shaun of the Dead (Edgar Wright, 2004).
Silver Linings Playbook (David O. Russell, 2012).
Sunrise (F.W. Murnau, 1927).
The Diving Bell and the Butterfly (Julian Schnabel, 2007).
The Full Monty (Peter Cattaneo, 1997).
The Ghost of Peter Sellers (Peter Medak, 2018).
The King's Speech (Tom Hooper, 2011).
The Lives of Others (Florian Henckel von Donnersmarck, 2006).
The Shining (Stanley Kubrick, 1980).
The Wonderful Story of Henry Sugar (Wes Anderson, 2023).
Toy Story (John Lasseter, 1995).
Wall Street (Oliver Stone, 1987).
War of the Roses (Danny DeVito, 1989).
Withnail And I (Bruce Robinson, 1987).

Television

Blackadder Goes Forth (BBC TV, 1989).
Blackadder's Christmas Carol (BBC TV, 1988).
Breaking Bad (AMC, ep. 1.1, 2008–13).
Bridgerton (Netflix, 2020–).
Dad's Army (BBC TV, 1968–77).
Downton Abbey (ITV, 2010–15).
E.R. (NBC, 1994–2009).
Fleabag (BBC TV, 2016–19).
Forbrydelsen: The Killing (DR1, 2007–12).
Game of Thrones (HBO Entertainment, 2011–2019).
La Couchette (Inside No. 9) (BBC TV, 2015).
Mad Men (AMC, 2007–15).
Modern Family (ABC, 2009–20).
Ozark (Netflix, 2017–22).
Schitt's Creek (CBC Television, 2015–20).
Squid Game (Netflix, 2021–).
Succession (HBO, 2018–23).
The Crown (Netflix, 2016–23).
The Office (BBC TV, 2001–3).
The Sopranos (HBO, 1999–2007).

INDEX

For Product Safety Concerns and Information please contact our EU
representative GPSR@taylorandfrancis.com Taylor & Francis Verlag GmbH,
Kaufingerstraße 24, 80331 München, Germany

Printed and bound by CPI Group (UK) Ltd, Croydon, CR0 4YY

08/06/2025

01897005-0015